Furred and Feathered Things

To order additional copies of this book, contact:
Xlibris
844-714-8691
www.Xlibris.com
Orders@Xlibris.com

ISBN: Softcover   978-1-6641-8557-9
       Hardcover   978-1-6641-8558-6
       EBook   978-1-6641-8556-2

Library of Congress Control Number: 2021914366

Print information available on the last page

Rev. date: 08/31/2021

ACKNOWLEDGMENTS

For reading all or part of the text I am grateful to Guilliana Appel, Peter Baverstock, Helena Bergallo, Enrico Bernard, Paulo Bobrowiec, Clarice Borges-Matos, Anderson Bueno, Maria Inês Burger, Zilca Campos, Ubirajara Capaverde, Renato Cintra, Tim Cluttenbrock, Norbert Dankers, Daryl Domning, Ceinwen Edwards, Gabriel Damasceno, Thaise Emilio, Louise Emmons, Carla S. Fontana, Jacitara Forsberg, Thierry Gasnier, Gordon Grigg, Robyn Hittman, Ivo Rohling Ghizoni, Claudia Keller, Viviane Layme, Richard Loyn, Luca Luiselli, Priscilla Mady, Anne Magnusson, Ramiro Melinski, George Monbiot, Anelise Montanarin, Tim Moulton, Tony Press, Rafael Rabelo, Emiliano Ramalho, Carol Ribas, Carlos Frederico Duarte Rocha, Enrique Rocha, Daniel Rocha, Ricardo Sampaio, Tânia Sanaiotti, Ruchira Somaweera, Valéria Tavares, Don Wilson, Grahame Webb and Barbara Zimmerman. Special thanks to Grahame Webb who not only corrected my memories, but provided invaluable photographs and texts for this and my previous books. For providing photographs I am grateful to Anne Andrew, Giulliana Appel, John Barkla, Helena Bergallo, Enrico Bernard, Norbert Dankers, Louise Emmons, Sue English, Bill Green, Gordon Grigg, Carolina Leuchtenberger, Albertina Lima, Richard Loyn, Dorothy Magnusson, Langdon Magnusson, Ramiro Melinski, Juliano Franco de Moraes, Roberto Novaes, Brandi Jo Petronio Nyberg, Ocirio Pereira, Fred Rocha, Tânia Sanaiotti, Walfrido Tomas, Grahame Webb and Graeme Wells. Suzan Murray provided the photo of Louise Emmons in the Foreword. The dugong design on the cover and used as a text separator was given to me by Dick Nuggarboi (deceased). I cannot express the importance of this symbol of our friendship.

FOREWORD

This fourth, taxon-themed memoir of Bill Magnusson's lifetime of interactions with animals and people, well complements the first three, as a compilation of sequential anecdotes chronicling the maturation of his thought via adventures during field research on birds and mammals, first in his native Australia, and later, in Brazilian Amazonia. I was invited to participate in the WWF forest fragments project that was based at INPA, in Manaus, and I spent half a year there; weekdays alone in forest camps, and weekends in Manaus enjoying fish barbecues and hanging about Bill's lab, where there was always plenty of tea and Vegemite (I wonder has the Vegemite habit spread among young Brazilians?), as well as an admiring flock of students. When invited to go with him to capture dwarf caiman in Reserva Ducke, I discovered not only the quintessential naturalist, but an original who walked barefoot in the forest, a habit entirely new to me. Each evening, the brittle spines of palms had to be dug from the feet. Palm spines do not dissolve in mammalian tissue, but work their way in. Bill fished a stingray with a machete from the canoe. It was delicious grilled on sticks over the campfire. To see mammals in the field, one must travel unperceived, and barefoot makes the least noise. However, in both Gabon, where I had spent four years, and in Peru, for another four, hunters wear calf-high rubber boots, perhaps as shields from snakebite, as well as from the ants and termites whose bites draw blood.

Bill's memory is remarkable. The stories in which I had some part are all exactly recalled, but for one forgotten event. The episodes along Bill's life in the field are thought-provoking and entertaining; he is a masterful and original writer, who engages us in each event, so that we are eager to discover its ending. His portraits of others are just. He is humble and modest, revealing his fears and setbacks as well as his insights.

The description and resolution of problems will be invaluable for students, who need to learn that Murphy's law applies to all field work with animals, especially with radiotelemetry. My PhD advisor, the late Bill Dilger, would advise us that the first 6 mo of a field project likely will be discarded, and observations need begin again when at last one understands the animals and place, uncovers the right questions to ask, and can work through solutions to setbacks. Bill's memoirs elegantly map the progress of learning by trial and error that is the field study of wildlife.

Louise Emmons

DEDICATION

Many friends and collaborators died while I was writing this book between February 2020 and February 2021. It was a bad year; some were taken directly and some indirectly by COVID-19, and some from other causes. All will be sorely missed. This book is dedicated to Aldevan Baniwa, Augusto Fachin Teran, Maria Aparecida (Cida) de Freitas, Marcelo Menin, Francisco (Chico) Pereira, Lúcia Toga and Richard Carl (Dick) Vogt.

CONTENTS

PREFACE

When someone says that the world is getting smaller, you normally think of modern communications technology, but the biological world is also shrinking. Although I have touched elephants, I have never seen a big land animal and neither has any other human. To understand that statement we have to go back more than 65 million years to the Mesozoic Era. It was a time of giants. If you had lived back then you would not have come up to the knee of a *Tyrannosaurus rex*, and it was small in comparison to the plant-eating dinosaurs. We can't imagine what it would be like to be near such a big carnivore, but a lamb looking up at a shepherd with an axe might feel the same way.

Some of the mammal-like reptiles got to what we would consider big sizes, but none of them were comparable to the largest dinosaurs and by the time of *T. rex* their descendants, which we call mammals, were pretty much all smaller than rabbits. The dinosaur lineages experimented with flight, and some even had four wings[130], but all the flying dinosaurs were comparatively small. Apparently, they could not compete with the Pterosaurs, a linage independent of dinosaurs that had bat-like wings. They were the largest flying animals that have existed, and if you had lived then you would have been a little taller than the calf of the largest species, which stood as high as a giraffe[130]. Although most of that height was due to the long neck, and their wing span was not much larger than some extinct birds, they must have had flying technology far in excess of any living thing today because extrapolations from the flying animals we know suggest that they could not have gotten off the ground.

We didn't get to see any of those great beasts because a meteorite hit the earth about 66 million years ago, resulting in a dust cloud that smothered the planet and killed all the pterosaurs and the big dinosaurs[6]. The only group of dinosaurs that survived was the birds. Today they are the most common vertebrates in terms of numbers of species and often of individuals in most parts of the world. There are estimated to be about 5,400 species of mammals and 18,000 species of birds, so dinosaur species outnumber mammal species by more than three to one. In that sense, the dinosaurs still rule the world, but the birds were never able to emulate the pterosaurs and produce giant flying creatures. The largest birds in the world, including those too big to fly, would probably have been snacks for the big pterosaurs.

With the extinction of the dinosaurs, the mammals were able to diversify and produce larger species[87], but even the largest of those would have been little more than inconvenient gunk between the toes of the largest dinosaurs. That was the situation in most of the world until about 50,000 years ago, but at that time a species of mammal called *Homo sapiens* that used projectiles rather than strength or stamina to kill its prey started to spread out of Africa. Within a relatively short period it had extirpated most of the larger land animals throughout the world[115] and we are witnessing the extinctions of the last of those species. Even the small vertebrates are disappearing[149], including those in places with apparently little human disturbance[172]. Humans are susceptible to miniscule species, such as bacteria and viruses, that use chemistry rather than brute strength to dominate their prey. Soon, almost all the biodiversity on earth will consist of humans, their domesticated hangers on, and the micro-organisms that feed on them will represent most of the wildlife.

We are subject to the shifting baseline, a concept originally attributed to Ian McHarg[118]. Basically, each generation sees the world as it is at the time and assumes that is the way it always has been, and the only way it can be. To really understand the modern world we need to look back at previous baselines and that is not easy technically or psychologically - we crave stability and imagine that it exists even as we feel the ground shifting under our feet. It took me a lifetime to see the full magnitude of the changes and it may be for that reason I was not very effective in staving off the most undesirable of them. Perhaps if I recount my story, some young mammologist or ornithologist will learn faster and be more effective than I was. Throughout the book I will use the common names for species, where they have them, but the same common name is often used for many different species, so I have provided a glossary linking the common names to the scientific names for those who are interested.

CHAPTER 1 - CHILDHOOD

Family picnics in the Royal National Park led to a life-long interest in wild things, like this black swan. Photo by Dorothy Magnusson.

When I was little, my parents often took me and my sister to visit our grandparents who lived in the suburb of Allawah close to Sydney's inner city. There wasn't much for kids to do and we waited for the news programs to end so that we could watch television. Conversations were often heated and revolved around subjects that were of no interest to little children, such as whether George Moore was the best jockey because he got the best horses or George Moore got the best horses because he was the best jockey. Basically, we just tried to keep out of the way.

One night, things changed. Someone had caught a ring-tailed possum and put it in a small birdcage. They said that they would give it to us to take home because we lived in an area that still had a lot of natural bushland where its chance of survival was greater than in the almost treeless backyards of Allawah. When I crouched beside the steel bars, the beautiful little creature looked back with huge eyes and I was hooked. For no logical reason, it felt very important for me that I would be part of its life, even if only for a few days.

One of my uncles saw me there and decided to play a joke. He said "We've decided not to let you take the possum; it'll stay here." I didn't know what to do. I knew that children must do as they are told unquestioningly, and that little men should not show their emotions in public, so I just walked out, found an empty room, hid behind the door and cried my eyes out. Somebody found me, comforted me and said that he was joking; we would be able to take the possum.

Apart from learning that one person's joke is often another person's pain, I had experienced something that is common to most people. They bond very quickly to other animals, especially mammals and birds that have the appearance or behavior of little humans. However, other species are not just little humans, just as children are not just little adults. You can admire them and love them, but you must treat them appropriately or you may hurt them. I have had a life-long love affair with the study of mammals and birds, and I suspect that much of that stems from irrational feelings, such as those I felt as a child. Nevertheless, despite that prejudice, mammals and birds have taught me a lot that is not in my scientific papers and this book is an attempt to pass some of that to you.

Photo 1.1 *Ring-tailed possums are common in Sydney suburbs. Photo by Bill Magnusson.*

When my parents moved to Yowie Bay on the southern outskirts of Sydney it was largely bushland. A man who lived at the far end of the street poisoned their dog, probably because he feared its aggression every time he had to pass our house. They were heartbroken, and my sister and I never had a dog as a pet when we were young because our parents thought that it would be too much of an emotional shock for us when it died. However, initially there was other wildlife, such as possums and echidnas, that used our back yard. I most vividly remember the tiny diamond spotted pardalotes that nested in holes over the fish ponds my father had constructed[95]. The tiny birds had rich orange on the body just forward of the tail and the white dots on their black wings made them appear almost luminescent as they flittered in and out of their holes.

My father eventually tamed the wilderness, replacing the rich bushland with well-groomed lawns, camelia bushes and cement paths, and left only a few scattered gum trees, which was more than most of our neighbors did. A few native birds, such as magpies, still occasionally used the lawns, and crimson rosellas came to eat berries of the introduced cotoneaster trees, but by and large the only common birds in Sydney in the late 1950s and early 1960s were introduced sparrows, starlings, spotted doves, and Indian mynahs.

My main contact with native birds when I was in primary school was through the species we kept in aviaries. Seeing my interest in wild things, my father constructed bird cages. One had a conventional design. It was about two meters deep and a meter and half wide. The first meter was enclosed by fibro-cement walls so that the birds could take cover in inclement weather and the outer part was covered by wire mesh. The other aviary was constructed of wire covered in cement to give the appearance of a natural rock dome. I kept budgerigars in the cement cage together with introduced java finches. The java finches were the only birds readily available that could survive with budgerigars, which have the disturbing habit of sidling up to a perched bird and biting off its legs.

The larger cage had native cockatiels, zebra finches, double-barred finches, star finches, diamond doves, and king quails. I enjoyed buying the birds because I imagined them in the wild, but captive birds soon lose their mystique for me and I never spent much time observing them.

My most vivid memories are of the baby king quails, which were small enough to get through the wire mesh and wander around the yard. The problem is that baby quails need their parents to warm them up regularly. I would find the little quails stretched out and immobile on the ground around the cage. They appeared to be dead, but if I held them cupped in my hand long enough they warmed up, reanimated and could be returned to their parents.

I had not long started high school when I found a baby spotted dove that had fallen from its nest, which was probably in a tall pencil pine growing beside the driveway to our garage. It had no feathers and couldn't stand on its spindly legs, which just stuck out from under its purplish brown belly. It could hardly even hold its head up,

Photo 1.2 *A diamond pardalote taking food to its chicks in an underground nest. This species no longer occurs in my mother's garden. Photo by Bill Magnusson.*

which had huge eyes and a wide beak adorned with bright yellow corners. It was a member of an introduced species, but I didn't think about the potential harm it might do to the native fauna and I just wanted to save it.

I improvised a nest out of a tuna can and rags, and I didn't realize that it was probably a much better crib than the jumble of sticks that most doves use for nests. The little bird was almost rigid with cold when I found it and I kept it cupped in my hands until it warmed up. Later, I put the nest in the living room close to a coke-fired heater where its lack of feathers wouldn't be a great handicap.

I don't remember what I fed it, but it did well, growing quickly and sprouting feathers that soon covered its whole body. Whenever I walked into the room it would stand in its nest and beg with its beak wide open. I didn't make much of that because it would sometimes beg when other people walked into the room. Despite its well-developed plumage, I didn't think that it could fly far enough to do something inconvenient, like falling into the heater.

I had not read Konrad Lorenz's books and never thought about the lack of suitable bird models for it to imprint on until one day when I decided to watch television in the lounge room. The little dove had been fed a few minutes before and it was sitting contentedly in its nest. I stretched out on the sofa and was almost dozing when it flew across the room, landed on the sofa and lay against me. It apparently thought that it was a human and should watch television. From then on, when I went into the room, the dove would fly to me and lay against me in a most unbirdlike manner.

Obviously, I became very attached to that dove and I would like to be able to give a happy ending. However, that was not to be. My father, noting that the bird was always in the house, decided that it needed some sun. No sooner had he put it on the lawn than currawongs, large native crow-like birds, appeared. At that time, they only came to Sydney in the winter, but when they did the smaller birds had to watch out. Within minutes, they had killed my dove.

The Society for Growing Australian Plants revolutionized gardening in Australia in the 1980s and many of the barren yards, including my parent's, were converted into beautiful parklands that resembled native bush. Many species, especially the grevilleas, provided nectar for species of birds that could find little nutrition among camelias and roses. Now, you can see honey eaters and parrots in my mother's garden, and the introduced species have disappeared or are very rare, but the diamond spotted pardalotes have not returned. There would probably be even more species, but the native noisy miners are very territorial[131], expelling many others, and the predatory currawongs, which used to be only seasonal visitors, now take advantage of the alternative food sources provided by humans to stay year-round.

Photo 1.3 A spotted dove in its native Indonesia. The species has been introduced to Australia. Photo by Bill Magnusson.

My lack of enthusiasm for caged birds resulted in me having a close relationship with another introduced species. The rock dove has been domesticated for thousands of years and their descendants, feral pigeons, are found in cities throughout the World. Their homing ability has resulted in their being used for fast communication, especially during times of war, and competitions are often held to see whose pigeons can return home fastest after being dislocated hundreds of kilometers. I was visiting a friend who showed me Blacky, a young bird that he was trying to get rid of. Pigeon fanciers generally either keep birds for racing or they develop inbred fancy lines that are esthetically pleasing to humans. Fantail pigeons fall in the latter category. They have too many tail feathers to fit snuggly behind the bird, so they form an arc that makes the tail appear to be as large as the body. This is beautiful or grotesque depending on your idea of what makes a bird attractive. In any case, they can barely fly. Individual pigeons tend to be valuable either to show breeders or to pigeon racers, but not both. Blacky was an all-black half fantail with a broad chest, product of crossing a racing pigeon with a fantail. He therefore had no value for either breeders or racers.

Perhaps because I have always been socially inept, and often excluded from groups, I sympathized with Blacky's predicament and offered to take him home. That was not very prudent because I already was not giving my captive birds enough attention and I had nowhere to put him. Nevertheless, I used discarded chicken wire to construct a makeshift loft about a meter wide and three meters long between my father's chicken coop and the back fence.

The improvised cage ended up with more inhabitants. I could not leave Blacky alone, so I found him a mate and eventually I acquired another two pairs. They lived in packing crates that I modified into nest boxes suspended near the roof of the cage. A sloping wooden stake allowed them to go to and from the ground without having to fly in the cramped quarters.

Sometime later, I found a pair of bantam chickens wandering around in nearby bushland. I "saved" them by bringing them home and putting them in the pigeon cage. They probably would have found their way home and it was little more than stealing, but it is easy to justify what you do when you are a kid. Putting bantams, which are renowned for their fighting ability, together with doves that are often erroneously thought to be peaceful, is not a good idea. Doves in general are like humans; weak and cowardly when confronted by another species, but cruel and aggressive with their own kind. Blacky was the dominant pigeon in the loft and probably had to fight to get that position.

I realized my mistake soon after I put the bantams into the enclosure. The cockerel started to walk up the sloping garden stake towards the pigeon nests. I need not have worried. Blacky met him half way and used his wing to batter the bantam off the perch and onto the ground. After two tries, the bantam never again approached the nest boxes. This gave me another reason to feel affection for Blacky; a half-breed dove that can defeat a pure-bred fighting cock is the stuff of legends.

The pigeons were different from the other birds I had in cages. I could let them out to fly around, have adventures, develop their personalities, and they would come back of their own accord. The problem was that one of the things they liked to do was sit on the roof of our house, where they pooped and left white streaks. My father was unimpressed and called the pigeons worthless road peckers. He said that they did not really have any great attachment to our yard and that he would show me what useless homers they were.

Photo 1.4 *Noisy miners are native birds that have adapted well to the urban environment, but they are extremely territorial and exclude other species. Photo by Bill Magnusson.*

We regularly visited my uncle who lived about 10 km away on the other side of Botany Bay, a wide body of salt water at the mouth of the Georges River. To get there, we had to cross the Taren Point Bridge, the only alternative to travelling dozens of kilometers up river to where there was another overpass. One day, shortly before leaving, my father went into the coop and stuffed the pigeons into a small box. Blacky, who had descended the pole to defend the nests was the first in and ended up crushed under the weight of the others. Dad said "You'll see that these road peckers won't cross water".

When we arrived at my uncle's house, Dad opened the box and almost all the pigeons took flight, making a beeline across the bay in the direction of our house. The only exception was Blacky, who fluttered, but could not get out of the box. Dad picked him up and threw him high in the air, but he just spiraled downward, apparently not being able to flap one of his wings. He smashed into the tiles on the roof of my uncle's house, bounced a few times and finally regained his balance to stand shakily with one wing drooped beside him. Dad said "He'll be alright" and went inside. I watched Blacky, but he had not moved by the time we headed home.

All the other pigeons were back when we arrived, but Blacky was not. My father's attitude to the pigeons changed a little after his failed attempt to show that they were road peckers, but he still didn't think that they were worth keeping. He revised his opinion of the pigeons six weeks later when Blacky walked in. By this time, he was able to flutter about 50 m before falling to the ground. While this might have been enough to escape an angry dog, it was obvious that he could not have flown across the Georges River. The only explanation I can think of is that he walked across the Taren Point Bridge!

Blacky's dislocated wing finally recovered and he could perch on the roof with the other pigeons, and dad no longer complained about the poop. He would open the coop to let them out and feed them if I wasn't there. Unfortunately, he left the door open one day and something too strong for even the valiant Blacky, probably currawongs or a cat, got in and killed him. Like me, he was just a nonconformist member of an introduced species, but he taught me a lot!

As a child I would regularly wander off to explore the local bushland, much to my parent's dismay when they had planned other activities. Most of the houses were on the higher, flatter areas and the steep declines were the last to be built on. I found a wombat hole in the bush near the bay and I was intrigued. I had never seen a wombat

Photo 1.5 *Feral pigeons are very aggressive to each other, but vulnerable to predators, such as this South American gray-lined hawk. Photo by Bill Magnusson.*

in that area, though they were common in the flatter grassy areas to the west. The hole may have been a "fossil" in the sense that the last wombat in the area may have died long before. I couldn't see far down the burrow, which was only a little wider than my shoulders, so I shoved my head into the darkness. There were new smells of earth and moisture, but I still couldn't see anything. Pushing with my legs, I advanced half a body length, but my arms were pinned between my torso and the walls of the burrow. That was when I discovered that I have claustrophobia, especially if I can't move my arms.

Desperation did not help because the only way I could get out was digging my fingers into the soft soil and inching backwards like a caterpillar. By the time I got out I was a physical and psychological mess. Perhaps it was good that I had not read the reports that say that wombats sometimes kill predators trying to get into their holes by pushing them against the roof of the burrow and suffocating them. It would have been a very ignominious death, the tombstone reading "Killed by a wombat"!

I looked for wombats in all the remnant bushland in our suburb and did not find any. I also didn't see any in the nearby National Park. It seemed that the environment was not good for wombats and I found it hard to understand why one had bothered to dig a burrow there. It had not occurred to me that the best places in terms of resources are not always the best places to live. Sarcoptic mange was introduced to Australian wombats, perhaps from feral European foxes. In the best places for growth and reproduction of wombats, where they have high densities, many or most suffer from the disease and end up covered in itchy scabs that must be very unpleasant. However, in places where the environment does not allow them to attain high densities, mange is rare and the wombats appear to be in good condition. Only much later would I come to understand the relationship between mammal densities and disease, and that rarity can be a refuge.

The only species of native mammals I kept were the brown antechinus, and the common dunnart. The brown antechinus is about the size of an overfed white mouse, and the common dunnart is about the size of a wild house mouse. The antechinuses I kept were all male and they didn't live long. I found out later that the males essentially have a time bomb associated with their huge testes, which together can account for a third of the animal's body weight. Males are so hyped up during the breeding season, and so overtaxed by trying to mate with as many females as possible, that the stress literally kills them and no male lives to see his children being born. As far as I know, dunnarts are not so oversexed.

Despite its popular name, I only captured one common dunnart. It liked to capture and kill its prey, which was probably its only diversion in the small cage. Keeping animals well and happy in captivity requires that you think about all their needs, including social and psychological requirements, but I was just a kid and spontaneously decided to keep the common dunnart when I found it under a rock while looking for lizards.

Photo 1.6 *Anthony Stimson showing a wombat to Jeni Magnusson. These large burrowing marsupials were probably never common in the sandstone country in the east of Sydney. Photo by Albertina Lima.*

I eventually found that the marsupials would eat prawns if these had the salt thoroughly washed off prior to freezing for storage, but before that I caught cockroaches and centipedes in the bush and stored them in the freezer compartment of my mother's refrigerator. The marsupials ate the dead food, and very often the cockroaches would come back to life, or at least twitch their legs, when they thawed out.

Planning to give my dunnart a treat, I brought back native cockroaches I had captured while looking for funnel-web spiders. Funnel-webs are Australia's, and probably the World's, most deadly spiders. Deadly for humans that is; the venom has little effect on most mammals[173]. They are mygalomorphs, which is the group that includes tarantulas. Although slightly smaller than a human thumb, they are intimidating because their huge fangs are about half a centimeter long when unfolded. If threatened, they flex the front part of the body back over the abdomen, wave their forelegs in the air and turn their fangs to point directly upwards. In that position it would appear to be impossible to approach them without being impaled on the fangs. I was fascinated by them and kept some in a disused aquarium near the dunnart cage.

Very tired when I arrived home after trudging through the bush all day, I decided to give the dunnart its cockroaches before having a shower. The dunnart was used to me giving it food and looked up expectantly when the lid was lifted off its cage. I opened the cloth bag and shook it over the enclosure, but instead of cockroaches a huge funnel web fell out; I had opened the wrong bag! Almost the size of the dunnart, the spider reared up exposing its deadly fangs.

Before I could react, the dunnart pounced on it, apparently impaling itself on the fangs, but it did not show any sign of having been bitten. When I looked closer, I could see that it had a spider leg grasped by each foot and it was flipping its prey over. The fangs closed on nothing and the spider stopped trying to bite when the dunnart snapped off its legs. My heart was thumping and I was trembling at the thought that I had handled the bag so carelessly, but the dunnart just sat on its haunches and munched on its dinner of spider legs as though it were eating pieces of chicken. Being an insectivore, which is a misnomer for animals that eat invertebrates, seems pretty unexciting until you remember that many of their prey are as large or larger than they are. A dunnart eating a funnel web is a bit like a lion trying to subdue a rhinoceros with venomous horns!

While at school, most of the mammals I interacted with were European rabbits. Although we kept some as pets, most were animals that we trapped and ate. My first memory of primary school is being in the class where the teachers explained the rules and our responsibilities. Never having been much of a rule person, I was talking to the student beside me when a huge hand descended on the back of my head and rubbed my nose into the desk; I was in no doubt who was in control. The hand belonged to Dick Yardy, the vice principal and the person that engendered the most respect in the school. Unlike the other primary-school teachers, who were basically city people that had little contact with the world outside the education system, Mr. Yardy had worked in country areas and had much more the demeanor of a farmer than a teacher.

Photo 1.7 *Small marsupials, such as this brown antechinus,*
have many small teeth suitable for catching insects, but not the
piercing incisors of rodents. Photo by Bill Magnusson.

As I was often in conflict with my teachers, you might have expected that my relationship with Mr. Yardy would be tense, but it didn't turn out that way; rabbits made the difference. Mr. Yardy had a large suburban block where he grew vegetables, and rabbits loved what he produced. He asked us if anyone had rabbit traps and I replied that my father did. He borrowed our rabbit traps and would often turn up with fresh rabbits or watermelons as thank-you gifts. I liked Mr. Yardy and sought him out about 50 years later. He had retired to a town on the north coast, given up the family farm and his main pastime was golf. Nevertheless, he still had the quiet competence and serious demeanor of a farmer, and I realized that the values he passed silently had a large effect on me at a formative age.

We mainly ate fish when we camped during my father's annual holidays, but he would often set rabbit traps, and I got a taste for fried rabbits, especially the kits, which were succulent and tender. The traps we used were leg-hold traps and only later did I realize how cruel they were, the rabbit often lying for hours with a broken leg and torn muscles before someone came along to put it out of its misery. Even box traps leave the animal stressed for many hours, so today I would probably only eat a wild rabbit if I could shoot it. I attended a conference in the UK in 2008, and we collected blackberries to make damper. Richard Vogt was a biologist with a culinary bent, and he suggested that we make a rabbit and blackberry dish to take advantage of the English countryside. He bought the rabbits at the local supermarket and we were surprised to find that they had been imported from China. I guess that it would now be almost impossible anywhere in the World to recreate the associations with eating wild rabbit that I had when I was a child.

Although I often saw kangaroos and wallabies bounding off into the bush when I was on holidays, they were just fleeting glimpses and I generally didn't develop any lasting memories. However, there was one exception. We had been fishing on a lake near Narawallee on the south coast of New South Wales. Early in the morning we heard the baying of a dog pack on the track of a prey animal. The baying continued throughout the day and it seemed impossible that the dogs had not caught what they were after or the animal had escaped. It was mid afternoon when we saw the pack and its quarry. The dogs were obviously domestic and not a feral pack. There were several breeds, but one was a beagle responsible for the baying, and probably the reason that the wallaby had not been able to throw off its attackers.

Wallabies will rush into tangles of brush when attacked by dogs. The dogs either risk being staked if they follow the wallaby or they have to go around, giving the wallaby time to get away. However, the beagle could pick up the scent on the other side and was relentless. Too slow and ungainly to catch the wallaby, it had to rely on the other dogs for the kill. In the middle of the afternoon, after the wallaby had been running or its life for about six hours, the dogs closed in. In a last-ditch attempt to escape, the wallaby jumped into the lake and tried to outswim the dogs, but a greyhound leapt

Photo 1.8 *We tend to underestimate the dexterity of predators on invertebrates until we meet an invertebrate as big as we are, like this model of a funnel-web spider in the Australian Reptile Park. Photo by Bill Magnusson.*

into the water, grabbed it around the neck and pulled it out for the rest of the pack to tear apart. Watching was a painful experience for a young child and perhaps explains some of my lack of sympathy for the people who let their pet carnivores kill wildlife.

My father had been a hunter during the depression years and told me many stories about hunting wildlife. He explained that dogs are smarter than kangaroos because they learn faster, which I do not doubt, but his example was unconvincing. He and his mates used "kangaroo dogs", which were nondescript mongrels selected for being larger and faster than the red and blue kelpies used on sheep and cattle ranches.

Dad said that the kangaroos, especially large males, were dangerous for the dogs because they would stand their ground, apparently leaving their bellies vulnerable. When the dog leapt to grab its throat, the kangaroo would hug it with its forepaws and use one of its hind legs to deliver a potentially lethal slash that could disembowel the dog. Dad said that only occurred the first time the dog attacked a kangaroo. The hunter would then shoot the kangaroo and stitch up the dog, which if it survived would use a different tactic on the next hunt. It would harass the kangaroo keeping out of reach of the deadly hind legs until the kangaroo ran, at which time the dog could trip it from behind and grab its throat when it fell. That was Dad's example of a dog learning and the kangaroo not!

When we visited the Abercrombie River, where Dad had spent many of the depression years, he told me a story about the time he'd tried a variation on the hazing scheme used by the dogs to try to kill a large wallaroo on a hill overlooking our camp ground. Wallaroos are small, but particularly thickset kangaroos with robust forearms. This individual was unafraid of the hunter and dad decided to try to kill it with his skinning knife. Removing the skin from a rabbit or possum is a delicate process, and the knife must be razor sharp, but not very big or you won't be able to manipulate it easily.

Dad's plan was simple. He would flick the wallaroo in the face repeatedly with a small branch so that it would rear back but would not be able to concentrate well enough to deliver a killing kick. That would allow him to get close enough to leap on the wallaroo, knock it over and cut its throat with his skinning knife. It almost worked. With the switch flicking in its face the wallaroo could not see where to kick and dad was able leap up, wrap his legs around the wallaroo's mid body and bowl it over. What he hadn't planned for was that the wallaroo did not lie still on the ground but used its massive hind legs to kick until dad's legs were only around its neck. Seeing that he was losing ground, dad slammed the knife down towards the wallaroo's throat, but its kicking put him off balance. The knife went deep into Dad's thigh, the wallaroo kicked free and ran off, and dad rolled around clutching his severely-damaged leg. For the rest of his life he carried a puckered scar to show that you shouldn't mess with buck wallaroos.

Photo 1.9 *Wallaroos are small, but powerfully built kangaroos with strong forearms. Photo by Bill Magnusson.*

I recount these stories to show you that my role models as a child were not academics that stood around posturing in university hallways, but simple and ingenious people who interacted directly with real the world and had a physical attachment to it. It is this primal connection between people and nature that I feel, and not the vicariant pleasures obtained from thumbs-up images on a smart phone.

Dad no longer hunted in the 1960s, but he loved to fish for trout in the Abercrombie River. I was a poor trout fisherman and I preferred the hour when it got too dark to walk the banks after trout and we would set lines to catch native Macquarie perch on the sandy bank of a deep pool. We would sit quietly watching the lines and a little "V" would slice through the water as a water rat, now often called rakali, swam parallel to the bank. Curious, the rat, about the size of a wild rabbit, would lift its head out of the water and we could see its oversized hind feet and sculling tail. Any movement on our part and it would dive like an otter, only to appear even closer the next time. We left fish heads near the water's edge and the animal would gingerly edge up the bank. Sleek and black on the head and back, it would sit with the fish in its mouth and show its bright apricot underbelly for a second, then flip back into the water, leaving hardly a ripple. These were some of the most enchanting moments of my childhood and I cherish them dearly.

Few people think of rodents when they think of Australia, but almost a fifth of the non-flying mammal species are rodents. Australasia was colonized by rodents in three waves. First came a lineage that includes all the endemic rodents except those of the genus *Rattus*, including *Hydromys*, the genus of the water rats. Next came the native species of the genus *Rattus*. All these species presumably got to Australia without the help of humans. Lastly, species of *Rattus* commensal with man, such as the house rat and the sewer rat, arrived in boats. My first scientific studies were on Australian rodents[91], but rodents affected my life in various other ways, not the least because of the emotional charge carried by memories of sitting with my family and watching water rats gliding through the Abercrombie River.

Photo 1.10 *Australian water rats, also known as rakalis, are common predators in rivers and streams. Photo by Bill Magnusson.*

CHAPTER 2 - HONORS

The architecture of Sydney University is impressive, but was intimidating
to a boy from the southern suburbs. Photo by Bill Magnusson.

I walked through the sandstone archway into the courtyard of the great hall. Gargoyles and other weird carvings stared down onto the trim lawns and neat paths that had been the meeting places of students for 120 years. I had received three years of undergraduate training at Sydney University, but I still felt a visitor, a stranger who could never be one with the hallowed traditions of the great University. I hurried down to the Zoology building. It was only 40 years old, but it still blended much better with the original buildings than many of the modern concrete and glass boxes that had sprung up on the university grounds.

I needed to speak with Dr. Alan Hodson, lecturer in Zoology and the man I had chosen to supervise the thesis project for my Honors year. I had been accepted despite a mediocre undergraduate record; I suspect because Alan had spoken on my behalf. I had participated in one of his courses and spent quite a few nights on his farm at Gosford, 70 km north of Sydney. A Ph.D. student, Norbert Dankers, was studying frogs on Alan's farm and I accompanied Norbert during his studies. Ostensibly, I was helping Norbert, but I suspect that the benefits he passed to me in the form of knowledge of the frog fauna were far greater than any he gained from my company.

Norbert introduced me to the idea of monitoring animals by their calls. He had lots of electronic gadgets and used recordings to determine the daily and seasonal variations in reproductive activity of frogs[53]. This only worked because Norbert had a deep understanding of the natural history of the species. Some species used up to four different calls, depending on the social situation. With the help of the University carpentry workshop, Norbert designed and built a small catamaran that could float over the reeds without damaging them, which he called "Elsie Bee" in Honor of Professor L.C. Birch. He recalls "One night we were lying on the small platform with a frog calling a few feet away. Suddenly we felt something like a small gust of wind, the frog gave a frightening scream we never heard before and it had gone. A big owl had flown over our heads and grabbed the poor frog." We still know little of the acoustic world of the creatures of the night, and how predators that use hearing to detect their prey, such as owls and bats, shape the communities of the night.

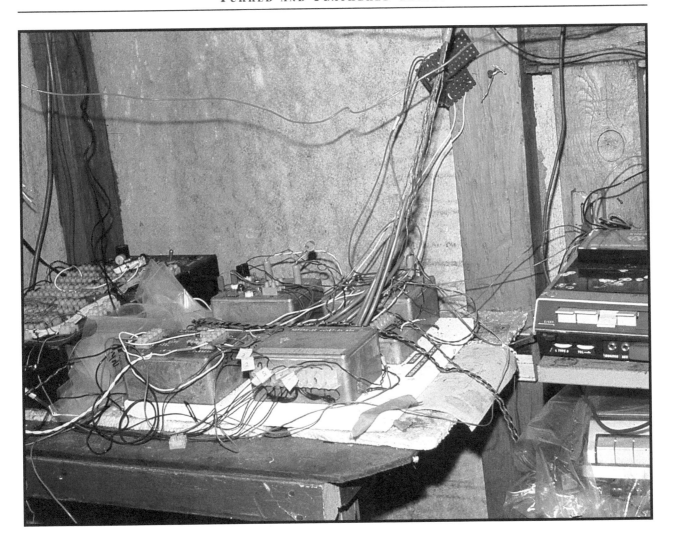

Photo 2.1 *Norbert introduced me to what was state-of-the-art equipment for acoustic monitoring in the 1970's. Photo by Norbert Dankers.*

Alan had an interest in mammals and had scattered traps throughout the bushland on the limits to his property. He hoped to study the native bush rat, but when he checked his traps, he found them upended without bait. After this happened a number of times, he sat a little way from his trap line to watch the recently-baited traps. He discovered that a rat kangaroo, more the size of a rabbit than a rat, was following him, carefully picking up each trap, shaking out the bait so that it could eat it, and then moving on to the next trap. As he didn't want to harm the little animal, he abandoned plans to study rats on his property.

Alan wanted me to study the effects of fire on the ecology of the bush rats in a nearby national park, but I didn't think that the project could be done in the nine months I had available. I convinced him that a comparative study of the water-concentrating ability of the bush rat, the swamp rat and the Northern Territory dusky rat would be much more appropriate for an Honors project[89]. I left the university that day content with my negotiations with Alan and confident of my ability to face the coming academic year.

The first setback to my plans was the refusal of the Northern Territory Wildlife Department to grant me permission to import dusky rats from the Northern Territory. They said that someone else was working on the species. This didn't bother me much as I still had the two NSW species to work on. I considered it a sensible decision to work on the physiology of these common species because I could complete the project in much less time than was available and I would not be subject to the vagaries of nature as would be the case in a field study. The first half of the course would be devoted to theoretical and philosophical studies and I planned to have all the animals and equipment ready by the start of the second term when I'd be doing full-time experimental work.

The little office allocated to the Honors students contained eight desks. That year, three women and five men were selected for the Honors course. Considering the sex ratio among undergraduate zoology students, the selection did not have a sexist bias. However, I soon noticed that I was a little different from the other students. People in the tea room commented that they sometimes had difficulty understanding my working-class slang. I was the only one of the eight who had attended a public school. All the others had attended private, generally religious, schools. Seeing that the vast majority of Australian children attended public schools, the system could not have been as egalitarian as it appeared.

We studied the philosophy of science and appreciated some of the latest mathematical developments which seemed to offer new ways of looking at ecological problems. The University of Sydney is one of the best and as undergraduates we had always been allowed to question dogma. In our final year we were expected to question authority, but it was not an easy step to take.

Photo 2.2 *As a teenager and young adult, Bill would often sit watching the forest on the other side of the valley to relax. Photo by Dorothy Magnusson.*

Professor Charles Birch was one of Australia's most famous ecologists, and his book coauthored with H. G. Andrewartha[8] still provides important lessons for beginning ecologists. He asked for an essay on the philosophy of science. As I questioned some of his published opinions and expected a reprimand, I prefaced the essay with a quote of my own invention: "He who sits out on a limb always sits higher than he who sits on a fence", and initialed it WEM. Professor Birch strode into the Honors room, beaming and distributing the corrected copies of our essays with an alacrity that showed that he was pleased with our efforts. When he stopped at my desk and dropped the essay in front of me he said, "Very, very good, but who is WEM? The Sydney Morning Herald has a section devoted to quotes by famous people and that quote is one of the best I've seen in a long time. We can send it in."

My chest swelled with pride and I said "Well, it's me, they're my initials."

"Oh!" he said, pondered for a few moments, turned and walked out. Lesson number one in communication: who says it is just as important as what is said. My chest deflated and I turned back to writing the next essay.

A little rivulet of water ran down the leaf, dropped past my collar and dribbled along my spine. I straightened up, shivered, dropped new bait into the empty trap and cursed fire, swamp rats and my over confidence. It was winter, July, and I still hadn't caught any swamp rats. The bush was wet with icy winter rain but the worst fires on record had ravaged the state that summer and the swamp rats had disappeared from all the places I had caught them so easily the year before. I trudged on to the next trap, flexing my fingers and hating the cold. The little aluminum box was closed and from its weight and smell I knew I had a rat. When I lowered the door to peer inside, two little eyes stared back. The handful of dark grey fur turned around revealing a short black tail and black feet, and I knew I'd caught a swamp rat. It swung around and the little face with stubby ears and beady eyes sniffed at the opening.

I let the door slam shut. There was no way I could collect 20 swamp rats for the experiment as I had planned, but I was determined to keep this one for some preliminary work. Fortunately, the bush rats had not been badly affected by the fires and I already had twenty to start the experiments.

Science is supposed to be white lab coats, petri dishes and Bunsen burners, but it didn't seem to be any of that as Janet and I sat on the floor and bent galvanized mesh with bloody fingers that had been spiked a thousand times by the coarse wire. Janet had been my girlfriend for several years. Small, with long dark hair, a round face and owl-like steel-rimmed glasses, she made a pretty picture as she sat among the pieces of cut mesh. However, it was midnight, I was tired, needed to finish another ten cages, and didn't have time to appreciate her beauty.

When I asked Alan where were the university's metabolic cages, he had just looked at me with a blank face. Nobody had studied renal physiology of rodents at Sydney University; I would have to construct the metabolic cages myself. I spent all of Alan's

Photo 2.3 *The only swamp rat I captured for my experiments in 1974. Photo taken with the aid of Sue English.*

research grant that year on galvanized mesh for the walls of the cages and stainless-steel mesh for the floors. Without Janet's help I would never have gotten them ready in time to start the experiments.

I even had to construct the trays to collect the urine, gluing glass rods onto Perspex plates that could be slipped under the wire cages. Time was ticking away and I still hadn't started collecting data. I had reviewed the literature about experiments on urine concentrating ability of rodents and decided to modify the general procedures to avoid what I considered to be two grave errors. The first change was to maintain the animals on different diets, one rich in protein and the other rich in carbohydrates. High-protein diets stress animals on restricted-water regimes much more than low-protein diets because the nitrogen in the protein has to be excreted in the urine. I decided that half my rats would eat crushed wheat and the other half would eat a combination of crushed wheat and soy bean. As no commercial rat diets with this mixture were available, I would make rat "biscuits" myself.

Most experiments on the urine concentrating ability of rats had simply completely denied them access to water. The experiment was essentially the urine-concentrating ability of dying rats. Besides being unnecessarily cruel it seemed to me that it might underestimate the capacity of moderately stressed, but otherwise healthy rats; the situation that would probably occur during drought in the wild.

I would reduce the water ration for each rat only a small amount below that which it drank without restriction. If it could maintain weight on that ration for three days, I would reduce the amount successively until I found the one on which it could no longer maintain weight; theoretically its limit. So easy on paper these modifications, but so difficult in practice. In 1974 there was a state-wide shortage of soybeans and nobody had soybean meal to sell. I wandered into Alan's office and stood dejectedly as he scribbled in his notebook. He finished writing, swiveled around on his chair and asked "What's wrong?"

I explained that I would have to change the project. There was simply no soybean to be had in the state. He thought for a moment, turned and picked up the phone. The person on the other end of the line replied "Yes, CSIRO has a few bags of soybean meal in stock. Yes, we'd be willing to let an Honors student have one for his research project." The impossible was possible and I hurried out to face the next problem.

I had been working all day making biscuits of the right shape, size and water content for the rats. I felt more like a baker than a scientist. Scratching bits of crushed wheat from under my finger nails and brushing flour off my trousers, I walked through the silent corridors. The more sensible inhabitants of the building were all home asleep or enjoying the delights of family life.

I flicked on the light in the controlled-temperature room in the basement that I had taken over for my experiments. The rats sat in individual cages that lined three of the four walls. The bush rats, looking like common house rats with slightly shorter tails, squatted timidly in the corners. The swamp rat wrapped its fingers around the mesh and bit at the steel. When I teased him, he squealed and tried to reach me by pushing his hands and stubby forelegs through the wire. All was well with the experiment and I could go home.

Photo 2.4 *One of the bush rats used in the experiments to determine urine concentrating ability. Photo taken with the aid of Sue English*

I flicked on the light in the controlled-temperature room in the basement that I had taken over for my experiments. The rats sat in individual cages that lined three of the four walls. The bush rats, looking like common house rats with slightly shorter tails, squatted timidly in the corners. The swamp rat wrapped its fingers around the mesh and bit at the steel. When I teased him, he squealed and tried to reach me by pushing his hands and stubby forelegs through the wire. All was well with the experiment and I could go home.

The steps up to the bridge over the roadway seemed steeper than normal and I was exhausted by the half-hour walk to the train station. Half an hour on the cold windy platform did not leave me feeling any better and the hour-long train trip seemed to take forever. The train only took me to within a mile of home and I trudged wearily up the hill, surprised that overwork and lack of sleep could leave me so weak. Everyone was asleep when I got in, so I hurriedly ate the plate of food my mother had left on the stove and dropped into bed.

Six-thirty a.m. Sunday and I had to get in to feed, water and weigh the rats. The experiments should have been over long ago but the rats kept losing weight, then stabilizing at a lower level. Some rats had stable weights after 40 days on water regimes that would have killed them had they been deprived all at one go. I swung my feet over the side of the bed and all the tiredness of the night before came back. My muscles ached and I had trouble focusing. I obviously had a virus of some sort but I was not about to be bedridden by the common flu, especially when my research depended on my presence at the university. It would only take me a couple of hours in the rat room to attend to the little captives.

Two steps and I fell on my face. The throbbing in my head didn't stop and I just wanted to lay on the carpet and sleep. My mother tucked me back into bed and called Janet. They went to the university, fed, watered and weighed the rats; chores that I had down to a fine art. What would have taken me two hours took them all day, having to learn and overcome in eight hours all the problems that I had faced during the previous months.

By Monday the virus had abated to the level that I was used to in bouts of the flu and I could attend to the rats again. However, I had been alerted to something I had not expected. The tension of the experimental and academic work was taking its toll physically and pushing me close to the limit.

My favorite form of relaxation was spearfishing. It didn't matter whether I caught fish or not. When I leaped off the rock into the surging sea the water washed the tension out. All would go quiet and I'd feel the power of the ocean flow through me, yesterday's bickering and bureaucracy left floating on the waves above. Unfortunately, it was winter and too cold to go snorkeling. Sometimes I'd drive out to a wilderness area near my home, and sit and watch the dark hills on the other side of the valley. If I sat long enough I´d feel the pulse of the universe in the blackness and I'd return calmer and rejuvenated. Generally, though, there wasn't time for anything but trains, rats and tension. I started to imagine that nothing more could go wrong. All I had to do was adapt my routine to the research and try to get some rest on the train; not many months to go.

Photo 2.5 *On the train home at night everyone was sleeping or engrossed in their own thoughts. Photo by Bill Magnusson.*

A train on the far platform thundered by, but I hardly noticed. I was thinking about the analyses I had to do. My arm was around Janet but it was a position of habit. There was no more feeling in my embrace than there was in my grip on the briefcase in my other hand. She looked up at me and asked "Do you think it's possible to love two people at the same time?" I didn't have time for silly academic questions like that. I replied "Of course it is." She nodded and I went back to thinking about experimental design.

Two weeks later when she said "Didn't you know I've been going out with Steve? I asked you about it on the train station", my world fell apart. It was true; I just hadn't paid attention to what she was saying. "Do you mind?" she asked.

"Of course not." I said, but I as I drove home my stomach contracted and I almost vomited. What did Steve have that I didn't? I was thin and weedy, didn't like to dance, couldn't hold a tune to save my life and thought parties boring. I didn't drink, smoke or do any of the things that sociable people do and now I was working 12 hours a day, seven days a week. Steve was tall, muscular, with long wavy hair that reached below his shoulders. He rode an enormous motor bike and was a member of the surf culture. He not only was the life of the university parties, he had friends in the surf and marihuana cult up the whole north coast of the state.

Janet having another friend to while away the hours when I was engrossed in my own selfish interests made perfect sense. I loved her and I could hardly deny her that, but all of a sudden I didn't get any rest while travelling on the train and I took much longer to get to sleep at night.

I let the few drops of rat urine fall into the well in the center of the dish. A few drops of reagent and I quickly covered the dish with a glass plate and sealed it with Vaseline. It would take many hours for the enzyme to convert the urea into gaseous ammonia and for this to diffuse across and be absorbed into the solution in the channel around the outer edge of the dish. The slightest error in measuring the reagents or sealing the dish and the results would be meaningless. I carefully collected the solution from a dish that had already been standing for the required number of hours. By carefully dripping reagent into it and measuring the amount of chemical necessary to make it change color I would be able to calculate the concentration of urea in the original sample.

I opened the stopcock and liquid glopped into the beaker. Too much! I watched the solution; it still hadn't changed color. Shaky hands only let two drops escape this time. "Take it slow Bill". The problem was that it was taking four hours per sample with this method. For the 82 samples I had it would take 328 hours just for the chemical analysis. There wasn't enough time to do all the analyses and, in any case, I didn't trust the results I was getting with these delicate chemical maneuvers.

Photo 2.6 *From the train I only saw blurred images of happy families enjoying each other's company. Photo by Bill Magnusson.*

One of the Ph.D. students asked "Why don't you call Roche Pharmaceuticals and ask them if there isn't a more modern method of analyzing urine? The technique you are using is the same they used a hundred years ago." I had no choice. All the other students had long finished their experiments and were busy writing up.

"Yes sir, we have just developed a simple urine-analysis kit that will be on the market next week. Give me the university order number and I"ll send you one immediately." The impossible had become possible again and I set up to do the analyses with the Roche kit, which was only slightly less finicky than the old method, but which, if set up in the right sequence, would take only 20 minutes per sample.

Pipette one for reagent one; move to the next tube. I sucked the reagent into the graduated pipette and expertly dropped the required amount into the vial. Sunday,

10 a.m., all reagents in order and the production line functioning. Janet and I were by ourselves in the laboratory, working flat out to meet the deadline.

Pipette 3, tube 3 and Janet handed me the fourth pipette. I didn't pay attention to which end of the pipette she had handed me, wrapped my lips around the wet end and sucked acid into my mouth. I coughed, spat and called Janet every expletive I could think of. When I stopped spluttering and swearing, I looked up and saw Charles Birch standing in the doorway. He looked shocked and just turned and walked away.

I felt bad because we had all become very fond of Professor Birch and grateful for the way he had patiently helped us learn throughout the year. I could apologize to Janet and, in any case, I think she understood the stress I was under. However, there was no way to explain to Charles and I just had to return to the endless chemical analyses with one more reason to feel irresponsible and inadequate.

This time I was at the podium. I looked out at the faces of the professors and graduate students. The Head of School was sitting at the front smiling and nodding as he did to give confidence to everyone, but most of the others were far away, busy with their own problems, and giving little attention to the less-than-professional presentations by the Honors students. I was nervous and unsure whether I'd be able to control my throat which was constricting involuntarily. In as loud a voice as possible I said "I think you all know the rat I work with", then I flashed up a photo of Alan Hodson. For a second there was a look of incomprehension on the bored faces, then the whole audience burst into laughter. I had their attention and everyone said that they enjoyed the presentation though I doubt that they remembered much more than the opening joke. Lesson number two in communication; it doesn't matter so much what you say as how you say it.

It was dark and I had difficulty concentrating as the mile posts flashed past. I had driven 300 km from Sydney to Canberra on Friday, then sat writing my thesis and handing the written sheets to my sister, Anne, to type as I wrote. We had finished late

Photo 2.7 *My family was critical to my finishing my honours degree.*
Front row, left to right, Anne, Joe, Kate and Peter Andrew. Back,
Dorothy and Ern Magnusson. Photographer unknown.

on Sunday and now I had to get to Sydney to meet the deadline of 9 a.m. Monday to hand in the thesis. I don't know if Anne realized the importance of the help she gave me on that last weekend. As a present I left the bush rat that I had longest in captivity and which was now too old and fat to release. It showed our appreciation by breaking out of its cage and eating holes through her boyfriend's suit.

In the dark on the final leg back to Sydney I had time to reflect on what I'd learned during that year, which I still recognize as the worst of my life. I wanted to continue with research but I knew that I'd have to do better or I wouldn't survive. I had found that it is possible for everything to go wrong despite seemingly well laid plans. I'd also learned that it is possible to do the impossible and right enough of the errors to get a worthwhile result at the end.

However, more important than the rest was that I had learned that doing research involves managing time. If you can estimate accurately the time you need to do each step, you'll be able to put it all together. This involves allocating time for the unpredictable as well, and more important, allocating time for personal life. If you can't integrate your personal life into your research you can destroy your curiosity, your will to learn, and possibly yourself. The wind on my face dropped to a soft breeze, the headlights lit up the big gum trees my parents had planted in front of the house many years before and I turned into the drive. A feeling of satisfaction swept over me and I knew that I had just completed a very important journey.

CHAPTER 3 - PH.D. CANDIDATE
SOUTHERN AUSTRALIA

Macropods, such as this Mareeba rock wallaby, are often
counted from light aircraft, but aerial survey is a dangerous
activity for wildlife biologists. Photo by Bill Magnusson.

When I started my Ph.D. studies I decided to take advantage of the researchers and students that were studying mammals to widen my experience. One student was Tony Press who initially planned to study broad-toothed rats. The species is an old endemic, one of the species that evolved from the first rodent colonizers of Australia. It appeared to be very rare, but Tony had heard that it occurred on Gloucester Tops in the highlands behind the central coast of NSW. I knew Tony as an undergraduate, but I had never spent time in the field with him. He was not very conventional and often not politically correct; descriptions that could apply to me, but his social life was much richer than mine and stories abounded about his ability to consume large quantities of alcohol.

I was pleased to have an opportunity to visit Gloucester Tops. The lowlands near the central coast that had not been cleared for dairy cattle were mainly covered in wet-sclerophyll eucalypt forest or paperbark swamps, but some areas had temperate rainforest, especially where the mountains met the plains. We camped at the base of the mountain, the only inhabitants of a national-park campground beside the Gloucester River. We set some traps, but caught only brown antechinuses.

At night, there were red-necked pademelons, small wallabies that usually live near humid forests, eating the grass around our tent, and I thought I saw a rat kangaroo, but it bounded off quickly. A short walk up the road revealed yellow-bellied gliders, gliding herbivorous marsupials not much longer than my foot in body length, but with long tails that hung down about half a meter. Their calls were strange, sort of a cross between a growl and a whistle.

More impressive were the calls of the koalas, which reverberated through the valley. We saw few, but their calls indicated that they were moving through the eucalypt forest at a rate much greater than would you expect from their sedentary behavior during the day, when they were generally motionless in the fork of a tree or slowly munching leaves.

The next day, we drove up the mountain, the mixture of rainforest and eucalypts giving way first to tall eucalypt forest with rough tree ferns, then scrubby open forest similar to that around Sydney. After about an hour, we entered open grassland with scattered snow gums and the occasional soft tree fern. The tree ferns seemed out of place among the cold-adapted sclerophyll vegetation that burned regularly and the temperature had dropped to way below that which I find comfortable.

Photo 3.1 *Red-necked pademelons graze on the grass in the camp ground near the Gloucester River. Photo by Bill Magnusson.*

The tree ferns were much more common in the occasional patches of southern-beech trees, which formed dense stands. The understory was like what you would expect in fairy tales, with colorful toadstools and the ground covered by ferns. The tree-fern trunks were contorted, apparently because falling branches from the beech trees regularly knocked them over so that they had to start growing upward again.

The broad-toothed rats were supposedly close to the banks of the upper reaches of the Gloucester River, so we drove out of the beech forest and down a steep road into the low heath near the stream. It was pretty chilly even though it was already about 10 a.m. The low bushes and sedges made an almost continuous knee-high cover. We spread the sedges and found tunnels, about the diameter of my wrist that crisscrossed the low-lying vegetation. We assumed that they were made by mammals and hoped that they would be the work of broad-toothed rats.

We set traps throughout the heath, and also in the surrounding sclerophyll forest, but had to return to the council grounds because camping on the upper part of the river was not allowed. Tony enjoyed the field work, which was rather incongruous because he had more the appearance and demeanor of a city street urchin than of a forestry worker. We searched for mammals again that night, but did not find any new species.

Cold winds from the south brought freezing temperatures to higher areas the next day and we rushed around to check the traps. There were bush rats in the traps in the sclerophyll forest and we caught a few dusky antechinuses in the tunnels. These diurnal carnivores are much like brown antechinuses, but larger and more thickset, more the size of a rat than a mouse. They often occur in swamps and heathlands, probably because they need cover to be active during the day and not get picked off by birds.

I was happy to catch the dusky antechinuses because I had never seen one before, but we caught only one broad-toothed rat. It had started to snow, but not that fluffy white stuff that accumulates on the ground and you throw around. The flakes were white as the fell, but as soon as they landed they turned into soaking icy drops of water, and neither of us had clothes appropriate for those conditions. We packed the traps into the back of the station wagon and started back, but the car wouldn't climb the hill out of the stream valley. The wheels just spun on the waterlogged clay and I got soaked, muddy and cold when I got out and tried to push.

The university car was in Tony's name and he had been driving, but I said "You're not getting up enough momentum – let me drive." I backed the car onto a flat spot and then raced it at the hill. It was like driving on ice. We careered up the hill, but I started to go off the road and was heading straight for a tree until I regained a modicum of control and the car swerved around it. That control just pointed me at a tree on the other side of the road and I swung the wheel again. We must have swerved around at least a dozen trees as we fishtailed up the road and I had a strong metallic taste of fear in my mouth when we finally came to a stop on the top of the hill, but the god of

Photo 3.2 *Megumi Yamakoshi looks toward the low heath that provides cover for broad-toothed rats and dusky antechinuses on Gloucester Tops. Photo by Bill Magnusson.*

inexperienced boys must have been with us and we didn't damage the university car. All because we didn't realize how cold the high country can be and the importance of snow chains, even if just to get through mud.

Tony did not find enough broad-toothed rats for a thesis and for many years the species was thought to be rare to the point of being endangered. However, when researchers started studying fox scats they discovered that foxes just love broad-toothed rats[69] and the species cannot be very rare or the foxes would have sent it extinct long ago.

Janet was responsible for an adult-education course at the university and asked me to help. This was a quick lesson in teaching a diverse class. The course could be used for entrance into the regular degree courses, so had to be of rigorous academic standard, but the experience of the students varied enormously, as did what they wanted to get from the lessons. One was a professional who had obtained a biology degree years before and just wanted to catch up. One was a house wife looking for an outside interest, and another was a man with an alcohol problem who lived on the street and had been directed to the class by the Salvation Army as a form of therapy. The backgrounds of the others were just as diverse.

The students quickly became friends and their problems became my problems. It was impossible not to be infected by the enthusiasm of the homeless man when he called you over to see what he had discovered under the microscope, and you soon forgot that he had not had a bath in a long time. One of the students lived alone in an old wooden house and had problems with rats that scurried through the ceiling and kept her awake at night. She said that she had contacted the Agriculture Department and used all the poisons that were legally available, but the rats just lapped them up and continued with no effects. I suggested that she use oleander flowers that carry a strong cardiac glycoside and are readily available in most Sydney gardens. She cooked meat with the flowers and put it in her ceiling. When the rats ate it all she put more for them, which they also ate. The petals killed the rats, but rather than being relieved she was just as agitated at the next lesson. She said that the smell of the dead rats was overwhelming and she couldn't find most of the bodies. Loneliness does not have a simple cure!

Janet and I lived at Bundeena, an isolated village surrounded by the Royal National Park, and we collected road kills on the way to and from university. The swamp wallabies often provided welcome meat for poor students, but we used many animals for dissections in the adult-education classes. I was surprised at the power of an echidna. It had been run over and killed, but before the impact it had flexed its strong back muscles and its internal organs were in an almost perfect state for dissection. Most of the major organs were in the places you would expect for a mammal, but the blood vessels did not follow any of the routes that were illustrated in our laboratory manuals for rat dissections.

Photo 3.3 *The rugged country around the Gloucester River is bitterly cold in winter. Photo by Bill Magnusson.*

The students were much more interested in mammals than the other animals we showed them and I asked Tony Press to help on a field excursion to the Blue Mountains where we would trap mammals. As at Gloucester Tops, the weather was miserably cold, with drizzly rain that soaked us. To keep the student's spirits up, I decided to light a fire and make tea, but the rain kept extinguishing the flames. Tony offered to protect the kindling by protecting it with his raincoat, but as soon as the fire started to take it became too hot for comfort and Tony would jump away. In the end, two of us had to hold him in place until the flames were stronger than the drizzle. Strangely, the uncomfortable conditions just seemed to cement the strong relationships that were developing among the members of the class.

One of the students, Robyn Hittmann, wanted to take her young son to see wildlife and I suggested Gloucester camp ground. I accompanied them and had a lesson in the strength of motherly love. Robyn hated leeches and from her reaction you would assume that they terrified her. Nevertheless, when her son started staring at a leach on her leg, she just said something like "Oh what an interesting animal!" and slowly picked it off and showed it to him; determined not to pass on her phobia to the next generation.

Robyn did not work directly with mammals, though she did complete studies in Animal Care Biology and Captive Vertebrate Management. She was also a member of NSW Agriculture's animal-care ethics committee and travelled to Thailand, Cambodia and Laos to help rehabilitate bears that had been rescued from the bile trade. More than forty years later, we still meet when I visit Australia, and I value the insights that her partner Clive has given me in relation to commercial chicken production.

I lost contact with Tony after I finished my Ph.D. and never went into the field with him again. However, I know that memory can be fallible, so I always check my stories with other people who were involved. When I started this book four decades later, I looked for Tony's address on the internet. However, the only Tony Press who worked with Australian mammals that I could find was one who had been Director of the Australian Antarctic Division, was currently Adjunct Professor at the Antarctic Climate and Ecosystems Cooperative Research Centre and held the titles ACE CRC. Knowing my friend's bohemian nature and lack of political correctness I knew that it couldn't be him. Nevertheless, it was my only lead and I sent a message through the Antarctic Division. I knew I had the right man when he replied "Hello Bill! How the f…. are you?!!!"

Craig Hamilton was studying rusa deer in the Royal National Park for his Master's degree[73] and he invited me to accompany him on field trips. I was interested because many writers had inferred that marsupials had only been able to dominate the mammal assemblages in Australia because they did not have competition from placental mammals. In fact, it is quite possible that placental mammals originally occurred in Australia, but lost out in competition with the marsupials. In any case, the placentals most often given as ecological equivalents of kangaroos and their kin are deer. Many species of deer have been introduced to Australia, but only six formed self-sustaining populations, and all of these are restricted to areas close to where they

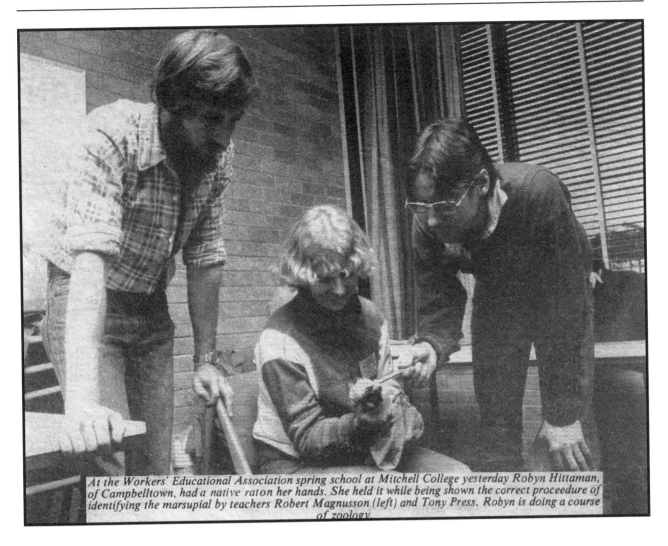

At the Workers' Educational Association spring school at Mitchell College yesterday Robyn Hittaman, of Campbelltown, had a native rat on her hands. She held it while being shown the correct proceedure of identifying the marsupial by teachers Robert Magnusson (left) and Tony Press. Robyn is doing a course of zoology.

Photo 3.4 *A report on our adult-education class published in the Western Advocate 5 September 1978 showing Bill, Robyn Hittmann and Tony Press.*

were introduced. None appears to be competitively superior to kangaroos. One of the most successful was the rusa deer; introduced into the Royal National Park, it spread about 160 km down the coast. It may have contributed to the extinction of fallow deer in the area and Craig thought that it might be having an effect on swamp wallabies. Based on habitat preferences, you would expect the deer to have more effect on red-necked pademelons, or parma wallabies, but these species had already disappeared from the park for reasons probably unrelated to deer.

Craig's study required that he capture and mark as many deer as possible. The deer were mainly found around the areas that had been farmland before being included in the park, probably because they are primarily grazers and cannot subsist only on rough browse as can the swamp wallabies. Most of the former farmland was heavily used by the public because the grassland was good for picnics and the best place for Craig to work undisturbed was around Garrawarra farm on the plateau overlooking Little Garie Beach. The Ranger Station was occupied by Ian Mahood, a National Parks and Wildlife Service Research Officer. Ian was on his honeymoon in an idyllic setting, but came out to talk to us when we showed up in the early evening.

Ian worked in the arid zone and he showed us a picture of himself holding a feral cat he had shot. Suspended by the tip of its tail at shoulder height, its nose was touching the ground! Apparently, the desert cats had evolved for large size in response to having to hunt rabbits and wallabies. Biologists can talk for hours when they get worked up about their subject and Craig and I were learning a lot, so we were in no hurry to start spotlighting deer. However, Ian's bride was not happy about us monopolizing her husband so soon after the marriage and subtly let us know. I thought she was being unreasonable as she had a lifetime to take advantage of Ian and we only had a few hours. However, Ian was killed in a helicopter crash while surveying rock wallabies shortly after and I still feel guilty about the time we stole from the young couple. Much later, and after undertaking a lot of aerial survey, I would discover that aviation accidents are the principle source of mortality for wildlife biologists[156].

Craig had a blow pipe with which he could propel hypodermic needles loaded with drugs to immobilize the deer. However, he only used the blow pipe after the deer had been caught in a Clover trap, which is just a wire box with a drop door on the front. As the drug was only a muscle relaxant, we had to work quickly to avoid capture myopathy. Being captured can so stress animals that they die hours, days or even weeks later even though they have recovered completely from the drugs. Therefore, captured animals must be blindfolded and handled gently.

The Clover traps were also dangerous for the swamp wallabies, but for a different reason. Macropods have what Craig called a self-destruct mechanism at the base of the skull. If they jump straight up and hit their heads on something overhead, which would probably never happen in the wild, the vertebra at the base of the skull cuts the spinal cord, killing the animal almost instantly. The net roof over the Clover traps was bad news for the wallabies and Craig tried to immobilize them as quickly as possible.

Photo 3.5 *Rusa deer are common in the Royal National Park. Photo by Bill Magnusson.*

I had often seen deer in the National Park, but seeing and holding an animal are different things. Close up, the deer are warm, their hair prickles, they smell of fermented grass, their lips are wet and their eyes are wide with fear. From then on, seeing them in the wild initiated a complex of sensations, smells and emotions that I had not felt before. Holding the wallabies had the same effect, though I already had a richer gamut of sensations associated with them because of the recently-dead individuals I had scavenged on the road to Bundeena.

Craig mainly analyzed feces to describe the differences between deer and wallaby diets, but he also had a license to shoot a few deer so that he could calibrate the feces against rumen samples, which better reflect what the animal had eaten. The problem was what to do with the body after the rumen contents had been collected, and I generously offered to discard the bodies in my freezer. I remember seeing my neighbor peering over the fence when I used the gum tree in our back yard as a support to hoist a deer up by its back legs so that we could gut and skin it. The deer provided plenty of meat, but to this day I do not much like venison. I find it too dry and stringy, but perhaps that's just because I don't know how to cook it. Now, I would probably braise it, or find someone who braises better than I do, but back then my culinary skills did not go past grilling or barbecuing.

The deer were mainly eating introduced grasses and had little overlap with the diet of swamp wallabies, but seeing them close up, inside and out, changed the way I saw mammalian herbivores. They were machines for converting vegetation into meat or feces, two delectable sources of nutrition, which you prefer depending on what you have evolved to eat. Small herbivores, such as deer and kangaroos, do this well, but not on the same scale as elephants or the extinct Australian diprotodon. I will come back to this subject in later chapters.

My Ph.D. supervisor was Graeme Caughley, a wiry New Zealander whose book[43] revolutionized population ecology throughout the World. To get a better idea of his personality, I suggest that you read his book, The Deer Wars[40], but I will introduce him with his own words[177]:

> "Let me describe myself to allow you, the reader, to gauge my motives and my view of the world. Confessions are not the best source of truth but they give clues, even if one must read between the lines. Socially I am inept. I go to considerable lengths to avoid meeting new people. I find it a strain. Charming I am not. Politically I am uncommitted.

> I am good at research, not as good as I would like to be but somewhat better than average. Research is not quite the activity that most people think. It is a blood sport in which the opponents are other researchers. It must be the cleanest sport in the book because the ground rules, agreed to by the great majority of participants, ensure that in the long run the best win. Even in the short run not too many injustices occur. The

Photo 3.6 *Swamp wallabies are common in the Royal National Park. Photo by Bill Magnusson.*

ultimate high in research is not the discovery of a new fact – that you do almost once a week – but in writing a scientific publication that changes thinking. If you are good you might achieve that with every tenth paper. But when you do it you know that you have done it, even before anyone reads it, and then you sit back and say to yourself 'try to shoot that one down, you bastards.' When congratulated for the incredible insight displayed by 'your book' the correct response is 'which book'; or if you lobbed this mortar shell in the form of a paper you can practise 'Oh, that old thing' or 'Actually, I am not quite certain that I got it exactly right.' Research is a very serious business, it is the cutting edge of science, but it is also great fun.

You also need to know something about my attitude to killing animals. Take the extreme case, the killing of a large whale by means of an explosive harpoon. It is not pretty, and I think I would like myself better were I to view it as an aesthetic and moral outrage, but I do not. It is not important that you agree or disagree with this viewpoint. The importance lies in your realizing that this is the way I am and in interpreting what I write in the light of that knowledge. I have no strong feeling for individual wild animals although paradoxically I cried when the family cat was run over. However I get very emotional about the suggestion that a population of wild animals should be exterminated. Hence I am a conservationist but not an animal-liberationist."

I am not sure about science being a blood sport that involves few injustices, but most of what he said would apply to me as well. I do feel for individual wild animals, a result of studying individuals, sometimes for years. However, I do not confuse the feelings I have for individuals, even much-loved pets, with the need to conserve species and ecosystems. Graeme was interested in counting animals, the first step in any population-ecology analysis. That is much harder than most people imagine because you miss most of the individuals when you survey, especially if you are counting from an airplane. As Graeme often emphasized, this even applies to animals the size of elephants. Many methods had been developed for correcting estimates based on the proportion of individuals missed, but they were hard to apply for counts from aircraft, which are necessary for counting widespread animals in remote areas, such as kangaroos in the Australian arid zone.

Graeme and I co-authored a paper that presented a method of correcting for the number of animals missed in aerial surveys[101]. It was an extension of an idea he had published in 1974 and initially I just provided the field data to illustrate it. However, Janet helped streamline some of the mathematics. When Graeme first presented the idea to me I was in Northern Australia and he wrote me a long letter outlining the method. However, half way through a complicated calculation he wrote "and it follows" before jumping to the end result. Janet and I tried to piece together the bit that was missing, but without success. I wrote to Graeme and asked him to explain "it follows", but that was in the days before email and it took many weeks for his reply to return. The "obvious" part he had left out occupied several pages of closely-spaced

Photo 3.7 *Graeme Caughley (center) with Geoff Ross (left) and Ron Sinclair (right) preparing the plane for aerial survey in 1978. Photo by Gordon Grigg.*

equations, but in the mean time Janet had found a simpler method that reduced the logic behind the method to a few paragraphs of mathematical reasoning.

The paper was originally rejected because we had not evaluated the precision of our estimate, a basic requirement for any statistic used in population ecology. I therefore contacted a Professor at the University of New South Wales and asked if he could help. He understood statistics and graciously invited me to visit him and explain the problem. The range of errors for any estimate based on combinations of counts is well known and the Professor showed me the formulas for the error in each part of our equation and how to combine them. At first it looked impossible to me because the calculations often filled several lines of his neat handwriting, but he said "We can rearrange the equations this way, which gives these terms, which are known to tend to zero, so they can be dispensed with." All well and good, but when I plugged my data into the formulas he produced, the estimates of the size of the probable errors were several times our estimate of the mean; that is, our method had almost no value for prediction.

I returned to Sydney University dejected, but Graeme said "These calculations assume that the errors of each part of the equation are independent, but they are linked by the survey effort. Let's try adapting the formula from the Petersen estimate and see what happens?" We tried it and used numerical simulations to show that the error estimates were reasonably accurate and small enough to make the method useful. This was an important lesson for me. Many times subsequently I have used numerical simulations to show that some mathematical methods are of little use to biologists, and that others that mathematicians denigrate often give useful results.

The paper was accepted and Graeme made me first author despite my small contribution. The double-survey estimate we developed is often used to correct density estimates in aerial surveys of wildlife, but not everyone cites our paper. Shortly after, researchers in the USA developed the same method and published it in another journal. Initially, I thought that it was still pretty impressive to be the co-discoverers of a method, even if there was no way to determine who had the idea first. At that time, I had not heard of Stigler's Law, which says that an invention is never named after its discoverer. In 1982, George Seber, famous as codiscoverer of the Jolly-Seber analysis, published a review of survey methods and I read it eagerly to see if he had mentioned our paper. He misspelled my name, but quoted our use of the technique in the middle of a long list of examples of the use of the Petersen estimate; we had reinvented the wheel!

I wanted to see Graeme's aerial surveys in action, but I could only participate for a few days, which would not make it worthwhile to be included in the main team. However, the surveys had to take advantage of small landing fields distributed throughout the outback. For that, the flight crew needed a backup car to provide transport from the landing field to the nearest town providing accommodation, and I volunteered as one of the drivers.

Photo 3.8 *Graeme Caughley (left) and Geoff Ross (right) using the double-observer method we developed to survey for kangaroos from a light plane. Photo by Gordon Grigg.*

The mallee country in the interior of Australia is harsh and the animals that live there must be well adapted to life with little water and often sparse food. Mallee is a term given to various species of eucalypts that coppice to form what is little more than a big bush with many trunks that rarely pass five meters in height radiating from an underground tuber. We arrived at our rendezvous a day before the plane and I convinced the three others in the car to drive out to a large stand of mallee so that we could search for native animals on foot.

Geoff Ross, Graeme's assistant, recounted the first incident "An emu that had been racing alongside our car for what felt like ages disappeared off into the mallee only to return to the road still running full tilt and crashed into the side of the car, got up shook itself and ran off back into the mallee, a full 5 minutes after we'd stopped and were unloading Elliot traps from the rear of the car! We were perplexed as to how to explain the dent to the university officials. Little did we know at that moment the episode would be overshadowed by the loss of our car keys."

We wandered into the mallee and were soon out of sight of the road, but I have a fairly good sense of direction and I was sure that I would be able to find my way back to the car by nightfall. My father had taught me to feel the sun on my ear to maintain a straight bearing, otherwise you soon start to circle. People who live in wild places, such as the Australian aborigines, probably automatically take into account the trajectory of the sun throughout the day, but city folk like me have to consciously adapt to the sun's movement to maintain direction.

It was hot and the bare red clay between the mulga trees provided little protection for even small creatures. It had baked hard, like a tennis court, so we zigzagged around looking for fallen trunks or mounds of leaves that might provide cover for small animals. I don't remember what we found, but it must have been interesting because we didn't get back to the car until it was almost dark. That was when Geoff realized that we had lost the car keys and there were no spares. This was not good for us because we were more more than 20 km from the nearest town, but it was worse for the aerial surveys. Planes cost a lot of money to maintain, and the likely loss of several days because of our folley in not bringing a spare key would bring severe criticism from the university professors. We had also not been authorized to take side trips for scientific tourism.

I started to follow our tracks back into the mallee. Three people walking through the bush together usually leave abundant sign of where they have been, but the hard clay showed no sign of footprints. I could see where grass or small bushes had been crushed, but we had been zigzagging around looking for animals so sign did not necessarily indicate our general direction of travel. In any case, we didn't know where we had dropped the keys and I had to check every loop. It seemed hopeless, but there were no other alternatives.

I figured that I had back tracked about as far as we had penetrated the mallee, but the light was fading quickly and I could barely see the ground even though I was bent over and sometimes even crawling to see the tracks. The spoor led into a large open

Photo 3.9 *The mallee country is harsh and there is little cover for animals. Photo by Richard Loyn.*

patch of hard clay where searching for signs in the half dark would be useless. I stopped and decided to give up, but on the other side of the open area I saw a mallee stem bent over so that it was almost parallel to the ground. I remembered ducking under it just before we decided to return to the car, so I walked across, and there were the keys. They must have fallen from someone's pocket when they slipped under the branch.

We met the plane and did not recount our folly to anyone, but the incident brought home to me how much modern science depends on logistics, and sometimes the most important aspects of those logistics can be as simple as making sure that you have spare car keys!

Much of what I know about aerial surveys comes from experience in research with Gordon Grigg, at that time a lecturer at Sydney University. We had surveyed for crocodile nests[102,103] and he was the pilot in the kangaroo surveys I described in the last section[70]. He invited me to take part in surveys of humpback whales in collaboration with Dr Bill Dawbin, a New Zealander famous for his studies of tuatara, the last remnant of an ancient reptile lineage that looks much like lizards, and research on the migrations of humpback whales[15]. I had lectures from Bill Dawbin as an undergraduate, but had never interacted closely with him until the whale surveys.

Gordon had laid out a zig-zag flight plan taking us alternately out to sea and then back towards land. As we had several observers, we would be able to use the double-survey technique to estimate the number of whales. Gordon had put tapes onto the wing struts so that we would count in a fixed strip and be able to calculate the area covered. The problem was that we found few whales. At that time there were several thousand humpback whales known to migrate up the east coast of Australia in winter, and less than a dozen southern right whales, which had almost been sent to extinction by whalers. The sea wasn't very choppy, but the waves and clouds continually produced dark shapes that could be confused with a whale. We had to concentrate despite the glare, so I was relieved when Gordon landed on a small grass landing strip in the middle of cattle pasture for our midday break.

We went to a small hotel for lunch, but I was disappointed when we found that they only served beer and nuts. Bill didn't seem to be put off by the prospect of a liquid lunch, but I was a teetotaler, and Gordon couldn't drink because he was the pilot. Seeing that we weren't satisfied with just a beer-nut lunch, Bill pulled out a small can of frog legs and gleefully set it on the table for us to share. It would have been churlish to let him know that we really wanted more than one frog leg and a handful of nuts, so we smiled as we munched.

We saw only a few whales on the way back, but Bill was very excited every time we saw a whale, and he didn't seem perturbed that the number of whales we saw was too low to allow any statistical conclusions. I appreciated his knowledge, but his lack of interest in statistics made him seem quaint and old fashioned to a university student who was constantly being evaluated on his ability to convert animals into data. Bill wanted to know how the whales chose their repertoire of songs as they swam along the coast, and how they collectively choose to change the songs between and within years[55]; questions we couldn't answer with the type of data we were collecting.

Photo 3.10 *Whales are easy to see when they display near boats, but are hard to locate from a plane when in the open sea. Photo by Bill Magnusson.*

It would be years before I realized that to really know animals you have to see them as individuals as well as numbers. Almost two decades later, shortly before his death, I visited Bill in his flat in Sydney. After several enjoyable hours discussing whales and whale songs, Bill unrolled old Japanese scrolls depicting whale hunting that he had recently acquired. They were long and stretched almost from one side of the room to the other. We sat cross legged on the floor to admire them as Japanese story tellers would have done in ancient times. The narrative was told by elaborate paintings and Bill lovingly traced his fingers over the designs as he explained the intricacies of catching a whale from a fragile open boat. He was not talking about concepts or numbers, but real people and real whales locked together in a life and death struggle. I wished that I had the wisdom to appreciate his insights when I first met him.

Photo 3.11 *Bill Dawbin disembarking on Stevens Island in 1973. Photo by Gordon Grigg.*

CHAPTER 4 - PH.D. CANDIDATE, NORTHERN TERRITORY

A rock painting of a thylacine in Kakadu National Park. The species has been extinct in the area for over 3000 years, but the aboriginal people still know its natural history. Photo by Bill Magnusson.

I collected data for my Ph.D. thesis[90] in Arnhem Land in the far north of Australia between 1975 and 1978 and I took the opportunity to learn about the tropical species that did not occur as far south as Sydney. Arnhem Land is a vast area reserved for the use of the traditional owners, and was one of the few areas in Australia where the aboriginal communities still lived much as their ancestors had. You can still see rock art in Kakadu National Park depicting a thylacine, even though the species has been extinct in the area for over 3000 years.

Grahame Webb, the field biologist in charge of the project, recounted the following story. "When I heard that there were rock paintings of thylacines, I got some colour photos of them and asked Jacky Adjaral did he know anything about them. He could speak multiple dialects and languages (about 15+ from memory), and started to give me the names for the animal in different dialects. When I asked him had he ever seen one, he said no, only the doctors could see them. I said 'well I'm a doctor - could I see them?', and he said no, only the clever doctors like old Anka! When I was with Jacky and Anka at Momega, Anka whose English was pretty basic, started to tell me all about their habits, but it was hard to understand. For Jacky, this was conformation that Anka could see them! So, I started a long but gentle questioning to find out if Anka himself had seen one with his own eyes. It turned out he had not, but had learned all about them from his father."

I was intrigued by the story and hoped to be able to take advantage of the aborigines' unique knowledge to find other species that were virtually unknown to modern science. I also started setting aluminum box traps of the sort that I had used to catch the rats for my honors project. The forest around Maningrida at the end of the dry season was more open than the forest near Sydney. The people set fire to the spear grass that dominated the areas between the scattered trees and the short regrowth provided food for kangaroos and made it easy to walk. I hoped to catch a northern quoll because I had never seen a wild quoll. These prettily spotted marsupials have habits and body form like weasels or civets and were once the dominant small carnivores in Australia, though all species are now rare and endangered. However, I only caught dusky rats, members of a species that also occurs in Papua New Guinea and Indonesia. Although I was pleased to see them in the wild, they were much like the bush rats I had worked on in the south.

Photo 4.1 *Anka (second from left) still knew the natural history of the thylacine thousands of years after it became extinct in the area. Photo by Bill Green.*

My thesis was on the ecology of crocodiles and I had little time to explore the dryland areas around Maningrida. Most of my time was spent in boats around riverine and mangrove forests, so I asked my aboriginal friends which species I was likely to find. They described a rat with a white tail and white marks on its body that lived in hollow mangrove trunks. It was likely a black-footed tree rat, but there were enough differences, especially the reports of white blotches on its back that I suspected that it might be a new species. However, no-one ever caught one for me. They also described what appeared to be a water rat, and that stimulated my curiosity. The same species of water rat I had seen as a child occurred in the region, but I couldn't imagine how it could survive in mangrove forests teeming with crocodiles, and it had a close relative, the enigmatic false water rat.

The false water rat had been described in 1889, but I had not looked carefully at the descriptions and naively assumed that it would look like a water rat. We sometimes saw rats swimming across the river, especially in floods, but all that we got close enough to identify were dusky rats, a species common on the floodplains, but not aquatic. We also saw some mouse-sized grey rodents in the mangroves during floods, but they dropped into the water and disappeared before we could catch them.

Other researchers had built a small wooden shed topped by a corrugated-iron roof to serve as a blind for watching crocodiles on the floodplain of the lower Tomkinson River. The construction stood in the middle of an open patch of black mud, but was close to mangroves and low sedges. Floods, sun and salt water combined to destroy the blind, and its components ended up strewn across the mud flat. One sheet of corrugated iron had fallen on the tangle of low sedges beside the river and I turned it over to see what small animals might be hiding under it.

Something had constructed narrow tunnels in the mud among the sedges and a mouse ran into the sedges before I could collect my wits, but there was another crouched in a small recess. It tried to hide under some sedges, which gave me the chance to pin it with my hand and scoop it into a cloth bag I carried for collecting snakes. I looked into the bag and saw that it was unlike any of the small native rodents I had seen in southern Australia; I was fairly sure that I had a new species.

Back at the research base in Maningrida, I constructed a roomy cage for the rat from a plastic crate and other bits and pieces. It huddled under a broken vase I gave it for protection and sniffed the air, presumably trying to make sense of its new home. About the size of an overfed white mouse, its main distinguishing feature was its head, which was more heavily built that that of a similar-sized mouse.

I had no idea what it ate, so I offered it a variety of foods, including peanut butter, nuts, bread, fruits and leafy vegetables; all good mouse fare. However, it would only eat the vegetables if I didn't give it animal foods, such as lizards, fish and crabs. One of the crabs I put in the cage was as big as my little furry captive and I just left it in the cage so that it would remain fresh until I had time to dismember it into bite-sized pieces.

Photo 4.2 *The interface between mangroves and sedge plain, like the site where we captured our first false water rat. Photo by Bill Magnusson.*

The mouse seemed curious about the crab and approached it slowly, bobbing its head from side to side when it got closer. This seemed to make the crab nervous, and it spread its claws wide open, wider in fact than the length of the mouse's body. So quickly that I could hardly see the movement, the rat bit at the crab's face and leapt backwards. The crab swept its claws forward, but they closed on thin air and the rat dived forward again and bit at the basal attachment of the claw to the crab's body, severing it in one quick bite. The crab now had only one claw, which it held up to one side. The rat repeated its lunge at the central eyestalks and when the crab swept its claw across in defense, the rat snapped it at the base. I would never have put the crab in the cage if I had thought that the mouse would attack it because the crab looked as though it could easily kill the rat with its heavy claws.

The rat then calmly walked around the unarmed crab, grabbed it from behind and flipped it over. The crab could do nothing as the mouse snapped off each of its legs. The little animal must have done this with great dexterity, because it is not easy to snap the legs off a crab, and the joints were as wide as the rat's gape. I watched as it ate most of the crab, with the exceptions of the tips of the claws and the hardest part of the shell, then waddled back to its shelter with its overextended belly dragging on the ground.

My captive was an accomplished hunter of any small prey I gave it, but its treatment of crabs was stereotyped and effective. Given that crabs are abundant on the floodplain where I collected it, I assumed that they must be its most common prey in the wild. Sure that I had discovered a new species, I searched the banks of the Tomkinson River, turning over any debris on the ground and searching the low bushes when the tide flooded the area, but to no avail. The traps I set caught nothing but crabs.

Janet was doing her Ph.D. on data she collected while travelling in a small ship during the dry season. Two months after we had captured the mouse on the Tomkinson River, the boat was anchored in Andranango Creek on Melville Island. The survey team included Graeme Wells, who was collecting data on mangrove forests for his Ph.D. thesis. Graeme found a mud mound at the base of a mangrove tree, and when they opened it they found a ball-shaped nest with three mice: a female and two young. Janet realized that they were the same species as the specimen I had in captivity. She wanted to keep them alive, but the leader of the expedition said that there was too much chance of them escaping; he told her to kill and preserve the adult, and the young died soon after. This was sad news for the little family, but now we could examine the skull. In those days, before genetic analyses became readily available, species identification was mainly based on skull characteristics.

The skull even led to the discovery of another specimen. Janet was collecting stomach contents from crocodiles, and about a month later she caught a crocodile on the Tomkinson River, 50 km upstream from where we had caught the rat under the corrugated iron. Among the things in its stomach were fragments of the skull of another individual of the same species.

Photo 4.3 *Graeme Wells taking notes on a mud nest of the false water rat at the base of a mangrove tree. A female and two young were found inside. Photo by Bill Green.*

We took all of the specimens, including my captive, back to Sydney and I looked for help to describe the species. Someone suggested I talk to Jack Mahoney, a specialist in mammals who worked as a technician in the first-year biology laboratories at Sydney University. Jack looked at the skull and immediately recognized it as being from a false water rat, the species I had been looking for! It hadn't occurred to me that the false water rat might be a mouse that was adapted to live near, but not in, water!

Jack had identified another skull in a museum collection a few years earlier. The species had been reported from the Northern Territory the year before[137] and Trevor Redhead graciously sent us a copy of the still unpublished manuscript. I also found a book[176] by Ellis Troughton who, apparently without ever seeing a specimen in the wild, and based only on morphology, concluded that the false water rat was a basically terrestrial rat specialized for feeding on hard-shelled aquatic prey.

With records from the eastern and northern coasts of Australia, and several unpublished records, it seemed that the species might not be as rare as people had assumed. Maybe it wasn't the lack of rats, but the lack of biologists in the mangroves that made the species appear to be uncommon. We wrote[100] "Because mangrove habitats on the coastal sections of most of the rivers between McKay in Queensland and Daly River in the Northern Territory are similar to those in which *X. myoides* [false water rat] have been found, it is likely that more intensive collections in these areas will show the species to be more widespread than previously thought." Subsequent studies have shown that to be true; the species has even been recorded from Papua New Guinea, and surveys for mud nests, similar to that which we reported, have even led to estimates of density[75]. For me, it was a lesson in how our impressions of the abundance of species often reflect more the behavior of the researchers than that of the animals.

I sent the captive specimen to Chris Watts and Peter Baverstock in South Australia because they hoped to find a mate for it and start a breeding colony. Unfortunately, they never did and it died alone in captivity. More than forty years later I received an email from Dean Portelli asking me about a false water rat in the Australian Museum that I had purportedly captured on the Goyder River in Arnhem Land. The Museum label was obviously wrong as I had never been on the Goyder River and Dean started sleuthing to track down the origin of the specimen. As my specimen was the only one known to have been captured about that time, I suggested that Dean contact Peter Baverstock to see if he remembered what had happened to it. Unfortunately, he didn't have any records of what had been done with the specimen and the origin of the Australian Museum specimen remains a mystery.

The exchange of emails did lead to Peter recounting the following story about the false water rat that reveals other details about its biology. He wrote "Actually I have a good *Xeromys* [false water rat] story (and there is not many people who can say that). In around 1973 I was staying at a B&B on Macleay Island - an Island in southern Moreton Bay. At the time *Xeromys* was known from only 15 specimens, the southernmost from Cooloola. Anyway, the B&B owners heard that I had some experience with animals, and asked my advice on how they could catch and kill this

Photo 4.4 The false water rat is a little bigger than a mouse and probably spends little time in the water. Photo by Bill Magnusson.

"rat" that kept swimming in their fish pond and eating their goldfish! "It's got these long whiskers" they said. I must say I took great delight in informing them that they were hosting one of the rarest animals in the world, and that the "solution" was to keep restocking their fish pond." I believe that Peter's story is the only report of the species catching free-swimming fish.

We know a lot more about the false water rat now than was known in the 1970s, but it remains one of the most enigmatic of the Australian rodents and I would love to have time to go back and learn more about it.

The Liverpool River had flooded, making a freshwater sea 10 km across, even well upstream of its mouth near Maningrida. I had been trying to save my equipment from the flood and I was heading home tired, cold and dispirited at the loss of my electronic thermometer. Only the tops of the trees marked where the main channel ran and the eddies buffeted the 7m boat and its powerful 50 hp outboard motor. All sorts of flotsam was swirling in the muddy water, but a short tube pushing against the current caught my attention. It was the nose of an echidna, swimming with most of its body submerged. I brought the boat around and used an oar to hoist the animal aboard. It appeared exhausted and just huddled against the side of the boat. As there was nowhere to release it, I took it back to Maningrida.

Echidnas are monotremes or egg-laying marsupials. In this sense they are primitive, but in all others they are pretty advanced. They can withstand extreme conditions and are able to subsist on a diet of ants. They can be found in the hottest deserts and in places in the Australian high country that remain under snow for months at a time. They are the only Australian mammal whose distribution extends from the tip of Tasmania in the south to Cape York Peninsula in the far north, and they can also be found in New Guinea. It may be that they are inferior, but they certainly don't seem to know that.

The echidna I had rescued appeared to be blind, but it got around well by using touch and smell. I fed it meat mixed with raw egg, which it lapped up. Echidnas are very strong, and the pens we had for crocodiles and other animals would not restrain it, so I let it go in my flat, which had 1m walls below all the windows. Two days later it was gone, leaving a hole in the window mosquito mesh. As most people do, I underestimated the echidna and thought that it would not able to climb the 2 x 4 inch wall studs. I added "expert climber" to my list of unexpected echidna capabilities. I hope that it survived and got back to the bush, but being an echidna in the middle of a township with dozens of expert aboriginal hunters does not bode well for survival.

Another animal that I found in the river during a flood was a baby nankeen night heron. These beautiful birds are rich brown colored with a black cap and two long tassels on the back of the head when adult, but juveniles are mottled brown with streaks on the chest. I fed it small fish and it grew quickly. At first I thought it cute that it would follow me around and I would quickly find it some fish. However, if I

Photo 4.5 *Echidnas have a wider geographic and climatic range than any other Australian mammal. Photo by Bill Magnusson.*

didn't have fish it would show its annoyance by pecking my heels aggressively, often drawing blood. As soon as I saw that it could catch fish in a shallow basin, I released it in mangroves beside the Tomkinson River. I hope it survived, but few animals raised in captivity or "rescued" after they have been injured survive when reintroduced to the wild. It is probably more a "feel-good" activity for the humans than something to avoid animal suffering or bolster dwindling wildlife populations.

I was spending most of my time on the river, and it became a second home. Each bend was different and patches of grass or trees on the banks that had blended into the overall landscape on my first trip became individuals living their own lives and harboring animals that needed them. Birds that perched on the same branches became regular landmarks and made me feel that all was as it should be. The brahminy kites were especially important, their brilliant white heads and breasts contrasting with their rich brown back and wings.

I was usually alone, but I did not feel lonely. I felt that they were my trees and my birds, keeping watch over my crocodiles and my river. I had particular affection for a pair of green pigmy geese that I always encountered on the upper Liverpool River. Of course, these feelings had nothing to do with reality. The true owners of the land were the aboriginal people, who had connections to the land that I could hardly imagine.

I realized this when I had aboriginal guides or gave people lifts up the river. Jacky Adjaral often showed me where to find crocodile nests, and it did not take long for me to realize that the world he saw and felt was much richer than mine. This was brought home to me when we gave a lift to Anka, a holy man with great knowledge of aboriginal lore; the man who told Grahame Webb about the thylacines. He sat with his grandchildren in the middle of the boat and would not let them close to the sides. At first I though he was worried that they would fall out, but he pointed to the steering cables that ran along the sides of the boat and he explained with gestures that they were dangerous. It was then that I realized that he thought that they were electrical cables. I jumped when another man accompanying us leapt to his feet, swung his shotgun over my shoulder and shot one of my pigmy geese. Both he and Anka were so happy when he plucked the bird out of the water. It was their bird and death was as much a part of their existence as life. My feelings were those of a silly city dweller, but that didn't make them any less real for me.

I often went into the bush with Nuggarboi, an old man with bandy legs and wide grin, and his son, Nalawade, who was about my height and well built, but had lost most of his fingers and toes to leprosy. Although they were experts with spears, neither was proficient with a shotgun. Their weapon was an old 16-guage held together by nails and fencing wire. As I was a better shot, they sometimes asked me to shoot a goanna for them if the big lizard was high in a tree and they hadn't brought their spears. I didn't like killing the lizards and I was even more reticent when they asked me to shoot a red-tailed black cockatoo. It was perched on the top of a mangrove tree swaying in the wind. My friends had spent a lot of time helping me and couldn't see how I could refuse without offending them. To say that I just wanted to watch the bird would have been unintelligible for them.

Photo 4.6 Jacky Adjaral (left), his brother Jiminmulla (right) and
Grahame Webb (center) in 1974. Photo by Bill Green.

I sighted down the barrel, which was at an odd angle to the stock and tried to follow the movement of the bird that was being buffeted by the wind. The shot knocked it out of the tree and Nuggarboi ran over and grabbed it gleefully. We would be many hours exploring a swamp with dense sharp-edged sedges that were often taller than we were, so Nuggarboi opted to hang the cockatoo in a small tree until we returned. He hooked its wings over two forks so that it was spread-eagled with its head drooping on its chest.

We had a very successful day and even though exhausted I was cheerful as we returned from the swamp, but there was a cacophony coming from where we had left the cockatoo's body. The bird had revived and, though badly hurt, it was calling weakly as it tried to lift its head and free its wings. The raucous calls were coming from a dozen black cockatoos that had heard its calls and came to help. They fluttered higher into the tree when we arrived, but peered down and alternately screamed at us and gave heart-rending wailing sounds as if in compassion for their fallen companion. Nuggarboi just trotted over, grabbed the bird and broke its neck, not even looking up at the rest. I was glad that he didn't ask me to shoot another one because I don't think I would have been able to after receiving such a scolding from the assembled birds.

A few months later, Nuggarboi, Nalawade, I and Fred, a botany student, were surveying for crocodile nests on the Goomadeer River, about 40 km east of Maningrida. Nuggarboi swung his gun past my head and shot at a water buffalo standing on the bank. We had not brought food and planned to live off the land, but a buffalo was much larger than we could possibly eat. The shot hit the animal mid body and it lumbered away from the bank.

The aborigines used solid shot to bring down large animals. They loaded the cartridges themselves, stuffing a lead fishing sinker into the open end. As they had no lessons in fluid dynamics they assumed that the best form for the lead would be long and thin, like a spear head. The result was that the projectile came out of the unrifled barrel tumbling and often taking an unpredictable trajectory. It carried a heavy punch, which would knock down a kangaroo, but was unlikely to penetrate far into the massive body of a buffalo.

I ran the boat into the bank and Nuggarboi and Nalawade ran after the buffalo. Three shots later, the buffalo was obviously distressed, but it was still on its feet and the aborigines had run out of ammunition. We had a 12-guage riot gun and commercial Brenneke cartridges with solid slugs. I didn't want to leave a suffering animal so I picked up the riot gun, but Fred asked "Can I shoot it?"

I agreed immediately, as I don't like killing animals, but I said "Shoot it in the head. The Brenneke won't penetrate the body, so you'll have to get very close to knock it out with a shot to the skull."

Photo 4.7 Red-tailed black cockatoos are highly social, sometimes gathering in flocks of hundreds. Photo by Bill Magnusson.

Perhaps because he was nervous of the buffalo, Fred shot from a distance, putting the only two slugs we had into its belly. I was pissed off because I should have taken responsibility, and now I would have to leave a suffering animal that we had no way to kill. Buffalo do terrible damage to the natural systems in the Northern Territory and the fewer the better, but that does not justify unnecessary cruelty.

I said that we'd have to go back to the boat as there was nothing we could do, but Nuggarboi said "No, I teach my son finish buffalo with knife", and he held up the knife with a thin ten-inch blade he used for cleaning fish.

Neither Fred nor I thought that it was possible, and we climbed into the only two mangrove trees that looked as though they were too large for the buffalo to knock over easily. The buffalo was on a small a patch of mud flat, but was surrounded by stands of mangrove saplings.

Nuggarboi gave the knife to Nalawade and motioned for his son to follow him. The old man was short and stood only as high as the buffalo's rump. Nalawade was taller, but his lack of fingers meant that he could not hold the knife in one hand, so he secured it between his palms.

Nuggarboi trotted in a wide circle to approach the buffalo from behind. I was nervous three meters up a tree, and there was Nuggarboi only a few feet behind the buffalo. He pointed to a spot beside the buffalo's spine just in front of its back legs. Nalawade sprung forward and drove the knife deep into the buffalo's back, which swung around, breaking the blade, and started to chase the hunters. They were dodging among the mangrove saplings, but I couldn't see how they could get away. The thin trees were a barrier to humans, but the buffalo just ran through them as though they were grass stems. Nevertheless, every time it swung its head to gouge them, they had dodged in the other direction milliseconds before. It looked like expert choreography; if either hunter had tripped the other, both would have died.

I have tried to cut the throat of buffalo calf with a moderately sharp knife and was unable to do it. I couldn't see how someone with no fingers could cut through the tough back hide, and now the broken blade was only the length of my index finger. Nevertheless, when the buffalo tired and stood still among the mangroves, Nuggarboi crept up behind it again, pointed to the spot that was now seeping blood and Nalawade drove the blade in again, this time maintaining pressure to slice down the animals back. He only opened the wound by a finger width before the buffalo turned and was after them again.

By now my feet were aching from being jammed into the fork of the mangrove's muddy branches, but there was no way that I would have had the courage to climb down onto the muddy ground where the enraged buffalo was chasing the hunters. I lost count of the number of times Nuggarboi crept up on the buffalo and Nalawade ripped at the gaping wound. Having shown how to do it once there seemed no point in Nuggarboi leading Nalawade in, but this show of courage and nimbleness seemed to be part of the lesson. If someone died, they would die together.

Photo 4.8 *Wild buffalo are now common in Arnhem Land. Photo by Grahame Webb.*

Finally, the buffalo started to get unsteady on its back legs, and I realized what Nuggarboi was planning, they were cutting through the fillet steak that runs along the spine. Without that, the buffalo lost control of its rear end and fell over. As soon as it did, Nalawade rushed in and used the opportunity to slash right down its side. We could not take most of the meat and had no way to preserve it, so Nuggarboi just cut out the fillet steaks and left the rest to the crows. As we walked away I thought I saw movement from the buffalo and said that it was still alive, but Nuggarboi said "No, that one dead." As we climbed into the boat, the buffalo bellowed and I said that it was still alive, but Nuggarboi just repeated "No, that one dead."

It was then that I realized the difference between dead for me and dead for the hunters. For them, the animal was dead when it had no more chance of living. The fact that it was still breathing was irrelevant. I understand their point of view, and I have no doubt that I would feel the same if I had to kill my own food everyday and felt at one with all the world, both living and dead. Nevertheless, the sound of that buffalo bellowing in agony haunts me to this day.

I was beginning to see that the differences between the way the aborigines saw the world and the vision of the white colonizers were much deeper than I imagined. We had money to pay aboriginal assistants and many people in Maningrida were eager for the opportunity to make some money, but they were mainly the younger men; the old men didn't seem to understand or want money. Nuggarboi was a prime example. He often came and suggested that we go somewhere in the boat, and it was always somewhere interesting for me. However, he refused the money when I offered it to him, even if I was paying somone else who accompanied us. It seemed that our outings were a present from a friend and that he would lose all pleasure if they were just a business deal. The deep friendship we felt was something that money couldn't buy.

Of course, I found other ways to reciprocate. If I knew that he was planning a trip up the Liverpool River, I would invent some reason that I had to collect data there so that I could give him a lift, but in general love and commodities do not mix. Things changed when a famous anthropologist visited Maningrida and stayed at our research base. He had written a book about Maningrida and was famous for detailing the complex marriage system of the local people that seemed to maximize outbreeding. His wife was an expert on one of the local languages. I was pleased to have the chance to learn from him and helped in every way I could. I thought that we had a very good relationship, but when he returned to Sydney he published a newspaper article alleging that the project exploited the aborigines and gave as an example the fact that I didn't pay some of the people that accompanied me in the bush.

The head of the project was obviously not happy about the adverse publicity and decreed that I could not take people with me unless I paid them. I remember the first time we came back from a trip and I pushed the money into Nuggarboi's hand. He handed it back and said "No!" I told him I had no choice and he had to take it. Tears welled up in his eyes, and stumbled off dejectedly. It seemed that all we had experienced and the love we felt came to nothing more than a few pieces of paper. I have rarely in my life felt such emotional pain at rejecting someone so close to me. I eventually got back his confidence and found ways of paying without having to put the

Photo 4.9 *Water buffalos look calm, but are extremely dangerous when aroused. Photo by Grahame Webb.*

money directly in his hand, but I realized that we had a value system that the white anthropologist would never be able to understand even though he was considered the leading expert on aboriginal social systems.

A special way of showing friendship in aboriginal society is sharing food. In fact, this is a behavior common to most human societies. Very often Adjaral or Nuggarboi would turn up at the front door with a huge piece of dugong meat and hand it to us with all the seriousness of a young man offering an engagement ring to his girlfriend. We were pleased that they were expressing their friendship and we cooked the meat as we would a piece of chicken or steak. The taste was good, but I always found the meat gritty and this took away much of the pleasure of eating it. I couldn't imagine why dugongs would accumulate grit in their flesh, but didn't think much about it after finishing each meal.

One day, I was on the beach when hunters brought in a dugong they had harpooned on the other side of the bay. They pulled it out of the boat and laid it on the beach with great difficulty. A dugong can be two and half meters and weigh up to 300 kg. The men were laughing and many people gathered to share the abundant meat. It had to be eaten that day because, except for us, nobody had refrigerators and all food had to be eaten fresh. Nuggarboi called me over to see the dugong close up. A long slash had opened the dugong's belly and he skillfully sliced of a large flap of meat that had once clothed the animal's ribs. The meat was covered in congealed blood, which didn't seem to worry anyone else who was carrying off pieces to the home fire. However, Nuggarboi knew enough about whites to know that they are finnicky about things they consider dirty. Therefore, he walked down to the water's edge and washed the meat where the small waves were breaking. It came out with no congealed blood, but I realized why the dugong meat we ate was gritty – we were eating beach sand!

We were sitting around the dinner table one night accompanied by a young boy who was the son of one of aboriginal elders who most helped the project. I'll call him Ricky, but can't give his real name for reasons that will become apparent. Ricky was close to the members of the research team, especially the biologist in charge, and he joined in the friendly verbal sparring of the group. We served dugong and Ricky ate it with relish. We were all surprised when he licked the knife after eating the last morsel and asked "What was that?"

Assuming that he didn't recognize it because of the way we cooked it, someone said "It's dugong". Ricky's complexion whitened and he said "No, not dugong! It's my dreaming, they'll spear me if they know I ate it." That is when we realized why he had never tasted dugong meat; aborigines do not eat their totem animals even if other members of their family are doing so. Ricky eventually calmed down and we convinced him that nobody would ever know that he had eaten the dugong. There were obviously complex relationships between the aborigines and the animals in their environment, and no simple rules applied to everyone.

Photo 4.10 *Dugong is a favorite food of the aboriginal people. Photo by Graeme Wells.*

That was as close as I got to knowing anything about dugongs in northern Australia, but surprisingly it would be my reputation as a dugong expert that would get me the job I have held for the last 40 years. I'll leave that story till later.

Another delicacy for the aborigines was flying-fox meat. Flying foxes are large bats that congregate in tens or hundreds of thousands in roosts during the day, spreading out at night to feed on nectar and fruit. At dusk, we often saw them flying lazily among the paperbark trees lining the river, and sometimes we saw uncounted thousands of them forming lines that darkened the sky as they flew out to sea. We couldn't imagine where they were going because there was nothing but open water between us and Papua New Guinea.

Bats probably first evolved soon after the extinction of the dinosaurs and pterosaurs, but the fine bones of bats do not fossilize well. The oldest known fossil bat is a little over 50 million years old. There is consensus that there are two major lines of bats, broadly corresponding to megabats and microbats, but there is contention as to whether some of the microbats we will meet in later chapters should be included with the megabats. Most of the megabats rely on sight to get around, whereas most of the microbats also use sonar for navigation. All classifications regard the flying foxes, which fly by sight, eat pollen, nectar and fruits, and form conspicuous roosting aggregations, as a distinct lineage. They are the principal bat frugivores in the Old World, whereas the frugivorous bats in the Americas come from a microbat lineage.

The bats we saw were mainly black flying foxes, though little red flying foxes also occurred in the area. A southern species, the grey-headed flying fox, is common around Sydney, and can be seen in fig trees in city parks, but I never took much notice of them when I was a kid; they were just silhouettes against the night sky. I got to see the northern flying foxes much closer when Adjaral offered me a delicacy. The hunters had killed many flying foxes at a roost and Adjaral handed me one with a beaming smile. It had been thrown into the coals to cook, which had singed off most of its fur, contorted the wings and legs backwards, and contracted its lips so that its teeth were showing in a permanent grimace.

Except for fish, white Australians usually don't look into the eyes of their victims as they eat meat, and I was no exception. It felt strange to hold the warm body and split the skin on its chest so that I could bite into the slightly cooked flight muscles. The flesh was oily and had a pungent smell, like a mixture of fruit and melaleuca oil. I certainly didn't find it very appetizing, but I couldn't disappoint my friends and carefully chewed the meat off all the bones. All the other game they gave me was delicious, but whenever I saw someone about to share the results of their hunt with me I hoped it wouldn't be flying fox.

Gordon Grigg's wife, Jan, worked in the Entomology Department at Sydney University, and Gordon asked if I could get her specimens of a species of nycteribiid fly. These flightless parasites never leave their flying-fox hosts, so the only way to get one was by collecting a flying fox. Janet also needed fur from flying foxes so that she could identify the hairs in crocodile stomachs. As the aborigines only ever brought

Photo 4.11 *A single dugong can supply food for the whole camp, but some people must not eat it. Photo by Graeme Wells.*

me cooked specimens, I would have to shoot one myself. This was feasible as we had a permit to collect any wildlife necessary for our crocodile studies.

Janet and I were travelling up the Liverpool River in an open boat when a flock of flying foxes took wing from the melaleuca trees that lined the bank. Flying foxes generally don't fly during the day, and I assumed that they had been attracted by the melaleuca blossoms that were exuding a heavy scent. I let go of the steering wheel and reached for the riot gun that belonged to the project. Its short barrel meant that it scattered shot over a wide area, which was good for collecting biological specimens at short range, but not so good when the target was 50m away, as were these flying foxes. I swung around, fired at a straggler, and it fell into the river.

I passed the wheel to Janet, who brought the boat around and headed towards the flying fox, which was bobbing in the current. My plan was grab it from the front of the boat, but the engine stalled as we got close and the Janet couldn't stop the boat as it passed over the flying fox, which disappeared under the hull only to surface again in our wake. Janet started the motor and turned the boat so that I could slip an oar under the flying fox and swing it into the boat. It wasn't dead as I had hoped it would be, but one wing drooped uselessly by its side.

As soon as it hit the deck, it scurried up the side wall of the boat and remained perched on the edge. It looked down at the river, over to us, down at the river again and then climbed back onto the deck, apparently preferring to risk its life with us than jumping into the river. I should have killed it immediately, but I looked into its big black eyes which seemed to crying for mercy and I couldn't. I said to Janet "We'll put in a box and take it back to the base. There we can collect the fur and the flies and I'll see if I can fix its wing."

The flying fox was easy to handle in the laboratory, but I was wary of its sharp teeth, which it showed whenever we got close. I had no trouble collecting the hair and parasites, but the shot had shattered the long bone on one wing, just past the finger with its long hooked claw that the bat used to climb. If it was to survive, I would have to amputate the end of the wing. That wasn't hard because the tip was attached only by the thin flight membrane. I pulled the skin down around the exposed bone and sewed it together as best I could, with Janet holding the struggling bat. It did not take long, but we only had local anaesthetic, so I thought that the shock might kill it.

I made a small cage with a wooden rod for the bat to hang from and left it till the next morning. Today you can find how to look after injured flying foxes and what to feed them on the internet, but in 1975 there was no internet, and few people looked after injured wildlife. I had no idea what I could feed it, or even whether it would eat, and we had no fresh fruit or flowers to offer. All we had was tinned fruit salad, which was not all that appetizing, even for us. Nevertheless, when I offered the bat a piece of pear it grabbed it and chewed on it for a few minutes before spitting out the pulp. Until then, I didn't know that flying foxes generally don't swallow the pieces of fruit they bite off, they just drink the juice and spit out the rest. At first he ate about half a can of fruit a day, but we reduced it to about a third of a can when I supplemented his diet with egg custard.

Photo 4.12 *Flying foxes usually hang in trees during the day. Photo by Bill Magnusson.*

Hanging upside down, which is right side up for a bat, it was two handspans long, its head was as long as my thumb, and its outstretched wings originally would have had a span of over a meter. Its teeth, especially the prominent canines, and sharp incisors looked more like those of a meat eater than a fruit lover. I had seen how dangerous rodents, such as sewer rats, could be when cornered and imagined that it might be hard to handle the bat. However, the flying fox, which we named "Fang", was always calm and seem to regard us as friends from the outset. This makes sense as we had rescued him from the river and and gave him food; I hope that he never knew that we were the demons that had knocked him out of the sky!

There was no-one to look after him in the Northern Territory, so I got permission from the Wildlife Department to take him to Sydney. It is now known that flying foxes can carry rabies-like viruses and people taking care of them should be suitably immunized, but no-body knew that in 1975. My mother fell in love with Fang immediately and said that she would look after him when I was travelling. At first, he seemed to do well in Sydney. The broken bone cut through the skin and I had to pare it off. This was obviously painful for Fang and he swung around, grabbed by thumb and pinched down on it with his massive teeth to let me know that it hurt, but as soon as he was sure that I realized that it was hurting, he released my thumb without damaging it and let me get on with tending to the wound. I have never seen such trust in any wild animal, or for that matter in any domestic animal.

This was not the passivity of a dove facing a superior opponent. Fang didn't like to be cooped up in the cage I made for him in our outdoor laundry, so I strung garden stakes so that he could climb out into trees in the garden during the day. My mother would call him down so that she could lock him in the laundry at night in case some predator, such as the neighbor's cat came after him when no-one was around.

My father generally didn't interact with Fang at first, but one night my mother was out and Dad decided to be helpful and put him in the laundry. The bat was in a small tree and didn't come when dad called, so he used a ladder to climb up. When Dad grabbed him by the legs to pull him off the branch, Fang drove his teeth to the bone in Dad's finger and used his wing claw to open a cut across his wrist. Showing great restraint, my father just climbed down the ladder, treated his wounds, and left the bat in the tree until my mother arrived.

In fact, Fang seemed to be able to look after himself in confrontations with cats and other domestic animals. The first time I saw a cat stalking him I was ready to come to his rescue, but as soon as he saw the cat, Fang started climbing towards it with one wing outstretched and his teeth bared. The cat ran off and never stalked him again. Even small dogs were not a problem. My Grandfather brought his little terrier on a leash when he came to visit. The dog was straining at the leash and barking at Fang, who was hanging in a low tree. I couldn't believe it when my grandfather said "See how brave my little dog is", and then bent down and released the dog, which was at least five times Fang's weight. I need not have worried. Fang took the challenge, dropped out of the tree and started to crawl towards the dog with teeth bared. The little dog turned and ran yelping out of the yard with its tail between its legs.

Photo 4.13 *Flying foxes rarely fly during the day unless disturbed. Photo by Grahame Webb.*

When I returned to the Northern Territory the first time, Fang's health took a turn for the worse. Large watery blisters formed on his wings and his good wing lost its terminal joints. My father would have killed him out of mercy, but my mother couldn't bring herself to let him do it. Today she would be able to call WIRES wildlife rescue, but no such organization existed in 1975. She called the zoo and the museum and anyone else that she thought might be able to help, but nobody had any idea as to how to treat the symptoms. The vets at the zoo said that she could take him there, but because of quarantine regulations he would never be allowed to leave. As they had no idea how to treat him, she thought that they were likely to euthanize him. She was desperate, but remembered that she had a similar problem; she would swell if she ate too much acid fruit. We had been feeding him on any fruits in season and thought that the more variety the better. When she put him on a diet of pear and banana, the only fruits she could eat as much as she wanted without swelling, his blisters dried, his wounds healed and he never again showed any health problems.

My mother took Fang to meetings organized by the Australian Society for Growing Native Plants and he became a celebrity. Everyone wanted to hold Fang, and Mum would have to take him away for a break every now and then. Nevertheless, it didn't matter how tired he was or if someone did something he wasn't used to, Fang trusted Mum's judgement and never showed any anger. Mothers would hold up infants so that Fang could take a piece of fruit from their tiny fingers, which he did delicately; probably inducing a life-long love of bats.

Fang was very social. If one of the family was in the yard, but not close to a tree, Fang would drop off his perch, crawl across the grass and then climb up the person's leg, finally holding on to their hair so that he could lick their face. Fang would even approach strangers if they were near his tree. That was alright if they knew he was there, but some people got a shock when a bat wing came out of a tree, hooked their hair and tried to drag them over so that their face could be licked.

Fang lived with Mum for 13 years, but one night she was called to the hospital where my father was terminally ill before she could put him in the laundry. When she came back, Fang was nowhere to be found. She searched the district knocking on doors and asking if anyone had seen a bat, which was complicated seeing that it was April Fool's Day. She also ran stories in the local paper, but no-one reported seeing him. It may be that he just wandered away to where nobody could see him, but he was so social that is unlikely. It could be that he was exploring a neighbor's yard and a large dog ate him, but the possibility that Mum still hopes for is that someone stole him to keep as a loving pet; he certainly deserved that!

Photo 4.14 *Fang with Megumi Yamakoshi en 1983. Photo by Bill Magnusson.*

Photo 4.15 *Fang with his adopted family; Bill, Dorothy and Ern Magnusson holding Michael (Joe) and Kate Andrew in 1987. Photo by Anne Andrew.*

CHAPTER 5 - MANATEE PROJECT MANAUS

Wild dolphins have become a tourist attraction in
the Amazon. Photo by Bill Magnusson.

I finished the requirements for my PhD in 1979 and I was looking for a job or a post-doctoral scholarship. There was an informal offer of a job to work on the hormonal regulation of fish reproduction, but my honors year had given me life-time immunization against lab work. There were few post-doctoral scholarships available and to get one you had to have the support of an established researcher. Things didn't look hopeful, but events were unfolding on another continent that I would only be able to piece together years later.

The Brazilian Institute for Amazonian Research (INPA) was looking for a specialist on Sirenia, the taxonomic grouping that includes dugongs and manatees. The head of their manatee project had left the country and they advertised for a substitute. The only candidate with a doctorate had worked on horses in the desert and the remaining manatee researcher at the Institute, a Canadian with a Masters Degree, was apparently happy to have him hired. However, an American Peace Corps volunteer was in his office when the Director was about to sign the invitation letter. She said that the Institute should look for a candidate with manatee experience.

The Director summoned the Canadian and said that he should seek further. The obvious place to look would have been the USA, which had the highest concentration of people studying sirenians of anywhere in the world, but the Canadian was wary of the Americans, and I would learn later that he was worried that an American with a Ph.D. would take over leadership of the project in which he had already invested several years. He told the Director that he didn't know of anyone in the Americas, but that he would contact an Australian, George Heinsohn, to see if he could help. Unknown to the Canadian at the time, George Heinsohn was an American who had established in Australia to study dugong.

I had been spending time attending conferences, and at one of those George Heinsohn was presenting a paper on aerial surveys for dugongs that seemed very interesting. Unfortunately, I saw that to hear the presentation I would have to sit through one by Helene Marsh on the dugong digestive system. I couldn't imagine anything more boring, but breaking into the session half way through would be embarrassing. Helene's presentation was anything but boring, and at the end I was fascinated by dugong intestines. In contrast, I found George's presentation somewhat lack luster and I got the impression that he was inferring that the dugongs were migrating out of the area when the water was murky and he couldn't see them. I didn't bother to talk to him after the presentation so I ended up never meeting him in person.

Photo 5.1 *Dugongs have a downward oriented mouth adapted for feeding on sea grasses. Photo by Bill Magnusson.*

Later, when a call for applications for Queen Elizabeth II scholarships was opened I remembered George's presentation and saw an opportunity. I wrote to him and said that I thought there might be flaws in his survey method and that he needed someone specialized in aerial survey to help him. Would he support my application for a QE II scholarship in marine science? Note that I never said that I was an expert in aerial survey, which I wasn't, but I had carefully worded it to give a false impression. My friends said that George Heinsohn would be offended that I had questioned his methods and never reply, but they didn't know George. Everyone who knew him said that he was not only sincere and dedicated, he was also humble.

George wrote back that a researcher in Manaus was "saying that his group is in immediate need of a Ph.D. ecologist to work on radio telemetry and ecology of the Amazonian manatee. The position would be a two or three year appointment. He asked if I knew of anyone suitable. I telexed back giving the name and address of one nearly finished Ph.D. student here (an insect ecologist who has helped us with dugong field work), plus your and Gordon Grigg's name and address as persons to contact. As a Queen's fellowship is difficult to obtain you might be interested in working on the Amazonian manatee."

OK, maybe I was better qualified than the entomologist who still didn't have a Ph.D., but they probably should have given the job to the horse researcher; my having dined on a few dugongs didn't make me any more qualified! Nevertheless, based on George Heinsohn's recommendation, I received a telegram inviting me to work on manatees in the Amazon, and I took the offer.

I was keen to see the exotic fauna of South America. My whole life I had only been exposed to standard mammals, such as kangaroos, echidnas and koalas, and everyday birds, such as kookaburras, lyrebirds and cockatoos. South America had rodents the size of pigs, anteaters almost as long as I was tall and cats big enough to eat people. There were also relatives of emus and ostriches that could fly, toucans with outsized beaks and tiny hummingbirds that weighed less than the last joint on my thumb. The Amazon is the most biodiverse region in the world, and Manaus sits in the middle of it, at the junction of the World's two largest rivers, the Amazon and the Negro.

Needless to say, I was quite lost in a new culture surrounded by people speaking Portuguese, of which I understood nothing. However, Robin Best, the head of the manatee project, picked me up at the airport in his orange Volkswagen beetle and took me to his house. Very tall, he had to bend over to fit in the beetle, but drove expertly among the cars that did not seem to be following any road rules. Three years older than I was and powerfully built, he had been a champion rower at the University of British Colombia and captain of the rugby team at Guelph. While a youth he had volunteered at the Stanley Park Zoo and the Vancouver Aquarium where his father was Director. During these activities as a youngster he learned how to manipulate and care for large aquatic mammals, such as seals and dolphins.

Photo 5.2 *South America has birds, such as this white-throated toucan, with no ecological equivalents in Australia. Photo by Bill Magnusson.*

The manatee project at INPA had been started by Diana Magor in 1974. Although she only had a bachelors degree and, according to contemporary reports[57], was not very good with paper work, Diana convinced Dr Warwick Kerr, INPA's Director, to invest heavily in the project. She had brought an orphaned manatee calf from Leticia and was soon tending to other abandoned calves. Diana liked to rescue orphaned wildlife and to spend time talking to manatee hunters, but did not have experience in reporting the results. This is common among wildlife enthusiasts and their contribution tends to be forgotten because they often leave few written records. However, without Diana, the INPA manatee project probably never would have existed.

INPA, or possibly just Dr Kerr, had a policy that projects should be led by a researcher with a Ph.D., and in June 1976 Daryl Domning was contracted to lead the project. He was primarily a paleontologist and the live animals were mainly of interest as hints about the past[57]. He carried out a number of morphological studies, but the manatee project took off with the hiring of Robin Best in October 1976. Robin brought in many scientific collaborators and by the time I arrived he had captive management and raising of orphaned manatees down to a fine art.

Robin talked about the current manatee projects, but I was jetlagged and I had trouble remembering the details. I woke late the next day and Robin took me to the INPA grounds, which were covered in low forest. He had office and lab space near the animal house that was used to provide mice to Institute's medical researchers, and there were large above-ground swimming pools on the other side of a narrow road which housed the captive manatees.

I had never seen a manatee close up before and expected something like dugongs or the huge warty West-Indian manatees that I had seen in documentaries about studies in the USA. However, the Amazonian manatees were smooth, like overinflated inner tubes, and less than three meters long; much smaller than other species of manatee. They were dark grey, except for striking white markings on the chest, though I could not see them very well through the water that was covered in grass and murky from the manatee poo.

Robin introduced me to student volunteers and some local people employed by INPA to cut grass for the manatees, and I tried to jot down their names in a small notebook before the jetlag swept away all the new information. He also left me to have lunch with Dr Warwick Kerr, the Director of the Institute who had hired me, but who was leaving that day to resume his position at the University of São Paulo in Ribeirão Preto. When Dr Kerr took over the Institute in 1975 it had only one PhD and one MSc. When he left in April 1979, it had 50 MScs and 60 PhDs. In those days, few Brazilians had Ph.D.s, and those who had obtained one somewhere else did not want to live in the Amazon. Dr Kerr was responsible for inaugurating four post-graduate courses in Manaus, which were among the first in Brazil. Much of what I have achieved in my professional life has been built on the foundations laid by Warwick Kerr; I will always be grateful to him and proud to have been one of his friends.

Photo 5.3 *Amazonian manatees have distinctive white patches on the belly. Photo by Bill Magnusson.*

When I arrived, many of the researchers were foreigners. Even today, when most INPA researchers are Brazilians, Manaus is the hub of Amazonian science and a cosmopolitan center. Many of the most famous ecologists of the last forty years have visited INPA. Soon after I arrived, Robin took me to a restaurant to have dinner with Philip Hershkovitz, at that time the foremost specialist in South American mammals, and Tim Cluttenbrock, famous for his long-term studies of deer on the English Isle of Rum. I don't remember the details of the conversations, but Tim surprised me by saying "Do you notice that you change your accent when you talk to Americans?" I replied that I didn't, but from then on I took note of the way people talked to each other. He seems to be right. When people with different English accents talk to each other they generally don't modify the way they talk, but when they converse with people from the USA they tend to simplify what they say and use a Californian accent, as though they think they won't be understood otherwise. There are so many subtleties to communication, and many of these are linked to our cultural heritages that I now spend a lot of time thinking about possible errors in communication when I prepare lectures or scientific papers.

Robin was interested in sloths, which resulted in my first trip onto the Rio Negro. Just like the rivers in northern Australia, the Amazonian rivers are subject to dramatic flooding. The difference is that the flooding is unpredictable in Australian Rivers. Heavy rainfall in the catchment can cause a river to flood within hours, and it is likely to return to normal level within a day or two. The catchment of the Amazon is larger than the continent of Australia. Heavy rains in one headwater might result in flooding while another remains almost dry, but the size of the catchment buffers the larger rivers from these unpredictable fluctuations. The big rivers, such as the Amazon and Negro, show a single flood peak each year, deepening the rivers by about 10m in the flood season and then gradually dropping to a minimum in the middle of the low-water season.

I had arrived in April, when the rivers were high. We drove to the bank of the Negro River, just a few kilometers downstream of Manaus, which is 1,200 km from the sea. There were ocean liners and oil tankers anchored offshore. The river was so wide that I could only just make out land on the other side, more than 5 km away. To someone used to rivers that you could throw a rock across in most of their freshwater reaches, it seemed more an ocean than a river.

The 5m-long aluminum canoe with 40 hp motor plowed through the waves formed by the wind pushing against the current. It was calm that day, but I would learn that violent storms often upturned 20 m-long boats if they were caught in the middle of the Negro River. What had been islands in the low-water season were now marked just by the tops of trees that were shaking in the current. This was where Robin planned to catch the pale-throated three-toed sloths, which could be reached easily from the boat. In fact, the first we came across wasn't in a tree, but was dogpaddling slowly in the middle of the river. Having seen pictures of sloths hanging from branches like wingless bats I hadn't expected them to be able to swim, but this one seemed to be doing very well until Robin plucked him out of the water.

Photo 5.4 *Three-toed sloths are common in Manaus,*
but hard to see. Photo by Bill Magnusson.

Robin's large hand held the sloth firmly from behind, just below its arm pits. The sloth spread its forearms, which were as long as its body, revealing the three long claws on the tips of its fingers. Its round head with large eyes moved slowly from side to side on its long neck, and it tried to twist its short hind legs to grab Robin's arm. Robin turned it around and put it on his hip, which it held onto like a toy koala. I say a toy koala, because you could not do that with a freshly caught wild koala without sustaining serious injury. However, three-toed sloths do not seem to have any effective means of defense once grabbed by a predator.

Robin directed my attention to the orange patch on its back that showed that it was a male and carefully rubbed a small piece of paper over it. To my surprise, the orange color came off on the paper. Robin wanted to collect moths off the sloth. Several species of pyralid moths live exclusively in sloth fur, which is coarse and often supports symbiotic algae. For some reason that nobody understands, sloths only descend to the ground about once a week to defecate and the moths then leave their host to lay their eggs on the sloth poo, where the larvae develop. Newly metamorphosed moths have to fly into the canopy to find another sloth.

Gene Montgomery, a researcher from the Smithsonian Tropical Research Institute in Panama accompanied us on the field trip and he explained to me that three-toed sloths were the highest-biomass mammals in the forest on Barro Colorado Island, the main study site for Smithsonian researchers. That is, the combined weight of sloths in the forest was greater than the combined weight of individuals of any other mammal species. I had spent many fruitless hours looking for koalas in eucalypt forest in areas where many were known to live, so I imagined that finding sloths would be even harder, given their cryptic appearance, infrequent movement and the dense rainforest canopy.

Gene said that only one person on Barro Colorado Island could find the sloths, a capacity that he had developed over many years. The researchers accompanied him and he pointed out the sloths, which the scientists then confirmed using binoculars. I asked if the person with that incredible ability was one of the authors on the paper and Gene said no, he hadn't contributed significantly to the science! I would find that attitude to be common among researchers, intellectual property relating only to laboratories and computers, with technicians and field scientists to be discarded after their critical input has been converted to numbers in a computer file[159].

We caught several more sloths in *Cecropia* trees, which are a favorite food of sloths. Considering the small size of the island, the density of sloths must have been very high. Three-toed sloths have little muscle tissue and what they have acts very slowly. Nevertheless, they use those muscles efficiently for climbing. Sloths were previously classified in the Edentata, a group that included species from the Old World that are only distantly related. It is good that they are now classified in the Xenarthra because Edentata means "without teeth", and the equivalent of canine teeth of two-toed sloths are proportionately longer in relation to the size of the skull than those of jaguars!

Photo 5.5 Robin Best with a male three-toed sloth. Photo by Bill Magnusson.

The only living Xenarthrans are sloths, anteaters and armadillos, and you might get the impression that it is a primitive group that has always consisted of a few hyperspecialized forms, like the echidna and platypus in Australia. However, until about 11,000 years ago, sloths were the dominant herbivores in the Americas[115]. There were many species, some of gigantic size, that lived alongside several species of mammoths and mastodons, giant bison, horses, camels, lions and other forms that we now generally only associate with Africa. None of these species survived long after the arrival of humans on the continent because they had not evolved with a tricky projectile-throwing carnivore.

The defense of the sloths, which was to rear back, spread their deadly claws and dare the predator to attack the soft underbelly, was particularly inappropriate when the predator had spears that could be launched from 10m away. A few species of giant sloths survived on Carribean Islands until about 5,000 years ago when humans invaded their last stronghold. The humans were much less effective at catching small burrowing animals and animals that lived high in the canopy of tropical forests, which is why we can still marvel at the sight of armadillos, anteaters and sloths.

When I arrived, Manaus had only about 400,000 people, and that was a lot more than it would have had if not for the interference of the military government. Worried that the forest might hide communist insurgents, the military strategists devised many plans to colonize and deforest the Brazilian Amazon. One of those plans was to make Manaus an industrial center, which would not happen naturally because of the lack of prime materials and distance to markets. Therefore, they declared the city a free zone where components could be imported without tax and assembled into appliances. Today there are about two million people in Manaus, but the economy is still driven by the free-zone factories. Fortunately, that has not led to as much deforestation as the military strategists hoped. Manaus imports most of its food requirements, so it has little hinterland devoted to crops and you can find relatively intact forest soon after you leave the urban limits.

Robin was trying to get me up to speed in relation to the local culture and took me to see the Opera House that had been built during the turn-of-the-century rubber boom, concerts given by famous Brazilian entertainers, and a few more seedy establishments. However, my limited capacity to communicate in Portuguese and my general lack of social know-how did not make the task easy. One of the students working with the project, Megumi Yamakoshi, helped me as much as she could, but it was an uphill battle. Sitting at my desk with my head almost exploding from trying to extract information from a book written in the 1800s, I threw it to one side and grumbled "I can't stand Portuguese."

Megumi was passing my desk at that moment and she said "Bill, that's not Portuguese, it's English!" I checked and she was right. It was written in that convoluted English with many thoughts and dozens of commas per sentence that was fashionable in the previous century, and it was just as confusing as the sophisticated Portuguese texts that people had been giving me to learn how "correct" Portuguese was written. In

Photo 5.6 *Giant anteaters can be over 2m long, and are now the largest Xenarthrans, but they are tiny in relation to the extinct giant sloths. Photo by Bill Magnusson.*

the end, I just learned Portuguese by talking to people, which means that I often say things that are completely understandable, but would not be considered grammatically correct in a school exam. That is, my Portuguese is no better than my English!

One of the most famous buildings in Manaus is the Municipal Market that was built with material imported from Europe and designed by Gustav Eiffel of Eiffel-tower fame, and Robin took me to dine at a restaurant associated with the market. We sat around tables assembled on the walkway overlooking the fishing boats that were moored waiting for permission to bring their catch to land. I had been brought up on fresh-caught fish and the deep-fried over-salted fish on our plates were not very appetizing. Robin, Gene and José, an official of IBDF, the Brazilian forestry service responsible for wildlife, were having a heated conversation that was lubricated with large quantities of beer, but neither I nor Megumi had much to contribute, so we just sat and listened.

After a few hours the conversation seemed to going in circles and I decided to walk home to Robin's house, which was only about 3 km away. Megumi said that she was ready to go as well, so we stood up to take our leave. I don't think that Robin was very impressed with my lack of social graces and he was probably wondering what he had done to deserve a teetotalling Australian. I had a problem though. Before coming to Manaus, I hadn't been wearing shoes very much, and the ones I was wearing had given me blisters. Therefore, I asked Robin if he could take my shoes in the car and I would walk barefoot. He didn't seem too pleased, but said that he would do it before returning to the animated conversation with Gene and José.

The next day I asked where were my shoes and Gene said "José got drunk and threw them in the river."

I said "In that case, José owes me a new pair of shoes."

Gene replied "No he doesn't. I held my knife to his throat and made him throw his shoes in the river."

I asked "Does that mean you owe me a new pair of shoes?"

Shaking his head, he answered "No, I realized what a stupid thing I had done, so I chucked my knife in the river with my shoes." Seeing that the conversation seemed to be going in the direction that I'd have to buy Gene a new knife, I just walked off to find out where I could buy new shoes in Manaus. I was no more socially competent in Manaus than I had been in Sydney and I could see that I needed to improve my social skills, but I didn't want to have to get drunk to do it.

At first Robin seemed content that I knew very little about aquatic mammals, probably because I let him know that I had no wish to take over his project. I volunteered for the menial jobs and let Robin make all the decisions. I had been employed to work on radio telemetry and ecology of manatees, but Robin knew far more about the ecology of manatees, or for that matter the ecology of almost any mammal, than I did, and he had invited Gene Montgomery to help with the telemetry studies. He also brought Jim Gallivan from Canada and John Kanwisher from the USA to help with studies of manatee physiology.

Photo 5.7 *Gene Montgomery, Robin Best and Bill putting a radio transmitter of a manatee, October 1980. Photographer unknown.*

Manatees are incredibly strong and, even though they can't get around without water to support their weight, one smack from their heavy tail could break bones. Robin and his team could get them into slings and haul them from one place to another quickly and efficiently and I generally just stood around trying to learn vicariously. Robin had constructed large tanks that were completely air tight so that he and Jim could measure manatee respiration. Getting the manatees into and out of the tank took planning and team work. My main contribution was to take some measurements at night when the others were asleep.

Robin had a project to introduce manatees into the Curua Una hydroelectric dam, which was about 600 km downstream from Manaus. Hydroelectric dams are often compromised by the large quantities of floating grass that grow in the reservoir, and manatees had been suggested as biological-control agents. The idea was to release manatees into the dam and monitor their activities by radiotelemetry. We would take them down river in one of INPA's large wooden boats, then truck them overland about 60 km to the dam. This required complicated logistics, but Robin had it all figured out. My job would be to radio track the manatees after they were released into the dam.

I had been very enthusiastic about this applied project in Manaus, but when I saw the dam I started to have doubts. Curua Una is a black-water river, which means that it is nutrient poor. There were floating grass mats in some places because of the nutrients released by the flooded vegetation, but the grass would probably die off naturally as the reservoir reverted to the river's natural black-water condition. I asked Robin what would happen to the manatees if the grass ran out, because trying to pass the turbines to get downstream would be fatal for them. Robin said that I wasn't to worry about that; while there was finance to study dams we would take advantage of it to learn more about manatees. Fortunately, at least in the first few weeks that I followed them, the manatees kept away from the dam wall. The dam now supports no aquatic vegetation and I don't know what happened to the manatees.

The trip was good for me because I met my future wife at Curua Una, but I had collected little data on the movement of manatees when Robin called me back to Manaus. The project needed more manatees and we would buy them from fishermen. This was technically illegal, but Robin said that we would be saving the manatees from being eaten, so it was legitimate. Manatees were common in the Lago do Rei, a lake in the middle of a large island just downstream of the junction of the Amazon and the Negro, which was less than 20 km from Manaus.

The main problem was that the water level in the lake was very low and the lack of flow meant that oxygen in the deeper parts was used up by the bacteria and other organisms in the mud, so the fish had to get their oxygen from the surface layers. Sometimes a cold front from the south would cool the surface water, making it sink and bringing the anoxic water to the top, resulting in huge fish kills. Nothing could be done about that, but the propellers of outboard motors could do the same, so SUDEPE, the organization responsible for fisheries, had banned motorized boats in the lake and set up a checking station at the mouth of the long canal that connected the lake to the river. I would have to convince the SUDEPE official to let us use an outboard motor in the canal in case we had to transport a manatee.

Photo 5.8 *A fisherman's home on Lago do Rei consisted of a canoe to cook, sleep and hunt, a tarpaulin to avoid rain and sun, and a pole to hang salted arapaima fillets. Photo by Bill Magnusson.*

It wasn't hard to get permission for me to enter the lake because I had INPA identification as a researcher. The SUDEPE agent accompanied us up the canal the first time, sitting in the bow and taking pot shots at the herons with his .38 caliber pistol. However, I found that I would need to spend several days in the lake before a fishermen caught a manatee, and my boat driver would have to make several trips to and from the lake by himself. As he wasn't a researcher, the SUDEPE agent said that I would have to get special permission for him. The problem was that I didn't know who could give such permission, and neither did the SUDEPE agent. I returned to Manaus, got some INPA letter-head paper, wrote a declaration of permission and borrowed everybody's stamps to put on lots of official-looking signatures. I then placed the fisherman's finger print at the bottom to seal the document. With this "official" letter, the SUDEPE agent agreed to let my boat driver in and out of the lake.

The fishermen used the same technique for catching arapaima, the world's largest scaled freshwater fish, and manatees. Both need to surface to breathe, but are sensitive to any disturbance. The fisherman would sit silently in the prow of a wooden canoe, harpoon raised, waiting for an arapaima or a manatee to surface within striking distance. This could take days, and the fisherman had to live in his tiny canoe because there was no dry land around the lake that was not separated by hundreds of meters of gooey mud. He had a small clay basin to light a fire and cook meals and barely enough space to lie down and sleep at night. I found it hard to sit in the small canoes and paddle without tipping over, but the fishermen had no problems; it was as though the canoes were extensions of their bodies. Silvino Santos filmed manatee and arapaima hunting in the 1920s[168] and you can still see his films on YouTube. The techniques used by the fishermen in Lago do Rei were exactly the same as those shown in Santos' films.

As manatees were caught infrequently, I had wait on the lake, living in an aluminum canoe with only a tarpaulin draped over a fallen tree as cover from the hot sun. Watching the fishermen, I started to have doubts about the capture technique to obtain manatees for research. The harpoons had long barbed tips that penetrated a hand width into the manatee, often passing into the lung cavity. Fishermen would normally kill the manatee by shoving plugs into its nostrils, but we would have to subdue a live thrashing behemoth. After two days, the fishermen towed over a manatee. They had used several harpoons to ensure that it did not break away and it had multiple wounds. When I got it back to Manaus, Robin christened it *Peneira*, which means sieve. Although I knew that there was a lot of illegal hunting of manatees, I doubted that the fishermen would have caught manatees in Lago do Rei if we hadn't been there because of the SUDEPE blockade on the entrance canal.

I spent a lot of time treating Peneira's wounds and he recovered. This gave me huge respect for the regenerative capacity of manatees. Deep wounds into the body cavity delivered in a stagnant lake seething with bacteria would have killed individuals of almost any other species of mammal that I could think of. Fishermen brought in other manatees for Robin's collection, but I didn't return to Lago do Rei.

Photo 5.9 *Arapaima fisherman, Lago do Rei in 1979. Photo by Bill Magnusson.*

Robin planned to build a large aquatic zoo in Manaus along the lines of the Vancouver Aquarium. He was negotiating the extension of the manatee pools with large glass windows for public viewing. One of the most valuable lessons Robin taught me was that projects need physical infrastructure if they are to be viable in the long term. It doesn't matter how important a conservation project is, a bureaucrat can eliminate it with one stroke of a pen if funding is restricted for any reason. However, if the project has extensive physical infrastructure the bureaucrats are afraid of a public backlash and have to support the project until alternative funding can be found.

Robin had other captive animals and the most appealing was a giant otter. Otters belong to the weasel family. Weasels and their relatives are famous for being able to kill prey much larger than themselves, but most are smaller than house dogs. Giant otters are the largest mustelids and can reach lengths of over a meter and a half and weights of over 30 kg. Robin's otter loved him, followed him around like a devoted dog, and often showed its affection by copulating with his leg. However, giant otters are dangerous animals and have killed both keepers and visitors in zoos. Many species of mammals, including humans, nibble their loved ones to show affection. The problem is that an otter nibble can be devastating for a human. After the otter nibbled his hand, and drove its canine tooth from one side to the other, Robin left the otter safely behind bars in its cage beside his office.

Captive animals are interesting and you can learn a lot about biology from watching them, but restrained animals soon lose their mystique for me and I was pleased when Robin said that we would be travelling up the Amazon to Tefé Lake to study dolphins. There are two genera of dolphins in the Amazon, and back in 1979 there was thought to be only two species. The tucuxi is shaped like the well-known bottlenose dolphin of Flipper fame, but is much smaller and doesn't get much longer than a meter and a half. The back and sides are light grey with a lighter or pinkish belly. They are fast swimming, often jump with body completely out of the water and they normally only eat fish.

Dolphins in the other Amazon genus, *Inia*, are called botos in Brazil. I will use this name as the Amazon River dolphin, as it is often called in English, could also be applied to the tucuxi. Some researchers have described other species from the Madeira and Araguaia Rivers, but most international organizations do not recognize them. There are similar complications with other Amazonian vertebrates. The problem is that populations of a species that are geographically isolated will develop unique genetic and morphological characteristics, but will interbreed freely if brought back into contact. Humans are a good example of such a species. Sometimes, only males can get around the barrier, leading to mixing of nuclear genes, but the mitochondrial genes, which are passed on only by females, remain distinct. This happened with people on the Indian subcontinent[138]. Similar differences are often used to classify non-human species as distinct, but a skeptic might say that this implies that the females are different species, but not the males! Here, I'll treat the boto as a single species.

Photo 5.10 *This boto was grey-white, but the tea-colored water of the Rio Negro makes it appear red. Photo by Bill Magnusson.*

Unlike the tucuxi, botos have a flexible neck, an elongated body and are not fast swimmers for a dolphin. Their dorsal fin is small and only slightly distinct from the body. They are much larger than the tucuxi, some reaching more than two and half meters in length, and it is the only cetacean in which the males are larger than the females. They are generally grey with patches of pink, though some individuals may be all grey or all pink. Other, only distantly related, river dolphins have similar morphology, which apparently evolved to allow them the flexibility to fossick among submerged vegetation in murky rivers. Botos eat a variety of fish and even turtles and crabs.

I had never spent much time observing dolphins, so I decided to use the trip up the Amazon on INPA's 18m wooden boat, the Marupiara, to learn something of their behavior. I sat on the bow and recorded the dolphins I saw in each segment of the 550 km journey. The major difficulty was in staying awake. The glare and the constant drumming of the motor made it hard to maintain concentration, especially when no dolphin had appeared for some time. It wasn't feasible to count all the dolphins or even estimate the number, but I could note the group sizes and whether the dolphins were near a confluence of the river with another stream or canal, or where the river was turbulent. The tucuxis were generally solitary, though occasionally in groups of up to four individuals near confluences. Most of the botos were in groups of up to about nine individuals. The botos were found in all classes of river turbulence, but the tucuxis seemed to be avoiding very turbulent and very still areas. The study was very basic, but the paper we published[104] it is still widely cited.

Tefé is a sleepy little town on the shore of a black-water lake that drains into the Amazon River. It has been a favorite collecting spot for naturalists for centuries because it gives access to the sediment-laden, so-called white-water rivers, black-water rivers, varzea forest inundated by white-water rivers, igapó forest inundated by black-water rivers and terra-firme or high-ground forest that is never flooded. Huge schools of fish, especially jaraqui, a pan-sized fish that eats bottom sediment, migrate along the banks of the lake. The fish call to each other and the fishermen can tell the species apart from the sounds they make. Jaraqui can't be caught on hook and line, and they usually swim too deep for small nets, which is why the Indians called the Negro River, and other black-water tributaries of the Amazon, rivers of hunger, even though there were literally tons of fish to be had.

Jaraqui will swim into gill nets, but when they do botos appear to cash in on the free meal. The fishermen do not begrudge the dolphins a few fish, but the botos usually take large chunks of net with the fish. Nets are cheap by city standards, but might cost a fisherman the equivalent of a week's wages. Understandably, the fishermen don't like dolphins and will often kill them if given a chance. The best way to catch jaraqui is with modern deep seine nets that can enclose schools and drag them onto the beach, and commercial fishermen from Tefé operated this way along the shores of the lake. It is much more difficult for the dolphins to damage the thick mesh of the seine nets, and dolphins are sometimes trapped between the net and the beach. Robin was hoping to take advantage of that to catch dolphins.

Photo 5.11 *Robin Best watches for dolphins as Zé Japonês (white shirt) and his fishermen pull in the seine net. Photo by Bill Magnusson.*

Robin hadn't explained to me why he wanted to catch the dolphins, but I knew that he wanted to catch a lactating female so that he could take samples. At that time, nobody knew the composition of boto or tucuxi milk. We travelled up the lake in a small boat owned by one of the chief fish wholesalers in Tefé, a man who went by the name of Zé Japonês. We tied off the small boat in some igapó forest and made our way to a small fishing village nestled in the forest on the hill beside the lake.

We would stay overnight with the fishermen and I was impressed by Amazonian hospitality. The fishermen's families fed us and provided us with places to hang our hammocks. Dinner consisted of fish baked on an open fire and farinha, the dry, gritty manioc meal that accompanies every Amazonian repast. Australians usually select fish that have few small bones, and many can't eat fish with any bones, but the most common Amazonian fish, such as jaraqui, have so many small bones that these have to be cut with many slices of a sharp knife, a process called *ticando*, before the fish is cooked. Even so, many small bones remain and you have to be very careful not to get one stuck in your gums. Robin once got one stuck sideways across his throat and it took me about twenty minutes to get it out with a pair of long pincers. Every time I would be about to grab it, he would gulp and the bone would move out of reach. He got angrier at each failed attempt and I couldn't convince him that it was his gulps and not my twisted sense of humor that was preventing me from grabbing the bone.

The family gave a demonstration of fish eating that could not be emulated. Even small children would put a large chunk of jaraqui in their mouth, chew it around for a few seconds and them spit out the tangle of small bones that had been stripped of their meat. When I tried it, I always got a sharp bone lodged somewhere in my gums. Even the farinha was hard to eat. I dipped my spoon in the bowl in the middle of the table and managed to get most to my plate, but there was a tell-tale line of crumbs across the table. Even getting the farinha from the plate to my mouth was not easy, and a ring of farinha dust formed in front of me. The family members would just put their spoon in the bowl and flip it so that a ball of farinha would fly through the air to the recipient's mouth, not a crumb hitting their lips or falling to the floor. I decided that it would take decades to master that art, but now, 40 years later, I would say that it takes longer!

The next day we sat on the beach, the fishermen watching for a school of jaraqui. One of the INPA fishermen with us was Sidoca, a small wiry man who only stood as high as my shoulder. Robin and the rest of the fishermen respected his knowledge and I was pleased to have him explain things to me, though my Portuguese was still rudimentary. Several botos were surfacing off the beach, apparently waiting for the fishermen to put out their nets. Sidoca said that you could tell the sex of a boto from the way it surfaced; females breathed with one smooth movement, whereas the males bobbed twice, as though they were curious about what they saw when they broke the water the first time. I could see that each dolphin either breathed with one or two bobs and I was eager to test his hypothesis.

The fishermen indicated that jaraqui were coming and prepared to set the seine net to enclose them. Normally they would avoid encircling a dolphin, but Robin asked them to try to catch the dolphins following the school. It worked and the seine

Photo 5.12 Tucuxi dolphins sometimes jump clear out of the water. Photo by Bill Magnusson.

formed an arc encircling the fish and the dolphin. I noted that it was surfacing like a male and then helped the fishermen haul in the net, which was incredibly heavy. Six strong men and I could only budge it about a handspan at a time, but the floats moved closer to the beach. Some of the jaraqui jumped over the net, but the dolphin just kept swimming in ever smaller circles.

When we dragged it onto the beach, the net had hundreds of kilos of jaraqui and one large dolphin, a male as Sidoca had predicted. I repeated the experiment many times, guessing the sex and then checking once the dolphin was caught, but I discovered that male dolphins are much more likely to be captured by the net than females, which are more cautious. I correctly identified the sex of all the animals, but as we caught nine males and only one female it was not enough to publish.

After a few hours, Robin had several dolphins on the beach and was busy measuring them and taking blood samples. I was mainly dragging in the net, but Robin asked me and the fishermen to help him carry a tucuxi that had been caught in the net further up the beach. When we got to the spot he indicated, he asked the fishermen to get a piece of net to put under the dolphin. When I asked why, he said that he planned to kill the dolphin to get bone samples and he wanted to be able to say honestly that he had worked on dolphins that had died in fishermens' nets. I was unimpressed and wandered off to talk to Sidoca.

We had to return to Manaus the next day, so we went back to Tefé. The Marupiara would remain in Tefé and we went to the airport to catch a plane. Despite being small, Tefé was, and still is, one of the most important staging points for drugs entering Brazil from Colombia. Therefore, the Federal Police closely examine all the passengers' baggage. Robin approached the inspectors and immediately started an animated conversation. He had a way of getting people on side quickly and giving the impression of honesty and sincerity that was extremely important for the fledgling manatee project. These were capabilities that I lacked almost completely.

It was only when the inspector asked what was in our boxes that I realized that Robin probably didn't have a permit for transporting dolphin carcasses. He said that the boxes contained clothes. I looked at the box, saw that it was leaking blood onto the table, and my heart missed a beat, but the inspector just shook Robin's hand and waved us on. Robin picked up the box, dragged a dry part of it across the drops so that it would not leave blood stains on the table and headed to the airline baggage counter. His coolness in potentially stressful social encounters impressed me enormously.

I wrote the paper on the dolphin surveys, but I had little interest in physiology or morphology, and I did not want to be involved in any more dolphin captures. Robin was also interested in the osteology of manatees, and the growing manatee babies offered an excellent opportunity to study bone development, but obviously Robin didn't want to kill his captive animals. Therefore, he got a used portable x-ray machine. The baby manatees didn't like being put on the x-ray table, so someone had to hold them in position while the x-ray photograph was being taken. Two young volunteers worked with the project and Robin had them restrain the manatees while he operated the x-ray machine.

Photo 5.13 *Handling large aquatic mammals is not easy and takes care and experience. Photo by Bill Magnusson.*

I knew that portable x-ray machines were hard to calibrate and could give dosages far above that needed for the image. Also, the x-rays could spread in any direction, so anybody nearby could be hit. An old machine that had been abandoned by a hospital was likely to be even worse than those that had been reported on. Robin had no calibration equipment and nothing to measure the radiation, so I told him that he shouldn't expose the students to such risk. At first he tried to convince me that I was worrying needlessly, but when he saw that I was not going to back down he became agitated and said "Alright then, I'll hold the manatees; someone else can operate the machine." Operating the machine without proper protective clothing was still dangerous, but at least the students wouldn't be directly under the x-ray beam, and Robin made it obvious that my opinions about the management of captive sirenians were not needed.

We returned to Tefé a few weeks later, but this time to take the Marupiara to Lago Amanã, where the local people said there were many manatees. At that time, the lake was of little interest to anyone, but Márcio Ayres proposed the now world-famous Mamirauá Sustainable Development Reserve near Tefé, and he and Robin realized Amanã´s potential importance in forming a corridor between Mamirauá and the Jaú National Park that another INPA researcher, Herbert Schubart, had been instrumental in setting up. It is because of visionaries like Schubart, Robin and Márcio that a large part of central Amazônia is protected from unregulated development.

I still did not have such wide vision and I concentrated on learning about the fauna of the lake. I took advantage of my companions to learn about caimans[94] and fish[95], and Sidoca would teach me much about manatees. He said that they migrated into and out of the lake along narrow canals, which is why they were vulnerable to hunters at that time of year. Although the water level was falling rapidly in the lake, there were still many manatees. Sidoca took me to a bluff overlooking the lake and said in Portuguese "See how many there are?"

I was on a hill hundreds of meters from any water and kilometers from the other side of the lake, so I couldn't see any manatees at all! Manatees don't surface like dolphins, they just slowly raise their nostrils to the surface for a few seconds and then drop back down with scarcely a ripple. I had difficulty seeing them in the pools back at INPA, much less in the middle of a gigantic lake. Sidoca patiently said "I'll show you," and explained where to look. I grabbed my binoculars and concentrated where he said until the manatee surfaced. They apparently weren't feeding or migrating because each one seemed to always surface at the same spot. I took out a notebook and mapped where each individual was. By making some assumptions about how often they surfaced, I was able to estimate the number of animals in my field of vision. The next day, Sidoca took me to another hill and we repeated the procedure. I couldn't see manatees by myself, but with Sidoca I could.

Photo 5.14 *We had to push the Marupiara out of Lago Amanã. Manatees are very vulnerable to hunters when the water level is low. Photo by Bill Magnusson.*

The water level was falling quickly and we literally had to push the Marupiara out of the lake the next day, but on the trip back I compared the area that I had covered to the rest of the lake. With some perhaps unjustified assumptions, I calculated that there were about 1,000 manatees in Amanã Lake. Extrapolating that to the rest of Amazonia indicated that there might be more than a million Amazonian manatees, which is not bad for a species thought to be in danger of extinction.

When I got back to Manaus, I took my calculations to Robin and suggested that we seek funds to survey the whole Amazon using Sidoca as a manatee-sighting machine. I thought that Robin would be happy to have me doing this as it would keep me out of his way. Our relationship had been deteriorating and it was obvious that I was contributing little to the manatee project as it was. However, Robin said "You realize that if your calculations are correct, we would have to remove the manatee's endangered status and that would dry up most of our funding?" I hadn't thought about that, and from the way he was looking at me I realized that I shouldn't continue the conversation.

The next day there was a note on my desk indicating that the head of the Fisheries Department, which was responsible for the manatee project, wanted to talk to me. I went to see him and he said "I've heard that you are not happy in this Department and we don't want anybody working unhappily, so I am willing to let you transfer to the Ecology Department." I went to see Herbert Schubart, the then Director of the Ecology Department, and he welcomed me with open arms.

I never again worked on dolphins or manatees, but my interactions with Robin came back to haunt me. He started a Ph.D. in England, but developed leukemia, apparently in the hip that he had held against the manatees when they were being x-rayed. Of course, the leukemia might have had nothing to do with the x-rays, but if it did, what if I hadn't interfered? If the students had held the manatees, maybe Robin would have received only a third the dose of radiation, and perhaps that wouldn't have been enough to induce leukemia. I'll never know, but I realized that even doing what I truly believed to be the right thing might have the wrong result. Robin's death was a huge blow to aquatic-mammal conservation in the Amazon, but the infrastructure he created still exists and the students he mentored continue to reveal fascinating facts about aquatic mammals, both in the Amazon and in other parts of Brazil.

Photo 5.15 *Lago Amanã was included in the central Amazonian corridor of conservation reserves in part because of the pioneering studies by Robin Best. Photo by Bill Magnusson.*

CHAPTER 6 - AMAZONIAN NATURAL HISTORY

Much of the Amazon wildlife lives in the canopies of the forest, like these red-and-green macaws. Photo by Bill Magnusson.

I set traps for small mammals on the INPA grounds, but the only species I caught was the common mouse opossum. The delicate little animal with huge black eyes fitted snuggly in my hand, but when I showed it to the INPA workers they jumped back and said in Portuguese "Be careful, it's venomous." I was getting to know something about the local animals that produce toxins because I had been bitten by a green vine snake a few weeks before and my hand swelled and hurt for about 12 hours, but I knew that there were no venomous South American mammals.

I called my assistants over to see that the little animal was quite harmless, but they insisted that it was venomous. It had settled into my hand, but I agitated it and let it sink its teeth into the skin between my thumb and forefinger. It had quite a strong bite for such a small animal and broke the skin, but it was not that painful. I said "See it's not venomous." A few minutes later, my hand started to swell and throb, just like the bite of the vine snake, and the swelling did not go down for hours. I don't know what caused the reaction, but I decided not to discount local knowledge so cavalierly next time.

Small marsupials which were more mouse like than the mouse opossum climbed in the low vegetation at night, but they never entered my traps. They belonged to a species that goes by the clumsy, but very appropriate, common name of delicate slender opossum. Although similar in overall shape, they are now put in a different family from the mouse opossum. I caught one by hand to photograph and I was surprised at how tame it soon became, but I didn't let it bite me!

South America has about 70 species of marsupials that eat fruit and invertebrates, and most of them are arboreal or semi-arboreal. However, it has no large marsupial grazers or browsers that would be equivalent to wombats, kangaroos and phalangers. Most people think of the Virginia opossum as the typical marsupial of the Americas, but large opossums represent only a small proportion of South American marsupials. My first encounters with the common opossum did not leave me very impressed. It looks much like the Virginia opossum and some authors consider it to be the same species. The common opossums were easy to catch because they fell into the 200 liter drums we used as garbage cans and they couldn't get back out unless the bins were half full.

Photo 6.1 *The delicate slender opossum curls up its ears when thretened. Photo by Bill Magnusson.*

It was easy to grab the opossum by the tail and gentle shaking prevented it from biting my hand. Although about the size of a cat, and with long rows of sharp teeth, it was one of the easiest species of mammal to handle that I have encountered. Common opossums are agile in trees, but they spend much of their time on the ground and their ambling gait does not appear very effective for avoiding predators. Their long sparse hair has various shades of yellow, brown and grey, making them look as though they have mange, and the pointed snouts do not evoke any warm human sentiments. All in all, adults are not very appealing.

Just about anything animal or plant that is easy to come by and digest is food for common opossums and they appear to be generalists in every aspect, adapting well to human disturbances. They appeared so generalized that I couldn't imagine how they could survive among all the specialized carnivores and frugivores that occur in

South America. However, they are one of the most commonly encountered species of mammal, with a huge distribution. It was much later that I discovered a spectacular specialization which might explain part of their success.

I was walking through the forest near Manaus in the late afternoon when I flushed something in the undergrowth and it made for a tree. I ran after it and saw a common opossum nimbly scrambling up a tree with a large snake in its mouth, which hung down about a meter on each side. I couldn't make out the species of snake, but many such large snakes in the area have venomous rear fangs.

I initially just regarded the observation as an exceptional event, but then I attended a herpetology conference where researchers of the Butantan Institute showed videos of common opossums eating South American rattle snakes[5]. The opossum just picked up the snake by the tail and started snacking on it, pushing it into its mouth as though it was eating a long sausage. The snake retaliated by repeatedly biting the snake on the head and body, but this elicited no reaction from the opossum, which just kept munching until it had eaten all the snake, including the deadly fangs.

According to the presenter, the opossum suffered no ill effects. However, the opossums are apparently only resistant to snakes from their own area. Putting a rattle snake with an opossum from rainforest, or putting a lance-head viper with an opossum from a savanna area, resulted in the death of the mammal. Perhaps it is the ability to eat deadly snakes from their own area that gives the opossums the edge over potential competitors in the forest.

My lack of knowledge of the natural history of the Amazonian plants and animals was frustrating and I took any opportunity to go into the forest with more experienced people. I had met Albertina Lima at Curua Una and returned to meet the people at the village downstream where she taught primary school. The village had been settled by Mundurucu Indians, who had been displaced from their ancestral lands in the state of Mato Grosso. The older women had fine tattoos over their heads and bodies. Albertina had been teaching in the one-room school for over a year and had good relationships with all the families. We stayed with Sr Germano and his family, who had a small farm overlooking the river. Sr Germano was much shorter than I was, but strongly built; his muscles testifying to many years cutting forest and planting manioc.

Photo 6.2 *This baby kinkajou found abandoned in the forest was cared for by a local family and rehabilitated to the wild. Photo by Bill Magnusson.*

The first night we were there, one of Sr Germano's sons returned from a hunting trip with a kinkajou. Although in the same family as coatimundis and raccoons, kinkajous are very different from their ground-living cousins. Like most species in the order carnivora, they eat a wide variety of foods, but most by volume probably consists of fruits. They have no direct ecological equivalent in Australia, but the little animal was thickly furred and reminded me of a small cuscus, including the prehensile tail. Its fur coat appeared to offer good insulation, so I was surprised to find a thick layer of fat covering the whole body when I skinned it. I would later discover that they have a low metabolic rate for their size, often enter into torpor before dawn and have to shiver to warm up in the morning. It is not unusual to see kinkajous when you spotlight in the rainforest, but these chance encounters would not have allowed me to appreciate how different they are from other species if I hadn't had a dead animal in hand.

I was delighted when Sr Germano invited us to go on a hunting trip with him to what he called the *centro*, which is "center" in English. It was apparently given that name because it was in the center of the undisturbed rainforest and far from any cultivated areas. It was my first chance to get into what I considered to be untouched rainforest, though I would later learn that people have been living in South America for more than 11,000 years, and have had densely populated settlements in the Amazon for over 2,000 years. It is unlikely that anywhere is untouched, which is why most researchers now refer to old-growth forest rather than use the term primary forest.

Sr Germano set off at a fast trot with his little white dog beside him. Albertina and I tried to keep up, but we, and especially I, slowed him down. The track had been cleared to the height of Sr Germano and his family, and Albertina was even shorter than they were. Whereas he could maintain a steady trot, I had to duck under vines and branches that crossed the track; an activity made more difficult by the aluminum-frame pack I was carrying. Sr Germano often had to wait while I untangled the pack from the undergrowth.

It was probably not much more than 10 km from the river to the center, but the track was tortuous and it took us about five hours to get there. Sr Germano stopped at a small clearing in the undergrowth where we would camp, then set off to check his *espera*, which means "wait" in English. This is just a seat made of poles tied to saplings near a larger fruiting tree. The *espera* looks more like a ladder with widely spaced rungs than a seat, but the hunter will often spend hours waiting for his prey to come to feed on the fruit under the tree.

If the animal comes at night, the hunter will only detect it by the rustle of dry leaves on the ground. Today most hunters use electric torches, but Sr Germano carried a kerosene lantern made from old powdered-milk tins. One can had only a hole in its lid for a thick cloth wick. A second had been cut open and bent around to make a parabolic reflector. When the hunter heard the animal, he would have to quickly use a match to light the lamp he was holding in one hand and then swing the gun around with his free hand to take the shot; all the while balanced on the thin poles.

Photo 6.3 *Sr Germano with the red brocket deer he shot near Curua Una. Photo by Bill Magnusson.*

Sr Germano returned before nightfall with a red brocket deer slung over his shoulder. He hadn't needed to use the lantern. I had never seen a South American deer before and I had imagined that it would be like the rusa deer I had seen in Australia, but this was smaller, weighing perhaps 20 kg. Palm leaves cut and laid on the ground provided a convenient platform and Sr Germano turned the deer on its back and slit open its belly. I remembered the grass-packed rumens of the rusa deer in Australia and I asked Sr Germano to cut open its foregut. Out spilled seeds of all shapes and colors, but no grass. This brought home to me the fact that few grasses grow under the rainforest, and those that do are generally not palatable to mammals. The role of deer in the forest was totally different from that of deer in more open areas; instead of being grazers they were browsers and frugivores.

The deer was warm and its sparse hair was spiky. The smell of blood and ruptured intestines reminded me of my experience with deer in Australia, and I started to see the South American species as more than names in a book. The muscle was too fresh to cook, so Sr Germano baked the liver over an open fire for our dinner. Sitting in the forest, looking into the coals, with a chunk of fresh-baked liver in my hand I was struck by the thought that you have to eat an animal to really know it.

The little white dog waited patiently for its piece of liver, which Sr Germano gave it after we had finished our meal. However, he shook his head and said that the little animal was useless as a hunting dog and that he would get rid of it when he got back. I had the distinct impression that getting rid of it was something much more permanent than just trying to find it a new home.

The meat would not last long in the tropical heat, so Sr Germano woke at first light and fashioned a back pack out of strips of bark and palm leaves. It was as effective as my modern aluminum and cloth pack that had cost me hundreds of dollars. Sr Germano would have to get the meat back to his house where it could be baked or smoked within a few hours and I knew that I would not be able to keep up with him even when he was carrying an extra 15 kg of deer carcass. In any case, I wanted to spend more time to learn about the forest far from settlements.

Sr Germano said that there would be no problem in our returning by ourselves as there was only one track and it was relatively straight. He disappeared into the undergrowth at a trot and we leisurely collected our gear and followed the track. There were initially many things to keep our attention, and we tried to identify the mammals and birds that scurried away as we passed by. There were so many things to see that we could have stayed in any one spot for hours, but we knew that we would have to keep moving to get back to the settlement before dark.

After about an hour, we came to a bifurcation in the track. Each path seemed to equally used and we could not distinguish Sr Germano's spore from that of countless animals that seemed to have walked each trail. We were far from the settlement and taking the wrong track would mean that we would be hopelessly lost. I was ready to choose randomly when the little white dog appeared far down the right fork. He sat there until he saw that we had seen him, then disappeared down the trail. The same thing happened at the dozen forks we came to on the way back. If the little dog hadn't come to guide us I would have had to abandon the tracks, head for the river, and perhaps take days to get to the settlement. I developed very warm feelings for our guide and I sincerely hope that Sr Germano didn't shoot him for being a poor hunter.

Photo 6.4 *The brocket deer's rumen was full of seeds. Photo by Bill Magnusson.*

Ever since my honors project I had wanted to study mammalian population dynamics, but that would take years of effort and is generally not appropriate for unemployed students without a Ph.D. After I moved to the Ecology Department, I decided to take the time to get to know the local mammals and select some for long-term studies. I had seen a mouse-sized rodent that was fossicking near the Director's office during the day soon after I arrived at INPA, but I couldn't catch any rodents on the INPA grounds, which were covered in relatively young regrowth forest. To increase my woefully limited knowledge of the natural history of the rainforest, I started spending most weekends at Reserva Ducke, a 10,000 hectare reserve on the outskirts of Manaus that was administered by INPA. Albertina and I would catch a lift to the reserve headquarters on Friday afternoon, walk four kilometers to our campsite on the bank of Acará Stream, spend Saturday and Sunday observing the fauna and flora, then catch a lift back on Monday morning to go to work. It would be our routine for over a decade.

I set mammal traps in the undergrowth, but they only captured one or two animals per 100 trap nights, a very low capture rate in comparison to what I was used to in Australia. Therefore, I was pleased when a Swiss researcher at the institute asked me to help a student who wanted to study rodents in Reserva Ducke for his Ph.D. thesis. I asked what experience he had and the researcher was offended. She said that the Herr Professor Doktor who had supervised his masters thesis was one of the World's most famous mammalogists and he would never send a student into the field unless they were totally prepared.

Humbled, I took the student to Reserva Ducke. We walked a few hundred meters along a road through the forest and I said that he could chose wherever he thought would be the best place to test his hypotheses. He looked confused for a moment and then said "But I need to put the equipment near the electrical outlets." I asked "What electrical outlets?" and he explained that he had used sophisticated equipment during his masters thesis and that this was possible because the fields he had studied in Switzerland had a grid of electrical outlets so that he never had to be more than 20 m from a socket. When I explained that we did not have a power grid underlying our forest he returned to Switzerland and I never heard from him again.

The trail to our camp had been made by an oil-exploration company many years before, and there were several other straight trails that had been put in by forestry workers studying tree phenology. I cut a trail along the stream to connect some of them and that gave me a circuit of a little under two kilometers where I could routinely search for mammals.

I knew that herbivorous vertebrates are often deficient in sodium because plants mainly use potassium for their physiological processes[76]; that is why ranchers often provide rock salt for their stock. I have seen huge trees felled by peccaries because they dug out the soil from around the roots to get to the salty loam. However, the piles of salt I put out did not attract any vertebrates, and I would learn later that sodium is usually only extremely limiting in the Amazon further from the sea. The only positive result of my efforts was to give the circuit a name; it became the *trilha de sal* or "salt trail" in English.

Photo 6.5 *The little white dog that led us back to Sr Germano's house. Photo by Bill Magnusson.*

The only common mammals I saw on the ground during the day were agoutis and acouchis; both are rodents in the family Dasyproctidae. Their overall body shapes are similar, but agoutis are larger, about the size of large hare, and lack tails. Acouchis are more the size of a wild rabbit, and have a small stub of a tail. Although they are rodents, they give more the impression of tiny deer as they forage in the undergrowth. The species of agouti near Manaus has a red rump and the acouchis have reddish heads. I generally just got a glimpse of them as they ran into the undergrowth. Sometimes, I heard collared peccaries as they ran off, but they rarely let me see them.

I occasionally disturbed a band of South American coatis, which made a ruckus as they distanced themselves, the juveniles climbing a short distance up trees to look back before jumping to the ground and running after the rest of the group. Coatis are carnivores that live in bands of 20 or more and have a varied diet that includes, fruits, bird eggs and even giant tarantulas. To study them would have required radios, and that was far beyond my budget in the early days.

One of the most unexpected encounters I had was with a Brazilian squirrel. The little grey animal was perhaps two handspans long when its tail was stretched out behind, but most of the time it carried its tail curled over its back. Its behavior was just like the squirrels in films I had seen as a child and the cartoon characters in Walt Disney movies. Its tail twitched compulsively and it jumped nimbly from tree to tree, only stopping to eat a palm nut it found on the ground and carried to a fork in an understory tree. I took the opportunity to move closer and it watched me with its huge black eyes as it gnawed on the nut.

I was surprised because I always associated squirrels with acorns or pine cones in frigid forests covered in snow in winter time. The little creature seemed out of place in a tropical rainforest. Only later I would learn that there are more species of tree squirrels in South America than North America, though the northern continent has many more species of ground squirrels, such as prairie dogs. There are even more species of tree squirrels in tropical Africa and Asia. Louise Emmons found nine species of squirrels coexisting in tropical forest at her field site in Gabon. It is only a minority of species of squirrels that live in oak trees and store acorns for the winter, but they have become "typical" squirrels because they play such an important role in children's entertainment.

I found few terrestrial mammals while walking at night, except for deer and pacas. Most of the larger mammals are quickly reduced to very low numbers in, or are excluded from, patches of forest that are hunted intensively by humans. After a few years, the catch consists almost exclusively of deer and pacas, and the last to go are usually the pacas. This is strange because pacas produce only one young at a time and do not have a large potential rate of increase, which is considered essential for a species to resist hunting.

Pacas look like like heavy-set agoutis, but are much larger and weigh up to 14 kg. Lines of white dots on their sides make them stand out when spotlighted, but probably camouflage them under natural light at night. I frequently found them close to my

Photo 6.6 *Agoutis, like this red-rumped agouti, are the animals most often recorded in line-transect surveys in the Amazon. Photo by Bill Magnusson.*

camp and I could get close to the juveniles, which did not seem to understand the danger behind the light. Adults live in burrows, but their usual method of escape was to dive into the stream. As the water was transparent, I could follow them as they walked along the bottom of the stream for ten or twenty meters, appearing much like the hippopotamuses I had seen underwater in Jacques Cousteau's films. After about five minutes, they would slowly emerge on the opposite side of the stream and creep up the bank, apparently unaware that the spot light meant that they were being followed.

Creeping seemed to be their principle mode of locomotion, and slow and wary seemed to sum up their overall behavior. An ornithologist friend from South Africa visited me and I showed her where she could photograph humming birds feeding on ground bromelias. Animals generally don't appear when you want to show them to someone else, or when you have a camera in hand, so I was happy to find a paca foraging at night within ten meters of our camp. I told my friend to walk slowly and I positioned her within five meters of the paca, which was eating fallen fruit. The light apparently bothered the paca, which picked up a seed, walked about two meters, and carefully buried it under leaf litter before creeping into the underbrush.

I was impressed because burying seeds is more typical of agoutis than pacas, and displaying such complex behavior in front of someone with a camera is unusual for a wild animal. However, I did not see any flashes from my friend's camera and I asked her if something had gone wrong. She replied "I didn't take any photos; I'm here to photograph hummingbirds"!

To find animals in the forest canopy in Australia, you generally go out at night. However, the only medium-sized mammals I found at night in Reserva Ducke were two-toed sloths, kinkajous and common opossums. Most of the canopy mammals were diurnal, and the only ones that were easy to see were monkeys. Presumably, two-toed sloths are more abundant, but I have rarely been able to see one in old-growth forest.

I knew that other species were present because I saw their tracks. Deer footprints crossed our trails regularly, but I only saw about one deer for each four hours of walking. I could take you to Reserva Ducke today and find tracks of South American tapirs, jaguars, and pumas within a short time, but I could not show you the animals themselves. I have walked a few dozen meters from my camp to a stream and when I returned minutes later there were jaguar prints on top of mine, but the cats never showed themselves. I have occasionally heard tapirs running off, but the only individual I have seen close up at Reserva Ducke walked past me near our camp. It is hard to imagine how an animal weighing over 150 kg can walk so silently and hide so effectively.

There are other animals that seem to be impossibly cryptic. I saw a giant anteater crossing a road in Reserva Ducke soon after I started to work there, but I convinced myself that it must have been an illusion because I have never seen another in well-developed rainforest, though I have seen many of these ungainly animals that fossick noisily in the leaf litter in savannas and dry forests. I have seen the enormous holes of giant armadillos near savanna areas, but have never seen either them or their burrows in continuous rainforest. Based on all my years in the forest I would say that giant

Photo 6.7 *There are many species of squirrels in tropical forests. Photo by Bill Magnusson.*

anteaters and giant armadillos must be absent or vanishingly rare, but camera-trap studies have shown that they are common in most of the Amazon forest. How they avoid detection by human observers is beyond me.

I started reading the literature on South American mammals and found that researchers divided them in two classes: small mammals were animals that readily entered standard-sized box traps and the other class consisted of animals too large for the standard box traps that were usually studied by walking line transects through the forest. Animals in the latter class were called medium and large mammals, but that classification would make an African biologist laugh.

South America's largest land mammal, the lowland tapir, would at most be considered a medium-sized mammal in Africa, and most of the "medium and small" mammals would be considered tiny there. It is an example of the shifting baseline. Ten thousand years ago South America had mammals to rival even the biggest animals in Africa.

My experience in Reserva Ducke and other forests made me doubt the many estimates of mammal densities based on line transects. There were powerful statistical methods for estimating the density of all individuals that were potentially detectable, but they would be useless if a proportion of the population was simply undetectable by walking transects. It occurred to me that hunting pressure in Reserva Ducke and other places I worked, even when they were nominally National Parks, was so high that if a segment of the population was not detectable by hunters the species would have quickly become extinct locally. I only knew they hadn't because I saw their tracks and feces.

I was fairly sure that most individual monkeys were at least potentially detectable, but I had trouble with how the researchers were using line-transect methods for even for the detectable part of the population. A line transect is basically a variable-width plot and statistics are used to estimate the proportion of animals detected in the plot. Nobody would use a single conventional plot as used by foresters to estimate the density of trees in a national park because they realize that there is great variability among plots. However, primatologists often estimated the number of monkeys in a park based on one or a few line transects, and they produced the variability statistics provided by the program to indicate the uncertainty associated with their estimates. The problem is that the estimates of variability are for hypothetical resurveys of that plot, not the variability between plots. Worse still, the methods required that 30 to 60 groups were sighted to develop the detection functions, and the primatologists didn't understand that the groups had to provide independent information. It isn't viable to walk enough independent kilometers to see 30 groups of most primates, so the primatologists just cut trails 2 to 6 km long and spent many days walking up and down the same short track until they had recorded 30 groups, which in many cases was just recording the same group thirty times!

Photo 6.8 *Pacas generally creep through the undergrowth, but may dive into water to escape predators. Photo by Bill Magnusson.*

After reading a new book on-line transect methodology by a respected primatologist, I wrote a review explaining all the statistical errors, but before I sent it off I posted a copy to Graeme Caughley and asked his opinion. In the era of snail mail it took months to get the reply, but Graeme was extremely negative. He said that I had obviously misread the book, which had been published by a leading US university press. He said that they would never let anyone publish a book with such obvious statistical errors. I threw the manuscript in the rubbish bin, but two years later, when I went to visit him, Graeme asked "Where did you publish that manuscript". When I said that based on his evaluation I had thrown it out, he said "But I read the book. I couldn't believe that anyone could make such trivial statistical errors; you should publish." It was too late for a review and by that time I had collected so much of my own data that I didn't have time to write about the work published by others. However, I did publish a general note on the problem 20 years later[93].

I wasn't using line transects for mammals because I was pretty sure that there was an undetectable segment of the population, but my suspicions would only be confirmed more than 30 years later when José Fragoso published a definitive study based on data collected in Guyana. I first heard of Joe when he wrote to me asking if I could be the Brazilian counterpart for his Ph.D. studies. He had Canadian and Portuguese citizenship, and had been working with the Goeldi Museum in Belém near the mouth of the Amazon. I wrote back that I didn't have the qualifications for the proposal and I didn't hear from him for several decades. In the mean time, Joe had been studying mammals, often with line transects, on Maracá Island in the State of Roraima. The island, which is in the middle of the Uraricoera River, is covered by seasonal dry forest and supports a wide range of mammal species. Joe was especially interested in the white lipped peccaries and he bought a plane to follow their wide movements outside the island[62]. Despite crashing the plane several times, Joe survived and accumulated a wealth of knowledge about "big" mammals. I didn't have much interaction with Joe in those days, but I remember returning from Roraima on a plane with him and his wife, Kirsten Silvius. I had developed a biodiversity monitoring system and the most frequently used field module consisted of two 5 km straight-line transects separated by 1km. I suggested that it was a good basic system for monitoring mammals, but Joe thought that surveys of one trail in the morning had a high probability of detecting the same group of monkeys as surveys of the parallel trail in the afternoon. I tried to use geometry to explain to him that was unlikely, but an hour of arguing did not convince him. As we got off the plane, Kirsten said "It's hard to know who's more stubborn, Australians or Portuguese." I asked for her opinion, but I won't give her answer in case it's not politically correct.

Joe planned to train indigenous people to use line transects to monitor their hunting resources, but met with political difficulties in Brazil. Therefore, he and Kirsten obtained funding to do a detailed study in Guyana, just across the border from Roraima[136]. They enlisted Indian hunters from 23 villages and carried out line-transect surveys of the "large" mammals[63,64]. As with previous studies, the Indians saw almost none of the larger species, such as tapirs and deer, within several kilometers of the village. Further away they saw more, but the number they saw only reached

Photo 6.9 *Nocturnal animals, such as this nine-banded armadillo, are rarely detected in line-transect surveys. Photo by Bill Magnusson.*

a plateau beyond about 6 km from the village. Other researchers had used similar data to show the "empty forest" and calculate how much hunting had reduced the populations of the larger mammals. However, Joe asked the Indians to also survey for sign and they found just as many tracks, feces and other artifacts in the empty zone as beyond it. That is, the species were locally extinct, but kept on making foot prints and defecating! Joe had difficulty publishing the paper despite its huge sample sizes and impeccable design. Other researchers who had made their reputations by using line-transect surveys were not willing to admit that they simply cannot be used to evaluate the density or distribution of hunted mammals unless you take into account the unobservable segment by recording sign or other indirect evidence.

I knew none of that back in the early 1980s and just used my walks through the forest to increase my knowledge of South American natural history. I saw crested eagles, which were about the size of Australian wedge-tailed eagles, but wedge-tails don't occur in thick rainforest. Crested eagles can maneuver through the thick canopy and tangled undergrowth to capture their prey. At night I saw spectacled owls that appeared much larger than any owls I had seen in Australia, and occasionally Amazonian pigmy owls that could have fitted into the palm of my hand. I often saw bright eye shines that I thought must have belonged to a mammal only to find that the eyes were attached to a greater potoo. During the day these birds mimic vertical broken branches and you can sit beside one on a log without realizing it. They bear an uncanny resemblance to the distantly related tawny frogmouth in Australia.

An astounding variety of toucans occurred in the canopy, the patterns on their huge bills often as spectacular as the gaudy colors on their bodies. Macaws and dozens of species of smaller parrots competed with the toucans for figs and other fruits.

On the ground, the South American equivalents of Australian brush turkeys are curassows and trumpeters. Although there tends to be only one species of each in the interfluves between major rivers, different interfluves have different species, each with its own distinctive colors or crest. Guans, which look like small curassows, hopped around in the trees and serenaded us with their loud calls. However, as a biologist I was more interested in the tinamous; fat little birds that looked like overgrown quails. I had to walk slowly and silently to get a glimpse of an adult, but I often found the bright blue eggs of the largest species. Tinamous are paleognaths, which means that their closest living relatives are flightless birds, such as emus, ostriches and kiwis. Most even share the same breeding system; females mate with and lay their eggs in the nests of several males. The male broods the eggs of his multiple partners and cares for the chicks during the first weeks of their lives. As the female lays her egg before mating with each male, he may not even be raising his own offspring!

Photo 6.10 *José Fragoso teaching students how to do line-transect surveys for animal sign. Photo by Bill Magnusson.*

I was still looking for sloths, but I rarely saw one, even on the INPA grounds where I knew that there were many. The sloths were supposed to always be in the *Cecropia* trees, but I often scanned all the *Cecropia* trees on the campus without seeing one. Presumably, other trees are more attractive to the sloths at some times of year. Most of the three-toed sloths I saw were crossing roads, or brought to me by people who had found them on the road. That is a hazardous undertaking for creatures that crawl slowly.

I saw a sloth in the canopy of a tree in Reserva Ducke on one memorable occasion. Albertina was with me and the joy we had in seeing a wild sloth high in the canopy was soon replaced by regret at a stupid prank we played on a student. Thierry Gasnier had worked with us both at Alter do Chão and Reserva Ducke and we were impressed by his energy and appetite. Despite being very thin, Thierry ate more than the two of us combined. While we were preparing dinner Thierry would often eat a packet of biscuits and two packets of instant noodles just to whet his appetite. We underestimated the power of all that latent energy.

The sloth was in a tree beside a rocky stream near our camp. Both Albertina and I had tried to climb that tree to catch frogs we were studying, but always to no avail. We could climb most of the trees, even those without low branches, with a *peconha*, which is a strap around your feet that can be used to provide lateral force to hold to tree bark. Indigenous people used strips of bark to make the *peconha* and we used a nylon belt. However, the sloth tree was covered in slippery moss, and even with the *peconha* we couldn't climb more than a few meters.

When Thierry asked if he could climb the tree to see the sloth close up, we smiled at each other and said simultaneously "Of course you can!" Thierry donned the *peconha* and started to climb. Just like us, he slipped on the moss. After climbing two meters, he slipped down one. That was the point at which we had given up, but Thierry summoned all his energy, climbed another two meters and again slipped down one. Any normal human being would have given up, but Thierry didn't stop. He kept shinnying up and gaining a meter or so even after each slip down. We were speechless as we watched him use superhuman effort to reach the sloth about seven meters above ground.

By using willpower, Thierry was able access the energy stored in his tissues, but to release that energy requires oxygen, and if we exercise too quickly our blood can't carry the oxygen fast enough and our muscles have to use anaerobic respiration. This does not require oxygen, but produces lactic acid, which is toxic if in too high a concentration. Just as Thierry reached the sloth, his lactic acid load reached a critical point and he fainted.

There was only one small branch between Thierry and the ground. It broke his arm when he hit it, but the impact knocked him sideways into the stream, which cushioned his fall. He had no other injuries and when we pulled him onto dry land we were shaking and perhaps as shocked as he was. Had he died, it probably would have destroyed our lives as well.

Photo 6.11 *A greater potoo. Photo by Albertina Lima.*

I remembered when I had been stuck in the wombat hole as a kid and thought it would have been ignominious to have been killed by a wombat. Being killed by a sloth would probably be just as embarrassing! Thierry is now a professor in the Federal University of Amazonas and we don't encourage students to climb trees without proper safety equipment anymore.

I have found two-toed sloths crossing roads, but have also found them on the beaches at Alter do Chão during the dry season. They presumably drag themselves across the sand to drink from the river. While it is easy to catch three-toed sloths, the two-toeds are a different story. They are much faster than the three-toed sloths and their large claws and canine-like teeth can cause terrible wounds. Catching one usually requires two people, each holding two legs.

Both two-toed and three-toed sloths have long legs used to hang from tree branches, so you might suspect that they are closely related, but the biochemical evidence indicates that they originated from different stocks. The three-toed sloths are placed in the Megatheroidea, together with many extinct ground sloths that included species as large as elephants. The three-toed sloths are placed in the Mylodontoidea together with many other large ground sloths. Both radiations produced both terrestrial and arboreal species, but only the arboreal species survived the arrival of humans in the Americas. The giant sloths died out so recently that you can still find their dried dung in caves in North America[115].

Many plants in Australia are adapted to pollination by vertebrates. I had seen a captive eastern pigmy possum when I was still at high school and the tiny creature with big eyes captured my attention, but I was never able to see one in the wild, despite spending many hours spotlighting banksias, one of their favorite foods. In 2008, I took Brazilian biologist Zilca Campos to the Royal National Park to see lyrebirds. We didn't see any, but as we walked down a track, less than 10 m from our car, we saw tiny creatures flitting in a vine tangle at three in the afternoon. They were feathertail gliders, a species that pollinates Australian flowers, but that is not supposed to be active during the day. I tried to get close to see what they were doing, but my attention was diverted by the screams of a crimson rosella, a common large parrot in the area. The rosella was in the claws of a currawong that was flying with difficulty through the understory holding a prey species that was almost as large as itself.

It was a good lesson in how a generalist predator, such as a currawong, could turn into a raptor, but I have never seen a currawong capture another bird that way before or since. After the currawong and rosella were out of sight, the feathertail gliders had disappeared. These were two very unusual occurrences, and I decided that Zilca was a good luck omen for natural historians. Nevertheless, I never witnessed Australian mammals pollinating flowers.

Many Australian birds are adapted to feeding on nectar and pollen. Some species of honeyeaters of the family Meliphagidae have brushes on their tongues for feeding from flowers, as do some parrots, known as lorikeets. Some of the honeyeaters and all

Photo 6.12 *Thierry Gasnier practicing capoeira. His energy was amazing. Photo by Bill Magnusson.*

of the lorikeets are dove-sized birds that have to perch to feed from flowers. A few of the smaller honeyeaters sometimes hover in front of flowers, but only for a few seconds. Sunbirds and flowerpeckers do similar things in other parts of the world. Before I left for South America, a friend told me that I would be impressed by the "zip – zip" of the hummingbirds, but I didn't understand what he was talking about until I saw one in the wild.

The tiny bird hovered in front of me as though examining the huge lumbering creature that was blocking its path and then it disappeared into the undergrowth in incredibly fast flight that could only be described as a "zip". There are many species of hummingbirds in Manaus, but I could only distinguish the small green ones with stubby tails from the slightly larger brownish ones with long tails known as hermits.

When I opened my bird-identification guide I was overwhelmed by the diversity of tiny creatures and realized that I would not be able to identify most of them during the short time they hovered in front of me.

I have recently taken to placing a camera on a tripod in front of a flower to capture an image of the hummingbird and allow me to identify it, but even so I only get blurred images of the wings beating at up to 80 cycles per second. In the early years, I just tried to identify the larger ones with distinctive tails and those I found in delicate nests on the extremities of palm leaflets. Apart from the high speed and affinity for flowers, I never thought that they might show more complex behavior.

Albertina changed my mind. We had been recording the behavior of lizards that lived high in the canopy, and Albertina often lay on her back in front of our shelter to watch lizards. One day she asked in Portuguese "Have you seen that the hummingbird mimics a butterfly and a leaf?" This seemed strange to me so I asked her where she got the idea. She said "Look at that cluster of leaves on the branch above us; it's a hummingbird nest."

A short time after I lay down to watch the nest about 10 m above me, a butterfly approached it in a zig-zag pattern with intermittent flaps of its wings. When it was close to the bunch of leaves it closed its wings and fell into the nest. A short time later, a leaf fell out of the nest and floated downwards, buffered by the atmospheric eddies as were other leaves, but when it got to about 2 m from the ground it turned into a hummingbird and zipped off into the undergrowth. It was then that I realized that the "butterfly" I had seen was a hummingbird beating its wings as slowly as the colorful insects, and that the "leaf" was a hummingbird falling without beating its wings at all. Both were incredible examples of behavioral mimicry that must have flummoxed predators looking for hummingbird nests, and I was impressed that Albertina had been able to see through the deception.

Albertina invited a bird expert to see the phenomenon. He carefully noted the speed of fall of the hummingbird and showed that it was similar to that of the leaves that were always falling from the canopy. He published the paper in the Journal of Ornithology[45] and I was surprised to see that Albertina was not a coauthor. He explained that she had not made any significant scientific contribution and therefore only merited a mention in the methods. I continue to wonder what "significant" means.

Photo 6.13 *Two toed sloths, such as this southern two-toed sloth, are faster and more dangerous when handled than three-toed sloths. Photo by Bill Magnusson.*

As a child I thought of crows and ravens as the principal scavenging birds. They were always present around dead sheep in the fields or on roads where animals had been struck by cars. There were no crows in Manaus, but black vultures ornamented the tops of houses like soot-encrusted chimneys. They could be seen everywhere, probably due to the inefficient garbage collection and the habits of people newly-arrived from the interior, where waste disposal generally consisted of throwing scraps out the kitchen window to be scavenged by wild or farm animals. I was fascinated by the large birds, which largely ignored the humans who considered them as useful cleaners. Some people even raised baby vultures with their poultry. These became very tame and attached to their owners, defending the chickens against smaller predators. Like the crows in Australia, they were intelligent and adaptable.

Although they are now most common around towns, black vultures obviously didn't evolve in an environment dominated by humans. Their natural environment in the Amazon seems to have been principally the shores of large rivers where they scavenged fish and other animals washed onto the banks. They generally can't be found in closed-canopy rainforest. We found nests of black vultures in tree stumps and rock outcrops, but near the rivers they were most common at the bases of large kapok trees. They took advantage of the large buttresses that often formed completely-enclosed box-like structures that could only be accessed from the top. The vultures flew off when we approached, leaving their eggs, or their chicks covered in grey fluff to the potential predators. However, few animals eat black vultures, which accumulate toxins in their flesh from the rotting animals they eat. This probably explains why they are so tame.

We calculated that the association of the vultures with the buttress roots was not a one-sided arrangement[98]. Black vultures have an incubation period of 32 to 39 days and adults roost on the buttresses at other times. Their feces must fertilize the soil around the trees and, based on data from other species, the chicks would require around 20 kg of carrion before fledging, most of which would be deposited at the base of the tree. This is a potentially important resource for the tree that could be used to increase seed production.

All South American vultures have bare heads and necks, but they are not closely related to the Old-World vultures, the similarity being a case of convergence in morphology of species that have the same way of making a living. Some of the New World vultures have a very good sense of smell and use it to find carrion, but Old-World vultures use sight to find carcasses[71].

Other vultures were more common in naturally open areas, such as the savannas of Pará and Roraima. I occasionally saw lesser yellow-headed vultures, but the most common were turkey vultures with spectacularly contrasting red and white colors on the head, and greater yellow-headed vultures, which despite the common name often had spectacular blue and red heads. These species, especially the turkey vulture, use their sense of smell to find carcasses, and it is reported that black vultures follow turkey vultures to find carcasses and then chase them off. All species frequently sat on fence posts, and the long lines of birds with their wings held open were a spectacular sight.

Photo 6.14 *In Australia, nectar feeding birds, such as this rainbow lorikeet, are generally large and perch to feed from flowers. Photo by Bill Magnusson.*

The largest South American vulture, and in fact the largest flying bird, is the Andean condor. They don't occur in Brazil, however, and the most spectacular Amazonian bird scavenger is the King vulture. I first saw one when driving down the escarpment from the Venezuelan border towards Boa Vista in the Brazilian State of Roraima. It was sitting in a tree near the road and I imagined that it would be a chance to get a great photo. However, that stretch of road runs through the Raposa Serra do Sol indigenous reserve and rice farmers trying to take over the reserve had recently burned down a village school in an attempt to intimidate the indigenous owners. We had no sooner stopped to photograph the bird than a pickup truck full of angry Indians pulled up to urge us on our way.

I have since got closer to one, but without getting the photo that this spectacular species deserves. The vultures are mainly immaculate white, with black flight feathers and bright red, yellow and black on head and neck. This is a bird of the forest and difficult to see. It is listed as least concern by the IUCN, but it worries me that I have seen fewer king vultures than harpy eagles; I suspect that they occur at very low densities. Other than the Californian condor, scavenging birds were generally thought to be of little conservation concern when I was a youngster, but now species of vultures are considered the most threatened group of birds, collapsing toward extinction[32], so all species should be monitored.

I was baiting mammal traps with a mixture of rolled oats and peanut butter, as I had in Australia, but I captured few mammals and initially I had no-one to suggest better methods. That changed when I visited the WWF Minimal Critical Size of Ecosystems Project, which is now run by the Smithsonian Institution and called the Biological Dynamics of Forest Fragments Project (PDBFF). At that time, they rented a house in the fashionable suburb of Parque 10 in Manaus. I don't remember why I went to the project, but I was talking to the project leader and was fascinated by the new Apple computers. I had never seen a mouse used to point and click before and everything seemed way more sophisticated than my simple laboratory equipped with a DOS operated computer that only accepted typed commands.

The office used to be a bed room, but the bed had been pushed across to one corner and I hardly noticed a slight woman with mousy colored hair sitting on it. When I was about to leave, she walked over and said "I want to talk to you about field work on mammals." I told her that I didn't work much on mammals and that the other people in the room could tell her much more about the conditions in the WWF reserves. She said "No, you're a field person; these people don't go into the field!" I looked around quickly because I knew that most of the people in the room considered themselves field biologists, but apparently no-one was listening. Her name was Louise Emmons and I would learn that she is one of the foremost field mammalogists in South America.

Louise studied African squirrels for her Ph.D. and had spent many years working in Cocha Cachu in Peru. She planned to study small mammals at the WWF reserves and had convinced the coordinators of the project to buy Tomahawk° woven-wire mammal traps, which were much larger than the Sherman° aluminum traps I had been using.

Photo 6.15 *Hummingbirds, such as this Purple-crowned Woodnymph from the Serra Nevada of Colombia, have transparent flight feathers and beat their wings up to 80 times a second. Photo by Bill Magnusson.*

We spent a lot of time talking and I invited her to see Reserva Ducke before she went into the field at the WWF reserves.

We camped on Acará Creek and walked the salt trail at night. I always walked barefoot and she said that she would too, even though I warned her against it. We had not been on the trail long when she asked "Do you see many deer?" I explained to her that deer were scarce in the reserve and that I only saw one for about four hours of walking. She said "That's strange; this is good deer habitat." She stopped walking, scanned the undergrowth with long sweeps of her headlight, and seconds later exclaimed "Ah! There it is!"

She was pointing at a deer sitting hidden in the undergrowth that was looking away so as not to give eyeshine. I never would have seen it if she hadn't pointed it out. For decades, she had been walking forest trails at night and this resulted in an uncanny ability to spot mammals and understand their subtle habitat requirements. I was fascinated by her skill and understanding of mammal natural history, but when we got back to camp I noticed that her feet were bleeding from the bites of the *Syntermes* termites, the soldiers of which have long blade-like jaws which lock into position when closed. I was used to avoiding them, but I remembered the painful bites I had received when I first started walking around the forest barefoot. I told Louise that I was sorry about the bites, but she said "It's no problem. I'm glad because I never paid them much attention before and now I am linking the termites to the type of soil and that may lead to an association with mammals." I suspect that there is no natural-history observation that Louise can't put into her model of rainforest functioning.

Louise invited me to see her work at the WWF reserves and I agreed. I had been to one of the reserves previously, but it was on a short trip netting bats with Don Wilson of the Smithsonian Institution. We set nets in the forest interior, but Don was unhappy with the low number of bats we caught and went to put nets in the regrowth at the interface between the forest and pasture, which gave much better results in terms of number of bats caught per hour. I remained in the camp with an assistant. The project did not permit researchers to walk around the forest alone, but my "assistant" was obviously afraid of the forest at night and it didn't take much to convince him to let me wander off by myself.

That led to one of the strangest experiences I have had in the forest. I was using a headlight powered by four AA batteries, which was state of the art technology at the time, but the weak yellowish light lasted less than an hour. I had a spare set of batteries, but that still limited me to about two hours in the forest; one hour going and an hour to get back to camp. I walked along the bank of a small creek that wasn't much more than a trickle for about an hour until the batteries ran out, whence I replaced them and started back.

The second set of batteries was getting low, but I wasn't much worried until I realized that I was passing a part of the stream that I had already walked along. As I had been walking upstream all the time, that didn't seem possible and I became nervous, unsure what was wrong with my mental map. My nervousness turned to panic when a peccary broke through the grass lining the creek and made straight for my legs. I shinnied up a sapling about the thickness of my arm and held on as long as I could before my hands started to cramp and I had to drop down.

Photo 6.16 *Black vulture chicks are raised in simple nests on broken tree trunks or directly on the ground at the base of a large tree or boulder. Photo by Bill Magnusson.*

The first thing I did upon hitting the ground was to look around for the peccary, which I saw had turned into a greater long-nosed armadillo, which the Brazilians appropriately call *quinze quilos* (15 kg). In an emergency you let your subconscious tell you what's going on and mine had confused the grey back of an armadillo in the faint light with that of a peccary. I had never seen a greater long-nosed armadillo before and decided to follow it, but it had been startled by my tree climbing and ran into the small stream and disappeared down an underwater burrow. I never thought that an armadillo might have an aquatic refuge.

I had accumulated a lot of unusual experiences and my heart was still beating rapidly as I followed my tracks back to the camp. I still can't figure out how I had managed to circle while apparently walking continually upstream, but Barbara Zimmerman, who studied frogs in the WWF reserves for her Ph.D., told me later that she had the same experience in the same place. Perhaps we had stumbled onto Indian sacred ground!

I camped with Louise in another part of the reserve and she planned to set the Tomahawk traps to catch small mammals. Instead of peanut butter, she used almost-ripe plantains as bait which she said were superior because most of the small-mammal species preferred them, and it took longer for ants to steal the bait. We arrived late in the evening and Louise said that we would set the traps the next day. After a quick breakfast of coffee and buttered biscuits she picked up two hessian bags, one for each shoulder, and pointed at another which she said I could carry.

The bag, which was full of Tomahawk traps, was very heavy, perhaps weighing fifteen kilos, and I stumbled along the slippery clay track after Louise. I would have called and told her to slow down, but that would have made me seem very wimpy as she was carrying twice the weight that I was. It took most of the day to set the traps and record information about the habitat around them. The next morning there were rats in the traps, which I recognized as spiny rats of the genus *Proechimys*. Their spines are not very long and you have to run your hand along the back from tail to head to notice them. *Proechimys* is a genus of hystricomorph rodents. This group colonized South America from Africa more than 40 million years ago, probably by rafting across the Atlantic Ocean when it was somewhat narrower than today.

Some histricomorphs, such as *Proechimys*, look much like the murid rodents of Europe and Australia, but their biology is very different. They don't "breed like rats". Instead of producing up to a dozen blind, naked, immature babies, spiny-rat females produce just two very large, fully-furred offspring that together may weigh a third as much as their mother. In general, *Proechimys* are very peaceful and I found them easy to handle in comparison with black or sewer rats, and I never worried about being bitten. However, I once kept one overnight in an upended Tomahawk trap. When I opened the trap to feed her, she leapt up and bit me. It was only then that I realized that she had given birth overnight and was protecting her babies.

The first hystricomorphs to get to South America were presumably similar to *Proechimys*, but they diversified into a wide range of forms. The largest today are capybaras, but some extinct forms were the size of hippopotamuses. Others, such as Patagonian maras, look like small antelope, and Old World porcupines share an uncanny resemblance to African porcupines, which are also hystricomorphs, but only distantly related.

Photo 6.17 *The king vulture is the most spectacular of the Amazonian vultures. Photo by Bill Magnusson.*

It is very difficult to separate the species of *Proechimys*, especially because adult size is not a good criterion. Female proechimys fall pregnant while still only half grown and continue to reproduce throughout their lifetimes. Jay Malcom, who also worked on mammals at the WWF reserves, took dental imprints of the animals he caught so that he could estimate their ages and determine whether they were still growing. This allowed him distinguish the species.

Louise took blood samples to prepare slides so that she could count chromosomes and differentiate some of the species. Some months later we were camped at Alter do Chão near the Tapajós River and Louise was capturing rats for chromosome analyses, and to prepare skins and skulls for museum collections. She did not kill the rats immediately, but injected them with colchicine. This chemical halts cell division so that you get lots of cells with easily recognized chromosomes, and it is not something that you want in your body. I had returned to camp late in the afternoon and Louise was frying rat carcasses over the open fire. I thought that it was a good idea not to waste the bodies after skins and skulls had been removed and eagerly chomped on the fresh fried rats, which reminded me of the rabbit kittens I had eaten as child. While carefully picking the last meat off a leg bone, I commented "These were very good, but I didn't think there were any rats that you hadn't injected with colchicine."

Louise replied "But there aren't any; I injected all these with colchicine." Seeing that I had gone decidedly white, she said "Don't worry, the heat denatures the colchicine." I believe that she was probably right, but I didn't eat any more of the spiny rats!

I would have liked to have spent more time in the field with Louise, but she put in a grant to study tree shrews in Borneo and got it. She had invited me to go, but found that her sponsors did not fund assistants. Most South American mammologists use her field guide to mammals, but I suspect that those who have not been in the field with her do not appreciate the decades of field work that gave her the experience to write that treatise.

Photo 6.18 *Spiny rats of the genus* Proechimys *are hystricomorphs and more closely related to capybaras than to house rats. Photo by Bill Magnusson.*

Photo 6.19 *Louise Emmons has spent much of her life studying tropical mammals. Photo by Bill Magnusson.*

CHAPTER 7 - PANTANAL

Jabirus are iconic birds of the Pantanal. Photo by Bill Magnusson.

After I left the Fisheries Department, I had little contact with otters. Giant otters had been hunted nearly to extinction in the areas close to Manaus, and the smaller Neotropical otters were hard to see. These can grow to a meter long, but a large part of that is tail. I was sitting in Reserva Ducke looking for turtles where a rock shelf had resulted in a series of pools much deeper than most of the brook. Looking downstream, I saw a plume of mud coming from under the bank, but it petered out and another formed closer to me. I stood up, but could not see what was causing the disturbance under the bank until an otter surfaced to breathe a few meters upstream. I had less than a second to observe it before it disappeared underwater and another plume of debris spewed from under the bank about 5 m further up.

That is the only time I have seen an otter in Reserva Ducke, though I have occasionally found their feces on logs beside the stream. I can count on one hand the number of times I have seen Neotropical otters in the wild, though there seem to be few places where you can't find their feces on rocks or logs beside the water. I would see quite a few giant otters in the Pantanal, which is an extensive flooded savanna on the border between Brazil and Paraguay, but for reasons not related to experience in the aquatic sciences; again it was due to my overrated reputation as a specialist in aerial survey.

Guilherme Mourão and Zilca Campos, two scientists employed by EMBRAPA, the Brazilian agricultural research organization, invited me to Corumbá in 1987 to help them plan their caiman studies and one of the projects involved aerial surveys across the Pantanal[125]. Aerial surveys only give very rough indications of the distribution and abundance of caimans because a large proportion of adults and all young are virtually invisible from a plane. However, Guilherme got funding for the surveys and we realized that other species, such as marsh deer, could be counted in the same surveys. Guilherme therefore invited another EMBRAPA scientist, Rodiney Mauro, to participate. Rodiney used the data for his masters thesis.

Marsh deer are large majestic cervids, a bit like the red deer of the northern hemisphere, but they are always found close to water. In fact, they spend most of their time in water deep enough to cover their hocks or even above their knees[116]. Occasionally they wade up to their necks to reach preferred plants. I was used to seeing deer creeping into the undergrowth, so watching these beautiful creatures in the open Pantanal was a treat for me.

Photo 7.1 *Marsh deer are elegant. Photo by Walfrido Tomas.*

The famous mammologist George Schaller together with the Brazilian biologist J. M. Vasconcelos had previously surveyed for marsh deer in the Pantanal and their findings were disturbing[157]. They reported that "numbering possibly as many as 7000 animals .... it is seriously threatened, following three bad breeding seasons, 1975–77, attributable ... to disease, perhaps brucellosis which is common in the cattle of the area. Heavy flooding has also taken a toll." Rodiney's estimate of the number of marsh deer in the Pantanal using the double-count method was 36,315 individuals[117], which indicated that it was very unlikely that there were only 7000 animals in the Pantanal in 1977 or that disease had limited their population growth. It was one of those good-news stories about wildlife that is becoming rarer each year.

After the aerial surveys, Guilherme and I collaborated in various studies, and he often recommended that students working with him should do their post-graduate studies at INPA. When he started long-term studies of giant otters I became involved vicariously through two Ph.D. students, both of which were called Carol. Carolina Ribas Pereira is agitated, of average height, looks at you with intense brown eyes and you can imagine her dancing in the Carnaval of Rio de Janeiro. Caroline Leuchtenberger is tall, more reserved, and her blue eyes would not be out place on the streets of Stockholm. The first studied the genetics of different family groups[139,141], which required her to catch them or try to get tissue samples remotely. Carol Leuchtenberger studied the behavior of the groups[79,80], especially their calls[81,83], and both studied the diet[84,140]. In fact, they often worked together and published jointly.

I mainly helped with the analyses, but you can't, or at least shouldn't, analyze something you have no feel for. Therefore, I accompanied the field work of both students in 2010. Unlike the Neotropical otter, giant otters are extremely social and live in extended family groups. They are generally hard to see in the Amazon, but they are concentrated into the small Pantanal rivers during the dry season. Each group has a stretch of river that it defends strenuously against other otter groups. As the Pantanal rivers are favorite destinations for amateur fishermen, and systematic hunting of otters has been repressed for years, the otter groups are used to people and you can observe them relatively closely without interfering with their behavior. Carol Leuchtenberger took me to see some of the groups she was working on.

Carol had radios on one member of each group, so she could find them quickly in the dry season when they were confined to rivers and their home ranges could be represented by lines on a map[79]. It was much more complicated in the high-water season when the groups spread out across the Pantanal and their home ranges became two dimensional[82]. It was the low-water season when Carol took me to see her study animals and she quickly located them with the signals captured by the huge antenna she held braced against the bottom of the boat.

We did not approach closely, but observed them with binoculars as they dived under the overhanging vegetation in search of slow-moving fish. I assume that they communicated vocally underwater because they moved as a group despite each member apparently searching alone. Giant otters have complex vocal repertoires[81], but you can

Photo 7.2 *Giant otters have permanent latrines where they dance on their own feces. Photo by Carolina Leuchtenberger.*

only hear the airborne sounds when close to the otters. Occasionally one animal, probably the dominant male or female, would lift its body high out of the water, showing the white marks on its chest, and look around, but it quickly went back to fossicking near the bank.

It would be nearly impossible to catch a giant otter when free swimming in the river, but Guilherme and the two Carols needed to get close to where otters were or had been around burrows and latrines. Giant otters spend most of the night in deep burrows dug into the bank, though predation threat from a jaguar and the presence of a large fish shoal apparently led to the otters being active for short periods at night[80]. By putting traps and nets to block burrow entrances, the team had been able to catch and afix radio transmitters to several animals.

The otters apparently don't defecate in the water, but climb onto the bank in specific locations to deposit their poop. These places are probably important for marking their territories because the otters do not just attend to their necessities discreetly; they dance on their excrement to spread it over an area of several meters, which becomes bare and stinking. That is, stinking to human nostrils. It probably just smells like home to giant otters, and many vertebrates use the latrines as a food source[78].

By collecting fish bones and other remains at latrine sites, the scientists were able to determine otter diets[84], and cameras installed at these locations revealed much about otter behavior[80]. Giant otters will even leave their dens at night to go to the toilet! Latrines are probably important for communicating clan membership and group size, but giant-otter disputes over territories are not only conducted remotely. When clans meet at territory borders, or when a larger group decides to increase its territory at the expense of its neighbors, fights can break out that lead to serious injuries and death.

The only predator capable of killing a giant otter in the Pantanal is the jaguar, and even this mighty beast of prey would probably come out second best if it tried to catch an otter in deep water. Therefore, other members of the same species are probably the most dangerous adversaries for giant otters. Long-term studies by Guilherme and his students have shown that their territories are dynamic, and that group size is important in determining the outcome of conflicts[82], much as it is in human disputes.

With the reduction in illegal hunting, giant-otter populations in the Pantanal are probably close to carrying capacity, and this has forced some groups into marginal habitats. Roads are constructed in the Pantanal by digging soil from trenches along the route and using this to form a rampart to support the thoroughfare. The holes beside the roads are called borrow pits and can be up to half a hectare in area. This is very good for tourism in the Pantanal, because much of the fauna concentrates around borrow pits during the dry season and can be observed easily from a car. Nevertheless, borrow pits are not ideal for all aquatic organisms.

As the water evaporates, borrow pits concentrate large numbers of dead and dying fish, which attract many animals, such as birds and caimans, that also defecate in the water. It is the sort of soup that you wouldn't want to drink. Giant otters would probably avoid such places in the dry season if they had a choice, but some of the

Photo 7.3 Carolina Leuchtenberger and Guilherme Mourão radio tracking giant otters in 2010. Photo by Bill Magnusson.

smaller groups don't. Either they disperse to the borrow pits or they will die in disputes with larger groups. Guilherme's students found that the otters can survive when things get bad by taking alternative prey, such as caimans, but they lose condition and the tissues around their eyes and mouth swell up and become red as yours would if you swam in the borrow pits at that time of year[140]. High densities of otters in the Pantanal are good for conservation, but not necessarily good for individual otters.

I got to see otters closer up when I went into the field with Carol Ribas. Some of her studies required tissue samples for genetic analyses, and the number of animals caught at dens was not sufficient. Therefore, she needed a method of removing tissue from free-living otters. One possibility was to shoot a hollow dart attached to a string into the thigh of an otter, recover the dart and use the tissue in the tip cavity for the analyses. This is great in theory, but getting close to a giant otter is not easy, and it would be too dangerous for the animal to aim at the head or neck, which are usually the only parts visible when it is in the water.

A professional hunter could be paid to do this, but that would have used up all of Carol's research budget long before she had enough otters. Fortunately, her partner, Gabriel Damasceno, had been raised in the USA and was an avid outdoorsman/ adventurer, amatuer marksman, and now gunsmith apprentice. Hunting native fauna is illegal in Brazil, as is the possession of high-powered rifles by the general population, which means that most hunting is done furtively at night using shotguns. In contrast, hunting is a multi-billion-dollar industry in the USA, with many hunters willing to pay thousands of dollars for the opportunity to shoot just one or two individuals per year of favored species. Gabriel did not need much convincing to help Carol get the samples she needed.

One group of otters surfaced near our boat and I was thrilled to see them so close. They lifted much of their forebodies out of the water to look around at this point, which was near the limit of their territory, but they seemed to be as interested in each other as they were in checking us out. Close encounters of this kind must have been common in the Amazon before the skin trade eliminated the species from the most heavily populated areas.

To get a shot at an animal out of the water, Gabriel would have to be positioned near a latrine long before the group arrived and that would take a lot of patience. We moored the seven-meter-long aluminum canoe about 20 m downstream of the latrine and sat silently as the hunter made his way along the muddy bank. Mosquitoes sucked our blood, but we had to be careful not to make any brisk movements that would clang against the side of the boat.

Gabriel scrambled along the muddy bank, perched between the water and the overhanging roots. When he was about 5 m from where he thought the otters would leave the water, he lay down in the mud with his rifle stretched out before him. He was dressed in camouflaged apparel similar to that used by soldiers in wartime and the sticky mud he had accumulated moving along the bank helped the disguise.

Photo 7.4 *Giant otters are highly social. Photo by Carolina Leuchtenberger.*

We had been sitting silently for over an hour when I saw Guilherme's gaze shift and I followed it to see slight movements near the opposite bank. The otters crossed the river as though intent on reaching the latrine and completely ignored us. Each animal surfaced only momentarily and I could not tell them apart, but Carol knew every member of the band and had given Gabriel strict instructions about which individual he was to try to get a sample from. He had not looked around, but lay staring at the place the otter would pass and give him a clear shot. I was a little uncomfortable in the boat and could only imagine how he must have been feeling, lying cold in the wet mud and unable to make the slightest movement to alleviate cramped muscles.

The otters must have been suspicious, because they spent a long time mulling in front of the latrine and only a few ventured onto land. I held my breathe as an otter loped up the bank in front of Gabriel and was relieved to hear the pop of the compressed-gas cylinder that indicated the dart had been launched. The startled otter ran back to the water and Carol ran across to retrieve the dart, but it had not collected any tissue. I think that Gabriel's aim was true, but the dart has to pull the fine line that attaches it to the reel on the gun and any slight angle other than straight on will make it ricochet off rather than biting into muscle.

Carol did not successfully collect any genetic samples while I was with her, but the experience was enough for me to have a new appreciation of the effort that went into every data point that was in her thesis. Scientific studies appear so simple when you read about them in journals and I suspect that most readers do not appreciate the years of work that field researchers, such as Guilherme and the two Carols, put in to get the data summarized in their tables and graphs.

Guilherme and Zilca Campos kindly took me to many interesting locations in the Pantanal over the years, but we spent most of the time at Nhumirim, EMBRAPA's research station in the Nhecolandia region. That part of the Pantanal is characterized by circular lakes, generally only a few hundred meters in diameter, spread over the floodplain. Like the borrow pits, the lakes concentrate wildlife in the dry season and the native species share the area with feral pigs and EMBRAPA's cattle.

Today, advances in technology allow spectacular scenes of tiny animals, but when I was a kid, film cameras rarely captured small details, so film crews pilgrimaged to Africa to capture scenes of mammals in action. Most of the children from that generation grew up expecting to see spectacular wildlife scenes when they travelled, and they are often disappointed in places like the Amazon where the biodiversity is abundant, but difficult to see. The Pantanal does not have any really big animals, and probably never had because it formed only about 10,000 years ago, long after humans had eliminated the South American megafauna. Nevertheless, it hosts many animals that can be seen from a distance and that are active during the day, such as Jabiru storks and capybaras, making it a Mecca for wildlife enthusiasts.

Photo 7.5 *Carolina Ribas and Gabriel Damasceno after an unsuccessful ambush. Photo by Bill Magnusson.*

The tiny patches of forest provide shade for nocturnal animals, but little protection from the probing eyes of would-be predators, such as humans. You can get close to tapirs, South American coatis and giant anteaters, and if there are not many animals nearby, you can quickly drive your car to where there are. In the early years, the costs of film limited my photography, but on recent trips I have captured long sequences of brocket deer grazing, jabirus displaying and capybaras interacting. There have been times of year, however, when there were so many mosquitoes that their buzzing and flying in front of the lens made filming difficult.

In the Amazon forest, I often go hours without seeing a mammal at night, and when I do the chances of getting a photograph are minimal. The first time I went spotlighting at Nhumirim I expected to walk kms from the base to see wildlife, but I hadn't gone 20 m when I saw a crab-eating fox. The little dog was looking for prey in the longer grass along the fence line and it ignored my light, even snapping at the insects that were apparently attracted to where the beam was focused. The same species occurs in the Amazon, but I have rarely seen it in the wild.

Another a few minutes and I saw a crab-eating raccoon foraging in the shallow water accumulated in a ditch. It appeared to be using its front paws to feel for food underwater, but I didn't see it catch anything. The common names of the fox and the raccoon do not mean that they have a predilection for crabs, it's just that freshwater crabs are among the largest and commonest invertebrates in many parts of South America. The raccoons forage alone at night in distinct contrast to the large group of coatis that I had seen in the same place during the day. I walked past the capybaras that had gone from spectacular to interesting to boring over the previous few days simply because it was hard to look somewhere without seeing one.

I hurried past pairs of small burrowing owls sitting in front of their holes and tried to get a close-up photograph of a brocket deer, but it crept into the undergrowth and I did not follow because of the tangle of spiny ground bromeliads that so often occupies the edge of the understory in Pantanal forests. A little further on I saw the rear end of a tapir doing the same disappearing trick. I was used to finding mammals in Australia from their eyeshines, but here it was not only the capybaras that reflected my light. A sweep of the beam revealed the eyes of dozens of caimans and nightjars that provided camouflage for the mammals.

I stopped in my tracks when I saw a huge jaguar walking down the gulley towards me and I started fumbling with my camera, which I had wrapped in a plastic bag in case it fell in the water. My headlight was state of the art for the time, which meant that it wasn't very good. When the cat finally got close enough, I saw that my "jaguar" was in reality just an ocelot, but it still seemed much bigger than the ocelots I had seen in the Amazon. I have long decided that I can't judge the size of animals without something near them as a reference. If my imagination can blow up an ocelot to the size of a jaguar, it can probably do anything. When I finally got the camera out I decided that it would be impossible to get a shot with that light and a 50 mm lens. Today, I would be able to get some nice footage with my little 30-times zoom camera and my 600-lumen led headlight.

Photo 7.6 *As in other regions with abundant wildlife, the Pantanal has many scavengers, such as this lesser yellow-headed vulture. Photo by Bill Magnusson.*

The impression of superabundant wildlife in the Pantanal is probably misleading because the wildlife has to concentrate around water during the dry season and around the few areas of high ground during the flood season. Nevertheless, it is an experience that shouldn´t be missed by anyone with a passion for mammals and birds.

***Photo** 7.7 Crab-eating foxes are common in the Pantanal. Photo by Bill Magnusson.*

CHAPTER 8 - ILHA DO CARDOSO

Hystricomorphs, like this *Trinomys iheringi*, are superficially similar to common rats, but they are more closely related to capybaras and porcupines. Photo by Helena Bergallo.

The only species of aquatic mammal that I encountered in Reserva Ducke was the Neotropical otter and I suspect that might have something to do with the presence of Schneider's dwarf caimans. These little crocodilians eat many mammals[105] and the biomass of the caimans in Reserva Ducke is probably higher than the biomass of all the mammalian predators combined[97]. It is easy to imagine how they catch pacas and other mammals commonly associated with water, but they also consistently eat monkeys and porcupines[105], which presumably rarely descend to the streams. Most aquatic mammals would have little chance of avoiding the ubiquitous caimans in the tiny streams.

In most parts of Australia you can find water rats and platypuses in small streams, and they are in most danger from terrestrial or aerial predators, such as foxes or birds of prey. Platypuses close their eyes when underwater and detect their prey with electrical sensors in their beaks. If they had aquatic predators, they almost certainly would have evolved to keep their eyes open when diving. They usually only remain on the surface to breathe for a few seconds, so you have to be very patient or very lucky to get a photo of one. The water rats eat mainly terrestrial prey, such as frogs, so they are alert for predators when hunting.

There are many streams in Brazil that have no dwarf caimans, so I was interested to learn if they had semi-aquatic mammals like those that occur in Australia. The opportunity to do so resulted from two chance encounters. In 1983 I met Helena Bergallo, better known as Nena, at a congress in Belém. Her future husband, Fred Rocha, had suggested that I talk to her and that started a friendship among our families that lasts to this day. About the same time, I met Tim Moulton, an expatriate Australian who was passing through Manaus looking for a job. There were no openings in Manaus, but Tim found a position as coordinator of research on Cardoso Island off the coast of São Paulo.

Tim organized Earthwatch expeditions to Cardoso Island, which is a State reserve. Earthwatch expeditions are staffed by volunteers, often retirees, who pay to go to interesting places to help with research, and Tim asked me to participate. Cardoso Island is very different from the central Amazon, which tends to be flat and covered

Photo 8.1 *Dwarf caimans even capture arboreal mammals, such as this bicolored-spined porcupine. Photo by Bill Magnusson.*

by sedimentary soils. The topography on Cardoso Island is rugged, with granite-like syenite peaks surrounded by extensive sandy flat areas beyond the beaches. Most of the streams have only tiny pools and consist mainly of fast flowing rapids and waterfalls. Broad-snouted caimans occur in the mangroves and adjoining plains, but do not penetrate far up the streams.

I had been walking up a small stream at night when I noticed something swimming along the bank towards me. My first impression was that it was a water rat because it was being propelled by a sculling tail, but I saw that its head was held high above the water. It ignored the light and when it was between me and the bank I could see that it was using its hands to rummage in holes and leaf litter, much as I had seen crab-eating raccoons doing in the Pantanal. It wasn't using its eyes at all to forage, and in that sense it was acting much like a platypus, but it did not grope any deeper than was possible without submerging its head.

I could now see that it was strikingly marked, with black patches outlined by broad white bands. The only mammal with similar contrasting coloring I knew of was the striped ringtail of northern Australia. It was easy to catch the animal because it appeared to be blinded by my light. I grabbed it around the neck and it opened its mouth, revealing spiky teeth similar to those of the common opossum. It was about the size of an Australian water rat or a wild rabbit, but its hind feet were even bigger in relation to its body than those of water rats, and the toes were connected by broad webs like those of a duck. It scratched me with the nails on its hind feet, but its hands were delicate, with long fingers like those of a monkey.

This was a yapok, a South American marsupial with a distribution from México to Argentina, but largely absent from large parts of the Amazon basin. It is the only living marsupial in which both sexes have a pouch. Strong closure of the backward facing mouth of the pouch allows female yapoks to keep their babies dry when swimming, and the males use their pouch to protect their genitalia when in the water, much the way humans males use togs to protect the family jewels.

Nena had asked me to supervise her Ph.D. thesis and here was the perfect study animal. Despite its broad distribution, very little is known about the population dynamics of yapoks or how they use streams. I was ecstatic. A beautiful enigmatic animal living in a subtropical paradise that was easy to capture and observe in the wild. What could be better? It wasn't difficult to convince Nena, and she started the project enthusiastically.

That was when reality hit. If nobody else had studied yapoks intensively there must be a reason. The idea that any animal with such a broad distribution could be so vulnerable to capture does not make sense. Nena did catch some, but they learned quickly. Instead of fumbling blindly into her hands, they just gave a quick glimpse of eye shine and then disappeared dozens of meters from where she was waiting. I insisted, but there was just no way that she could catch enough to justify a Ph.D. project. Yapok biology remains a must do project for my next reincarnation!

Photo 8.2 *The yapok is a semi-aquatic marsupial that uses its long fingers to capture prey. Photo by Bill Magnusson.*

All was not lost, however. Nena being an inveterate mammologist set traps around the streams and captured four rodent species. Three of them, *Nectomys squamipes*, *Euryoryzomys russatus* and *Akodon cursor*, are sigmodontine rodents, presumably descendants of ancestors that entered South America from North America when the two continents came into proximity. The fourth was an echymid rodent *Trinomys iheringi*, which is descended from an African ancestor, like the *Proechimys* in central Amazonia. They would be the focus of her Ph.D. thesis and Nena collected data from February 1993 to January 1995.

Like many of my students, Nena fell pregnant during data collection. Maybe I should open a fertility clinic! My wife Albertina conceived on almost the same day and was also doing her Ph.D., but Albertina had already collected most of her data and didn't have to drag heavy mammal traps around slippery terrain with a swollen belly. Numbers of captures and trap nights do not allow you to evaluate the personal struggles that each researcher has to face to generate the data. There were no holes in the series of data on rat reproduction that Nena collected despite being engaged in her own reproductive activities.

Nectomys squamipes is often described as a water rat because it is rarely found far from water and it has been reported to forage in a manner similar to that of the yapok, feeling for submerged prey while swimming with its head out of water, but Nena's trapping data indicated that they spend much of their time up to 40 m from the stream[18]. Nena did not sample prey availability in the stream, but survivorship of *Nectomys squamipes* was lower when there were few fruits available, so this species probably depends as much or more on food sources on land as those in the water.

The sigmodontine rodents all bred in the warm wet season, though they did not peak in the same months. Only the echymid, *Trinomys iheringi*, reproduced most of the year with a peak in the cold dry season[17], reinforcing my conclusion that the contribution of African hystricomorph rodents to biological diversity went far beyond just providing some large species. Despite their superficial morphological similarity, hystricomorphs like *Trinomys* and *Proechimys* are ecologically very different from the northern-hemisphere rodents and their descendents.

The largest extant herbivorous and carnivorous Brazilian mammals, the tapir and the jaguar, are now extinct on Ilha do Cardoso. What effects this will have on the ecosystem and the other mammals is unknown. The small rodents and marsupials survived the loss of the giant sloths and other megamammals, and it is likely that they will also survive this recent defaunation, but it worries me that there are no long-term studies under way to confirm this prediction.

Photo 8.3 Nectomys squamipes *is common around streams in the Atlantic forest. Photo by Helena Bergallo.*

CHAPTER 9 - ALTER DO CHÃO

The savannas near Alter do Chão contrast with the high forest
in surrounding areas. Photo by Bill Magnusson.

Albertina took me to Alter do Chão in 1980. It is a small village on the bank of the Tapajós River near the outflow of Verde Lake. Alter do Chão is in a dry belt that divides eastern and western Amazonia, so it is surrounded by dry, often deciduous, forests and patches of savanna, rather than the thick rainforest found in most of the Amazon. The principal economic activity of the people that live in the area is tourism and Alter do Chão is often called the Carribean of the Amazon. Enchanted by its beauty, I told Albertina that I would find something to study there, and those studies continue 40 years later.

A masters student, Tânia Sanaiotti, was looking for a thesis topic and I suggested that she look for possible projects at Alter do Chão. Tânia liked birds and introduced me to two very contrasting systems. She studied the swifts that roosted in the Manaus petroleum refinery and that must be one of the most unnatural systems imaginable. The refinery, especially at night when Tânia went to capture the swifts, looked like a scene from a horror movie. The tangle of chimneys and ducts emitted jets of steam at various points and the smell of hydrocarbons was overwhelming. The steam produced ghost-like wavering shadows in the refinery lights. The birds, however, apparently found the refinery very attractive and at the height of the annual migration hundreds of thousands roosted on the hot and often vibrating pipes. The only advantage for the birds that I can imagine was the lack of predators. Socially roosting birds are adopting cities in increasing numbers throughout the world. Rainbow lorikeets roost communally in Miranda, the nearest shopping center to my childhood home, but they were not there when I was a kid. White-winged parakeets fill the trees in busy thoroughfares in Manaus and other species nest communally in other Brazilian towns, but I do not know of any studies of this global phenomenon.

Although she supervised some graduate monographs about the refinery birds, Tânia decided on a much more aesthetically pleasing landscape for her masters thesis[152]. There is a peninsula between the Tapajós River and Verde Lake that has large patches of savanna and one of the most conspicuous birds in the savanna is the rusty-backed antwren. These tiny birds, a bit smaller than a sparrow, regularly hop into the upper branches of patches of bushes within their territory and sing stridently to warn off competitors. By catching them and putting colored bands on their legs, Tânia would be able to map their territories.

Photo 9.1 *White-winged swallows are common on the beaches of Alter do Chão, but there are many more species of birds in the surrounding savannas that most tourists never see. Photo by Bill Magnusson.*

In December 1984, we gridded a four-hectare patch of savanna with twine and Tânia used the grid to make a detailed map of the patches of bushes scattered among the expanses of short grass. Six pairs used this area and Tânia estimated the home range of the focal group to cover about 3.2 ha. Although the antwrens were extremely territorial in relation to conspecific individuals, they did not appear to interact with other species.

Tânia's study alerted me to the importance of understanding the biology of your study organisms. Another species, the white-fringed antwren, occurred in the dense vegetation at the interface between the forest and the savanna. We could tell the two species apart by coloration and their calls, but we had to look closely. The simplest way to distinguish the species was based on where they foraged. If the bird was using isolated bushes in the savanna, it was almost certainly a rusty-backed antwren. If it was on the border of the forest you could assume that it was a white-fringed antwren. The bushes in both places looked similar to us, but the birds obviously thought them very different.

I realized how difficult it is to distinguish species when you have no information on their ecology when we went to the Smithsonian Institution in Washington to check our identifications. There are many subspecies of both species of antwren and when I took a series of different subspecies of the rusty-backed antwren from the museum drawers and placed them side by side I realized that if I put a specimen of the white-fringed antwren in the middle of the series it would not stand out at all. That is, there was more morphological variation within species than there was between species. This was in the days before genetic analyses became readily available, so the limits of the species had been defined based on uncountable thousands of hours of observation by dedicated ornithologists, and they got it right!

Tânia was later joined by Renato Cintra, an ornithologist working for INPA and several post-graduate students. One of our principal questions related to the effect of fire on the savanna fauna and we found that fires affected the availability of fruits for birds, especially during the main breeding season[154]. Renato and Tânia showed that the annual fires had little short-term effect on the bird assemblages[47], which is to be expected because the savanna birds are presumably adapted to surviving frequent fire. However, one of Tânia's students, Lais Coelho[49], showed that the vegetation changes associated with the absence of fire for more than a decade completely changed the composition of the bird assemblages; species associated with grasses, such as the grassland sparrow, disappeared and forest birds colonized the area.

Fire so dominated the ecology of the savannas that it took me a long while to realize that this may be a relatively recent phenomenon. Many similar areas in Africa do not support regular fires because the large herbivores, such as elephants and rhinoceroses, create bare patches of ground that impede the spread of fire. When the large "bulldozer" mammals were extirpated by humans in Australia and South America, fire became the major controller of vegetation structure in the semi-arid areas.

Photo 9.2 *A rusty-backed antwren on its nest in a bush in the savanna. Photo by Bill Magnusson.*

It was at Alter do Chão that I started realize how much birds dominate vertebrate assemblages. One of the best ways to catch birds, especially in savannas, is with mist nets. The fine mesh is difficult to see and snares unwary birds. You need special permission to use mist nets and band birds, and to obtain it you generally have to prove that you gained experience with approved birders. Tânia and Renato were authorized birders and I accompanied them on many occasions.

It was relatively easy to set the nets in the late evening, though the bundles of aluminum poles were heavy and the nets had to be hooked to the poles in exactly the right way or they would tangle and not unfurl the next day. Getting up before dawn and setting off without a reasonable breakfast was the worst part for me. I generally don't feel alert without at least some bread in my stomach and caffeine derived from coffee or tea circulating in my blood stream, but birders generally don't seem to have these needs and I know of hotels dedicated to birders that don't offer breakfast until 10:30 in the morning.

It is in the last hour of darkness that most birds seem intent on making their prescence known by participating in the dawn chorus. There are a number of hypotheses for why birds call in the early morning and I don't know which is presently favored by ornithologists, but two appeal to me. One says that groups of birds, which may consist of just a pair or a large flock, have to recognize each other with their calls when foraging, so they remind each other each morning. The other is that female birds take about 24 hours to form the calcareous shell after the egg is fertilized by the male. Therefore, couples interact in the early hours so that the female can lay the egg early the next day. Whatever the cause, birds are obviously very social, garrulous, and are planning ahead, even if unconsciously.

I knew the four hectares of savanna that Tânia had mapped like the back of my hand, so I could get to the nets without leaving my groggy just-up state. However, I had to be alert when opening the nets. Little sticks from the ground or tiny leaves on the shrubs tangle the nets if you aren't careful, and the four layers of net separated by thicker lines had to be extended just the right amount or the net would be too taut and the birds would bounce off. By time the last net was open, we generally had to rush back because the birds were starting to move.

Moving along the open nets wasn't easy when they passed through patches of bushes or near trees. If you got too close, buttons on your clothing, your watch or other equipment would snag on the net and you would have to waste time to untangle it. It was best to use a minimum of clothes and avoid any fasteners that could catch on the net.

The first few minutes after dawn were the most hectic. The savannas on the peninsula in front of Alter do Chão were mainly covered by a short tuft grass about a handspan high, so it was relatively easy to view each 12 m net from one end, but sometimes that would reveal three or four birds tangled in the mesh that had to be freed before they hurt themselves. As there were at least ten 12-m sections to inspect, stopping to remove birds could leave others further along unprotected, and the small

Photo 9.3 *Tânia Sanaiotti checking mist nets in the savanna of Alter do Chão in 1985. Photo by Bill Magnusson.*

savanna hawks were not averse to getting a free meal in the form of a gift-wrapped bird. The hawks could tear the net and we rarely caught one, but the occasional hole in the net indicated that they had dined there.

I am not a birder and do not normally carry binoculars so, other than the obvious ones, such as parrots and toucans, my bird categories were generally limited to small green, small brown, large white that you eat and large black that you don't eat. However, close up I could see that there was an astonishing variety. Tânia and her students were experienced birders and could generally remove a bird from the net in less than a minute. They would work out from which direction it had hit the net and approach from that side. By careful turning they could free the legs, which they held while slipping the mesh off the wings.

The first time I accompanied the birders I sat beside Tânia as she carefully measured and banded a yellow-bellied elaenia. It seemed easy to identify from its light-yellow belly and white bars on its wings, so when we reached the next bird I said in Portuguese "Look, it's a yellow-bellied elaenia."

Tânia said in Portuguese "No Bill, it's a lesser elaenia."

After making many errors at identifying species of elaenias, I decided that I should limit myself to identifying the birds to genus, and I assumed that most of the birds with the common name elaenia because the looked alike would be in the genus *Elaenia*. However, when I pointed to a bird in the forest near our camp and said that it was an *Elaenia*, Tânia said that although its common name was elaenia, it was in the genus *Myiopagus*.

Going back to using common names, I identified an elaenia in the net, but Tânia said that it was a brown-crested flycatcher. Looking through the field guide, I found dozens of pages with greenish yellow birds with white bars on their wings. That's when I gave up. Either I would become a dedicated birder and do almost nothing else, or I would depend on ornithologists to give me a glimpse into the incredible variety of tropical birds – I chose the latter course.

Many of the birds concealed their most spectacular features when they were foraging or tangled in the net. If lots of things want to eat you, it's best not to show off too much, and I assume that is why so many species have converged on the same cryptic colors. However, if you are near a potential partner, you want to stand out from the crowd. Therefore, most of the species have special songs or dances or crests that can be tucked away when not needed. In the Amazon, the most spectacular example of hidden colors is probably the Amazon royal flycatcher whose crest usually just appears as a tiny knot above the neck, but which can be spread out in a spectacular red fan five times the width of its bearer's head.

Birds are difficult to identify when you have them in hand. To identify them free-flying in the field you have to have decades of experience wandering the through wild areas with binoculars in hand, and that is what Renato had. After a decade at Alter do Chão, he could often identify the local birds with only a fleeting glimpse. I joked that often I only saw the vibrating branch where the bird had been and an

Photo 9.4 *A stripe-necked tody-tyrant. There are many species of yellowish tyrants and flycatchers in and around the savanna near Alter do Chão. Photo by Bill Magnusson.*

ornithologist would say "Yes, but when the branch waggles that way it's a ……. ." Renato's experience allowed him to publish papers that included species that never entered mist nets[46]. It also meant that relatively fast surveys could be made of the forest fragments scattered through the savanna[48].

Extension of our studies on the peninsula of Alter do Chão to the savannas of the region was mainly based on planning by Ana Albernaz for her PhD thesis. Ana had studied the silvery marmosets in forest fragments on the peninsula in front of the village of Alter do Chão for her masters degree[4]. Her supervisor was officially a French researcher, but he was a botanist and never visited Alter do Chão. We often saw the marmosets on the edges of forests, though they rarely entered the savanna.

The marmosets have brilliant white fur on most of the body, but their tails are black and the bare skin on their faces and ears is brownish orange. About one and half handspans long and less than half a kilo, they are not very big, but get around in groups of six to twelve individuals. You would expect the white color to make them conspicuous, but we usually only detected them because of their piercing cries or the movement of the branches as they jumped from tree to tree. I often tried to follow them, but one would always spot me and cry out, and the band would disappear into the forest.

The marmosets often visited the same trees, but they were low on the trunks rather than high in the canopy where you would expect them to find fruits. When I looked at the boles, I found almost circular holes where the bark had been gnawed away, and many were still exuding gum, the sticky sap that some species of tree produce to avoid attacks by boring insects. I rubbed my finger in the transparent resin, smelt it and rubbed it on my tongue. The gum was aromatic and had a slightly sweet taste. I hadn't realized before that monkeys might milk trees for their sap.

Many people have studied the home-range sizes of primates, usually by following a group continually until the monkeys become habituated to the presence of the researchers and presumably act naturally. This gives detailed information on each group, but limits the number of groups that can be studied and much of the information is redundant. If a group is feeding in a fruit tree, they will probably still be there for the following minutes or hours, so dozens or hundreds of observations may only give information about preference for a single tree.

Ana started following groups intensively, but found it hard to habituate the groups. When she obtained radio transmitters she put them on four groups and only recorded the location of the group once per day, before they had registered her presence. By varying the time of day it was located, she was able to accumulate a large number of independent observations for each group.

Photo 9.5 *Ana Albernaz setting a trap for silvery marmosets in 1990. Photo by Tânia Sanaiotti.*

Many of Ana's conclusions differed from those generated by the continuous monitoring. The monkeys did not use many of the areas they had used as she was following them when they could not see her. More importantly, they ceased activity at about 2 p.m. when they were followed continuously, but remained active until 5 p.m. when not influenced by the presence of a researcher.

Ana's study revealed the need to take into account variability among groups. Home-range size variation in monkeys has often been attributed to differences in climate or other factors that vary over large geographic areas. However, the groups studied by Ana were all in a small region with no variation in climate, but had home ranges that differed by up to six times in area. Ana found that although silvery marmosets do not have strong morphological adaptations for eating gum exuded by trees, they rely heavily on that resource during the dry season when few fruits are available[4] and that the relationships between food availability and home-range size varied among groups. She only radio-tracked four groups, so there is likely to be even more variation in the biology of the species.

Ana did not return specifically to the monkeys for her Ph.D. thesis[3], but designed a sampling plan for all the savannas and forests in the area. This resulted in us installing forty sampling modules in savannas, 26 in forest fragments and six in continuous forest. Each module had four parallel sampling transects that were 250 m long and separated from each other by 50 m. These would allow standardized sampling of all elements of biodiversity in the region[109] and change almost everything we thought we knew about the functioning of the savannas.

The patch of savanna we had been studying on the peninsula was covered mainly by a short bunch grass not much higher than my ankle, but most of the other savanna areas in the region had much larger areas of tall grass that came above my waist. It wasn't only the savannas that were different, the surrounding forest and the forest patches within the savanna varied from place to place. There were many mammals in the forest that we never saw in the savanna, such as two-toed sloths and red-bellied titi monkeys. I was crossing a small patch of forest during the day and was not expecting to see many mammals when I came upon an ocelot stretched out on a horizontal branch less than two meters above ground. I carefully circled so as not to disturb it, but it ignored me, staring with the disdainful look that all cats seem to have. Obviously, I didn't have my camera with me or it would never have left itself so exposed! I have never since seen an ocelot so close during the day.

Many researchers had studied the number of species that occurred in forest fragments in relation to island-biogeography theory. This conjecture was originally based on oceanic islands and modelled the number of species based on probabilities of colonization and extinction. The theory basically postulated that the species density would be higher on larger islands that were close to the mainland. It is important to note that the theory makes the prediction that species densities will be higher on large islands. This goes beyond the obvious fact that if you survey more area you will find

Photo 9.6 *Silvery marmosets are common near Alter do Chāo and frequently eat gum in the dry season. Photo by Bill Magnusson.*

more species. It says that in the same areal extent, such as in standard-size plots, there will be more species on larger islands.

Extrapolation to habitat islands, such as forest patches, separated by unfavorable landscapes required many more assumptions, but that wasn't what what worried me about its application to mammals and birds. Basically, none of the fragments at Alter do Chāo, or for that matter that had been studied elsewhere, were large enough to support a viable population of any species of mammal or bird. If they occurred in the area, individuals must be using many more than one fragment. In a broader context, the Canadian researcher Leonore Fahrig has published several papers suggesting that it is the quantity of suitable habitat in the landscape that is most important, and not the size of individual fragments.

The site we had studied most intensively was nested within a larger area covering a bit more than 100 km² of savannas inderdigitated by patches of forest. This landscape had been patchy for at least 150 years because the English naturalist Henry Bates[16] had commented on the forest fragments when he visited the area in the 1800s. The area was close to the center of the Tapajó Indian nation that had occupied the area for at least 7000 years, so the landscape we see today may have existed for thousands of years. This offered a valuable opportunity, because one of the strongest criticisms of island-biogeography theory applied to forest fragments was that the patches that had been studied in recent agricultural landscapes had been isolated for such a short period that there had not been time for the species to come to a new equilibrium.

Renato Cintra carried out visual surveys of birds in 19 forest fragments and six sites in continuous forest. This was only possible because Renato had a decade of experience in the area and was able to identify the birds from their plumage or calls, and did not have to use mist nets. He surveyed the plots in 1999 and 2000, and the results were similar in both years. Basically, the density of bird species was related to fragment size, as predicted by island-biogeography theory, but distance to continuous forest and distance to other fragments had no effect. Even though the number of bird species per plot was lower in individual fragments, eight out of every ten species found in continuous forest could be found in the fragments, so the fragments contributed to the conservation of birds in the region[48].

Outside the savanna area, there were larger forest patches immersed in a matrix of cattle pastures and small farms that dated to about 30 years before our studies. Further up the Tapajós River were areas with little deforestation that had been included in the Tapajós National forest. These areas were contiguous with large areas of forest, but people from the local communities hunted them intensively. One of Albertina's students, Ricardo Sampaio, realized that these areas offered an opportunity to study the effects of forest fragmentation on the mammals larger than 2 kg that could be detected by line-transect methods[151]. He included squirrels and silvery marmosets, which are slightly smaller, presumably because he recorded them in most sites. Realizing the limitations of day and night visual surveys for active animals, Ricardo complemented them with surveys for tracks, feces and other signs, and interviews with local people.

Photo 9.7 *Silvery marmosets gnaw holes in trees to get the nutritive gum that exudes from the wounds. Photo by Bill Magnusson.*

Ricardo did not see any silky anteaters, short-eared dogs, bushdogs or greater grisons, but local people reported the silky anteater in continuous forest and a few reported the short-eared dog and the bush dog. I knew that the greater grison still occurred in the area because I sometimes saw a pair in our principal study area. They were wary and I could see why they would be difficult to detect in short-term studies. These species are considered rare wherever they occur, but all have large distributions. Camera-trap studies are starting to reveal the distribution of bush dogs[144] and short-eared dogs[146], but the other species probably require new methods of survey. Silky anteaters live on vines high in the canopy, and most individuals are detected when trees are cut during logging operations. Little is known of the ecology of greater grisons, but they are thought to occur at low density and are rarely encountered in the wild.

The main conclusion from Ricardo's study was that most of the larger extant forest mammals can survive in fragmented landscapes, but hunting eliminates the most susceptible species from the areas with easy access. Large-bodied species, such as tapirs and white-lipped peccaries were not seen in the fragmented areas and informants said that they rarely occurred there. The two largest monkey species, white-nosed sakis and the white-cheeked spider monkey were considered extinct in the three areas by most informants, but I have often encountered both species further into the Tapajós National Forest. White-cheeked spider monkeys seem especially vulnerable to hunters. They often sit in trees directly above you and throw sticks and feces at you, which is not a good strategy if the object of their disdain has a shotgun.

Based on their distributions, Ricardo predicted that there would be 39 species of mammals in the size range he studied, and he found evidence of the presence of almost all of them. All were found or reported to occur in the area with continuous forest, nine out of ten of these species were in the area with recent deforestation, and seven of every ten in the highly fragmented area.

None of those species could survive if confined to even the largest fragments, so they must have been dispersing among suitable habitats. Many of those surviving in fragmented areas are heavily hunted, and those that do not are mostly those with low reproductive rates that are easily overhunted. If local people focused only on the species most resistant to hunting and left the others alone, it is likely that most of the species in the region would recolonize the disturbed areas. That is, it appears to be hunting rather than fragment size that limits mammal occurrence; island-biogeography is largely irrelevant.

As I ran down Ricardo's list of species I realized that I had seen almost all the species in the region, except for the giant armadillo and the silky anteater. However, I rarely saw more than a few species in any one day. Most species are very good at avoiding humans, which is why they persist. My general impressions as to density and distribution of mammals were heavily biased and of little use for making conservation decisions. I would have to rethink the methods, and especially the scale of study, but more of that later.

Photo 9.8 *Silky anteaters live on fine branches and vines in the canopy and are rarely seen. Photo by Bill Magnusson.*

All these conclusions were made in relation to the species that mammal researchers in South America call "medium and large" species, but what about the others? When Cristiano Souza in 2000[167] and Clarice Borges-Matos in 2015[30] studied small mammals in the forest fragments of Alter do Chão I had a chance to find out. Small mammals are generally caught in aluminum or wire box traps, or pit-fall traps made from large plastic buckets buried in the ground. The box traps tend to work everywhere, but some species are reluctant to enter them and are much more readily captured in the pitfalls. For some reason that I have never been able to figure out, pitfall traps capture few small mammals in some places, such as Reserva Ducke, but capture as many or more individuals as box traps in other places, such as Alter do Chão. Elildo Carvalho used pit-fall traps in the forest fragments of Alter do Chão to capture lizards[39]. The traps were extremely inefficient for lizards, but captured many small mammals, which led to the theses by Clarice and Cristiano. Clarice used 30 aluminum box traps, 30 wire box traps and eight 60-litre pitfall traps in each of 16 forest fragments and two plots in continuous forest. Half the box traps were set on the leaf litter and the other half in trees about two meters above ground.

Some of the forest patches were surrounded by regrowth and some by open savanna, and this factor turned out to be the most important in determining the composition of small-mammal assemblages, with much smaller effects of patch size and patch isolation. We don't know why, but rodents, which were generally the larger species and ate mainly fruit, dominated in the patches surrounded by regrowth. Marsupials were most abundant in forest patches surrounded by savanna, and most of them were small and mainly insectivorous. To understand why, we would probably have to carry out long-term studies of each species, but I have run out of years to do that in my lifetime.

Wandering around forest fragments and supervising student theses had only given me a general idea about the ecology of mammals in the forests of Alter do Chão, but soon after being introduced to the area by Albertina I started a long-term study of rodents in the savanna that would change most of my preconceptions about mammal population dynamics.

The savannas of Alter do Chão have patches of bushes and small trees scattered among the grasses. Often these form around large termite mounds, which probably increase nutrient availability and possibly protect young plants from fire. I first went to Alter do Chão in 1979, but I saw few mammals in the savanna. I would occasionally find collared anteaters walking in the savanna at night and I was surprised to find one asleep during the day, lying on the ground, but curled around the base of tree. It was in 1983 that I first saw a mouse-sized grey rodent near the base of a termite mound at ten in the morning. It saw me and disappeared into one of the ventilation shafts at the base of the mound. Careful inspection of the cleared area around termite mounds revealed two more of the grey mice. Based on this, I wrongly concluded that the species must be associated with termite mounds.

We had carefully mapped the plot for the studies of the antwrens, but I needed aluminum box traps and I didn't have funds to buy them. I asked the Director of my Department and she said that the institute only had money for repairs, and could not buy traps, which were considered "permanent goods". One of the institute's technicians had a boat-repair company and the capacity to produce aluminum products. I showed

Photo 9.9 *Clarice Borges-Matos studied the small mammals of forest patches near Alter do Chão. Photo by Juliano Franco de Moraes.*

him a commercial trap and asked if he could make the parts. He assured me that he could, so I put in a request to repair 100 traps and asked for all the parts necessary for those traps. It worked, and I was overjoyed when I received the boxes of parts, which I then had to assemble. We are still using most of those traps 40 years later!

I tried several configurations, but for most of the study we put the traps 20 m apart for two days, then moved them 10 m to cover the intermediate positions for another two days. The grid started out as 150 m by 200 m, but we eventually extended it to 300 m by 340 m and covering 10 hectares. Initially, I put the traps exactly on the grid points on our map, but it soon became clear that the rats almost never entered traps sitting on leaf litter in the clumps of bushes, or put close to termite mounds. They only readily entered traps set among clumps of grass with bare ground between.

We used peanut butter mixed with oatmeal, but the ants quickly took the bait, so we supplemented it with half a Brazil nut, which resisted the ants much longer and gave the rats something to eat when they were in the traps. The only form of permanent marking we had was toe clipping, and I was worried that it might traumatize the rats, even though we did it quickly with sharp scissors. The first rat I caught twisted violently in the cloth bag as I tried to subdue, measure and mark it. It was small enough to fit comfortably in my hand, but very strong, with sharp claws that dug into my skin and gave it leverage to try to twist its head around and drive its incisors into my fingers.

I released the rat, content that it hadn't been able to bite me, and it ran into the grass. As I cleaned and reassembled the trap, I thought about the trauma it must have felt and wondered if it would ever again go into a trap. I had only walked a few meters when I heard a trap door slam shut two positions further back. Not wanting to leave an animal in the trap and exposed to the sun, which was climbing higher in the sky, I went back to see what I had caught. It was the same rat! This time it just lay calmly in my hand as I inspected it and its cut toe, and when I put it on the ground it hopped off slowly, as though I didn't pose a great threat.

That behavior: desperate struggling that sometimes resulted in bites on the first capture and extremely calm on subsequent encounters, was the standard for almost all the rats we caught. They quickly became what mammologists call "trap happy" and I had to reduce the number of days in each trap session so that the rats didn't become obese. Only one rat of several hundred showed signs of infection of the cut toe, and that cleared up within a few days. It appeared that I had the perfect site to study the population dynamics of the rats because they were abundant, readily entered traps and did not seem to change their behavior much due to handling.

We soon found that rats rarely entered traps after seven at night or before six in the morning. A few were active in the middle of the day, but leaving the traps open in this period led to captured animals suffering heat stress and a few died. Therefore, we only opened the traps between six and nine in the morning and four and seven in the evening.

Photo 9.10 *Marsupials, such as* Marmosa murina, *were common in forest patches surrounded by savanna. Photo by Bill Magnusson.*

Unlike most savanna areas, which have many species of small mammals, the savanna had only one resident species, the hairy-tailed bolo mouse. We occasionally caught individuals of *Proechimys* species and juvenile common opossums that somehow managed to squeeze into the traps, but these were never recaptured and were presumably just passing through. This is good, because I can just call individuals of the species we studied rats or mice and you'll know which species of savanna rodent I am talking about. I have never heard anyone use the common name "hairy-tailed bolo mouse" given by the IUCN!

We started by looking at the natural history of the species. Most people think of rats and mice as a relatively homogeneous group that differs mostly in size, but there are many specialties among rats, including species that hop on two legs like kangaroos and species that use their prehensile tails to hang from branches like monkeys. Some, called voles, have small eyes, short tails and are active at dusk and dawn. Northern-hemisphere voles are in the subfamily Arvicolinae of the Cricetidae family. The swamp rats I had tried to study for my honors thesis are in the family Muridae, but also had these characteristics. The mice in the savannas at Alter do Chão are in the Cricetidae family, but are not closely related to the arvicoline voles. All these species have probably converged on the same morphology because you don't need large eyes if you are not active at night, and a long tail, which is good for balance when jumping, is of little use in the cramped tunnels under thick grass. Although the hairy-tailed bolo mouse has a huge distribution, the Amazonian populations are isolated from those in the more southerly areas, and a study of animals from Belém in the eastern Amazon indicated that they might be morphologically distinct[88].

Ângelo Francisco studied the diet of the savanna mice by sorting through the feces left in the traps[65]. Mouse poo is basically just green or brown mush and Ângelo considered all the unidentifiable fragments under the microscope as vegetation and the chunks of chitin as coming from invertebrates. He could identify some of the bits of invertebrate exoskeleton and estimated that the mice were eating mainly centipedes, beetles and termites, which accounted for 92% of the particles. Most of the rest were from spiders and bugs. There wasn't much seasonal variation in the diet, but the rats ate more invertebrates in the wet season after a fire passed through.

We knew that the mice sometimes ate fruit because the feces were often stained purple by the fruits of *Declieuxia fruticosa*, a small herb that also colored our lips when we ate the fruits. Small rodents are usually not very effective seed dispersers because they tend to chew up everything they ingest and we were unable to find a reference to any rat or mouse that disperses seeds that it ingests. Therefore, we were surprised to find seeds of a shrub, *Miconia albicans*, in the rat feces[99]. The fruits of this species are green, pea sized and mushy when ripe. There are several other species of *Miconia* in the area with fruits that are generally similar, except that they are dark colored.

Tânia had found the seeds of the other *Miconia* species in bird feces, but birds apparently weren't eating *Miconia albicans*. Lizards ate small fruits of other species, but ignored the fruits of *Miconia albicans* that accumulated on the ground under bushes. We tried the fruits and they were sweetish, even when we ground the tiny seeds between our teeth. However, there must be something unpalatable in the fruits. If not, other animals would eat them and the rats would grind up the soft seeds, which are full of nutrients to sustain the seedlings after they germinate. The seeds of this species pass through the digestive tracts of the mice and most of those we found in the feces germinated, indicating that the mice may be important dispersal agents for the species, which is an unusual mouse-plant interaction.

Photo 9.11 *The first hairy-tailed bolo mouse I saw was in a hole in a termite mound and it took me a long time to realize that the species rarely uses these refuges. Photo by Bill Magnusson.*

We also identified a predator on the mice from food rejects. Owls tend to swallow small prey whole, which means that they ingest a lot of things, such as feathers, fur and claws that are difficult to digest. Rather than trying to pass all that through their intestines, they regurgitate what they can't digest easily, producing pellets similar to the fur balls that cats regurgitate. A Stygian owl had a roost in a large tree on the periphery of our study grid and Tânia investigated the pellets under the tree to see what it had been eating; most of the prey were savanna mice.

We found the nest of another owl of this species about ten km distant. The nest was on the ground under tall grass and had two fluffy chicks that stared up at us when we got close. For some reason, I hadn't expected the owl to nest on the ground, but it makes sense for a savanna species. I often saw the owls perched in trees during the daytime and assumed that they were sleeping, but as much of their prey consisted of diurnal mice, my assumptions about their habits were probably wrong.

The highest rates of growth and reproduction of the mice were at the end of the dry season, when rainfall and availability of fleshy fruits were at a minimum[65]. Presumably, it was an increase in dry seeds or invertebrates at this time of year that benefitted the mice. This was an important lesson for me. For humans, the end of the dry season is stressful, with high temperatures, low humidity and frequent fire, but the mice just loved it. The savanna lizards also had the highest growth rates and gonadal development in that period[92].

Our studies indicated that the mice avoided the forest and even small patches of bushes in the savanna. However, this gave a misleading picture of the importance of trees and bushes for their diet. We knew that they ate fruits of the bushes, and the invertebrates they ate transited freely between clumps of bushes and grasses.

To know whether their primary sources of food came from food chains based on grasses or bushes we needed a way to track the flow of carbon through the system. Fortunately, this is possible using stable isotopes. Most of the carbon in the atmosphere is in the form of ^{12}C, which means that each atom of carbon has 12 neutrons in its core. However, some of the carbon is in the form of ^{13}C with an extra neutron. The different forms are called stable isotopes because they do not decay quickly and produce gamma rays as do the isotopes of some elements, such as uranium.

The isotopes of carbon have similar chemical reactions with other elements, but ^{13}C is heavier and this affects its uptake by plants, and consequentially its incorporation in tissues. Different groups of plants take up ^{13}C and ^{12}C differently, so by studying their ratio, called $\delta^{13}C$, you can determine whether the carbon was derived from bushes and trees or tropical grasses. The isotope ratio changes little as you move up the food chain, so it is possible to determine whether the carbon in the tissues of an animal, such as a beetle, centipede or mouse, was originally fixed by a bush or a grass.

We took a tiny piece from the end of the tail, or used the toe clips to determine the isotope ratio of the tissues of the mice we caught. Surprisingly, they were much closer to those of the bushes and trees in the area than to the common grasses[107]. Therefore, despite spending most of their time among the grasses, which presumably gave them

Photo 9.12 *Bill Magnusson baiting traps and Tània Sanaiotti observing birds. Photos by Tània Sanaiotti (left) and Bill Magnusson (right).*

protection from predators, such as owls, most of their food came from sources that originated among bushes and trees. The balance between tree-bush clumps and grasses was essential for the survival of the mice in the savanna.

We trapped the mice regularly from February 1986 to January 1989 and this allowed us to map the home ranges of many of them. Analyzing animals as numbers is very different from seeing them as individuals. You lift the trap from the grass that is still wet with dew. From its weight, you know whether you have an adult or a juvenile. When you tip it into the cloth bag you can tell by its jumping whether it is a new capture or an already marked animal. If it is a new adult female, you feel a flutter in your stomach because you know that it probably means that the mouse you expected to find at that trap site has died. Few animals lived more than 7 months, but a few were still going into traps 16 months after first capture[106]. The older individuals would generally just lay back like a rag doll, totally relaxed as we took their measurements.

I checked the literature and found that the short life span was typical for mammals, which generally have much shorter lives than other vertebrates of the same size, unless they live in trees or can fly[13]. Larger species live longer, but generally not as long as large lizards, turtles and crocodiles. Basically, mammals live fast and die young. Birds of similar sizes live even faster and die much older, but so do bats, which is the only order of predominantly flying mammals.

The home ranges of the female savanna mice did not overlap, indicating that they are strongly territorial. This is typical of rodents, especially those with vole-like habits. Female savanna mice are smaller than males when not pregnant, but full-term gestating females weigh as much as males. Because they are in a perpetual cycle of gestation and lactation, adult females probably need a lot of food, so they defend their territories against potential interlopers. In contrast, adult males probably have more than enough to eat, so they are more worried about finding receptive females that can help them pass their genes along to the next generation. Trying to defend a large territory with many female home ranges would probably yield fewer babies than simply covering as much ground as possible in the hope of finding females during the short period that they are neither pregnant nor lactating, so male home ranges overlap extensively.

In contrast to studies in central Brazil, the number of mice in the area appeared to be relatively constant, and we did not record zero densities, as happened in most previous studies of the species, even though they were short term and rarely covered more than two years. This was one of the major conclusions of the paper we wrote[106], and an affirmation I would come to regret.

Photo 9.13 *The fruits of* Miconia albicans *were rarely eaten by birds or lizards, but were favorites of the savanna mice. Photo by Bill Magnusson.*

Once we knew enough about the basic biology of the savanna mice, we could reduce the effort on each sampling grid and cover more areas. We used 31 of the 40 savanna plots Ana Albernaz had marked throughout the region. Viviane Layme carried out most of the study and used the data for her doctoral thesis. We only collected data in each of the approximately four-hectare plots during two days in each trapping session, which we knew from studies on the peninsula was sufficient to catch most of the mice on the plot. Trapping over a larger area was more complicated socially, and we had to get permission from landowners. Nevertheless, some of our traps were still stolen and sometimes several people claimed ownership of the same block of land. Preparation and planning took more time than the field work.

This study was also physically more demanding. The plots were generally a minimum of several kilometers apart. Some could be reached by road and others only by boat. To cover the whole area within a reasonable time it was necessary to trap two or three plots per day. This meant that we had to rise very early, drive or pilot to where we could leave the car or the boat, walk hundreds of meters or kilometers through waist-high grass to get to the first trap, and cover the one kilometer of trap line in each plot quickly so that all the traps would be checked before the sun rose high enough to overheat captured animals. It was worthwhile however, because the data showed that studying only one plot gave a biased impression of the population dynamics of the rodents.

We had previously collected data on the vegetation structure in the plots and Viviane set pitfall traps made of plastic bottles with their tops cut off to catch invertebrates. She carefully separated and weighed the invertebrates that constituted most of the rodent diets. There was no evidence of an effect of vegetation or fire, but the density of mice in a plot was strongly related to the amount of invertebrates in that plot, corroborating some of the conclusions from our study on the peninsula[77]. Nevertheless, we realized that just studying the density of rats ignored the "dynamics" part of population dynamics.

The most obvious and embarrassing result was that no mice were captured in our primary plot on the peninsula in this period. The species had gone to local extinction, just as it had been reported to do in previous studies. Careful reanalysis of the data indicated that the mice had been decreasing in density for most of the period we studied them. I remembered a classic paper by Graeme Caughley[41]. He used the data he, his collaborators and students collected on pasture growth and kangaroo densities to model the effects of rainfall on the population dynamics of kangaroos in the Australian arid zone. The surprising result was that random rainfall in the desert, which could go from deluge to nothing in a single day, acted through pasture growth to cause long-term cycles in kangaroo numbers that had peaks more than 40 years apart. The kangaroos were sometimes at high densities when there was little pasture and at other times there was more than enough grass to eat, but there had not been enough time for the kangaroo numbers to build up. The suitability of environment conditions was not reflected by kangaroo densities, but by their rates of increase.

Photo 9.14 *Stygian owls are major predators on savanna mice despite being mainly nocturnal. Photo by Bill Magnusson.*

We decided to investigate the savanna-mice rates of increase instead of densities, and Ivo Ghizoni used the data for his masters thesis[67]. The mice were obviously declining throughout the study area during this period, but the degree and sometimes direction of density changes varied among plots. Nevertheless, reductions in density were less in plots where invertebrate availability increased and was also related to the vegetation structure, an effect we had not been able to identify when we studied only density and not density change. Fire had no detectable effect on the mice, and neither it nor vegetation structure were related to changes in invertebrate densities. Therefore, food seemed to be the driving force behind changes in mouse densities.

I was worried that the decline throughout the area might have been because we had been capturing the rodents and suggested that Ivo survey other areas as well. He installed six new plots in the general area that we had been studying and two on the other side of the Tapajós River, which is 16 km wide at that point. Densities in the new plots were as low or lower than those in the plots we had been studying intensively, so we concluded that the declines were not because of our interference.

Albertina continued monitoring the extent of fire in all the savanna plots, and we continued monitoring the density of savanna mice in the plot on the peninsula. The number of rats capture in the dry season fell from 20 in 1985 to two in 2016. The plot did not burn during the last 9 years, but fires were frequent in other plots. We suspected that the changes in mouse densities might be related to global climate phenomena. Densities of rodents were known to be affected by changes in rainfall induced by the Southern Oscillation Index (SOI), a measure of the difference in sea-level pressure between Tahiti and Darwin, which reflects differences in ocean temperatures.

SOI affects local rainfall, but there is variation in local rainfall due to other factors. Louise Emmons had speculated that smoke from dry-season fires might reduce dew fall, and hence water availability for savanna rodents, an effect that would also be related to local rainfall. We tried to put all these factors into a model to explain variation in density of mice in the plot on the peninsula. The model explained most of the differences in rates of increase between years, but the effects were complicated[108]. Increases in SOI increased local rainfall, which reduced the amount of fire in the region, remembering that the peninsula plot did not burn in this period. Mouse rates of increase were positively related to the amount of regional fire, an effect opposite to that predicted by Louise Emmon's hypothesis.

We detected no direct effect of local rainfall on rodent rates of increase, but there appeared to be an effect of SOI independent of local rainfall, something we could not explain because the effects of SOI on rodent densities had been interpreted as due to its effect on local rainfall in all previous studies. It may be that the savanna mice are favored by increased air pollution due to burning, but we cannot imagine how. Basically, this study just indicated that there are complex effects of global climate on local rodent densities that we know nothing about. Just about everything in our model was correlated with everything else and this makes it hard to isolate individual effects. A change in weather conditions might take a long time to change invertebrate availability, and so might not affect rodent densities for several years. We obviously needed many more years of data to sort out the various interactions, but we have captured no savanna mice in the peninsula plot since 2016.

Photo 9.15 *The savanna mice used areas with little leaf litter and rarely strayed far from grass cover. Photo by Bill Magnusson.*

As the peninsula plot has not burned in recent years, changes in vegetation may explain the absence of savanna mice, but Albertina trapped eight other plots distributed throughout the Alter do Chão savannas in most years between 2010 and 2019. Considering all plots together, there was no effect of SOI or local rainfall. Overall, there was a tendency for a reduction in density, with peaks in 2000, 2004 and 2013[110]. However, variation in densities of mice was similar in some plots, but not in others. The plots formed three clusters, both in terms of geographic distribution and synchrony in rates of change. This makes sense, because mice in individual plots do not form a population in any sense, and are influenced by immigration from neighboring plots.

When we grouped the data from each clump, the results were different. Density variations in one clump were related to SOI, but those in the other clumps were not. The similarity among adjacent plots became obvious when we animated the data by making a sequence of maps with the density in each plot represented by the size of the point indicating its position[111]. Over the 19-year period, we could see the density of mice increasing in one part of the area while it diminished or remained constant in others. Rather than a single population, we had three populations, or as it is described in the scientific literature, a metapopulation.

Most studies of small mammals are carried out in a single plot of one to four hectares, but our studies of savanna mice indicate that different localities in the same region might have different population dynamics of rodents, some responding to global effects, such as SOI, while others do not. We are also wary of conclusions from studies undertaken when a species has very high densities. This makes it easy to study and facilitates statistical analyses. However, many species are at low density most of the time and the factors important for maintaining the species in the system may be very different from those that affect its population dynamics when at high densities.

We have no doubt that the savanna mice we studied are limited by invertebrate availability when they are at high densities, but that might not explain most of the fluctuations in density. Global effects, such as SOI, and local rainfall may affect some areas, but not others. We suspect that the metapopulation dynamics of the mice are mainly affected by other factors. A prime candidate is disease. The asynchronous fluctuations in density among clumps of localities is what might be expected if disease is a limiting factor, high densities favoring disease transmission and low densities leading to local extinction of the agent causing the disease. New colonizers would find a disease-free environment that permits high rates of increase, but when densities become high enough for disease transmission again, the population will go into drastic decline.

These are only hypotheses, but with the appearance of new pandemics, such as COVID-19, it is becoming important for us to understand possible epidemics in native species, because some agents, especially viruses, do not respect the limits between wild species and humans.

Photo 9.16 *Albertina Lima holding a recaptured savanna mouse that no longer feared humans. Photo by Albertina Lima.*

Photo 9.17 *Fire has drastic short-term effects on the fauna, but is necessary to maintain the savannas. Photo by Bill Magnusson.*

CHAPTER 10 - THINKING BIGGER – RAPELD

Tapirs are common in the forest, but generally too big for jaguars. Photo camera trap Projeto Jaguar.

Our research at Alter made me see the importance of large-scale studies and looking at landscapes rather than individual research plots. We had also learned that it was important to be able to integrate the information on mammals with that of plants and physical factors, such as soil fertility and fire. However, the experimental design we had used in the savannas had limitations for studies in other areas, especially those with rugged topography. In 2000, we installed a modified system in Reserva Ducke, which basically consisted of a grid of trails linking uniformly-distributed plots. The trails were straight, one kilometer apart and installed by a professional topographer. The first plots were one kilometer apart and the center line of the plots followed the altitudinal contours to reduce within-plot variation in soils and distance to the water table. We called the system RAPELD because it could be used for rapid surveys (RAP) and maintained for long-term ecological studies (LTER). The abbreviation for LTER in Portuguese is PELD (*Projeto Ecológico de Longa Duração*).

The initial grid in Reserva Ducke was eight by eight kilometers and covered 64 km^2, but that was generally too big, even for LTER sites near academic centers and we eventually opted for five-by-five kilometers (25 km^2) for large grids. That size is very small to capture variation across Amazonian forests, and we settled on a smaller configuration with two parallel five-kilometer trails separated by one kilometer and ten uniformly-distributed plots when we needed a system that could be replicated over large areas. The spatial standardization permitted comparative studies that had never been possible before, and allowed integration of mammal data with data from other biological groups and environmental measurements[52,109].

RAPELD overturned just about all our preconceptions about the functioning of Brazilian ecosystems; we hadn't realized how something as simple as lack of access could bias impressions about the distribution of fauna. Our straight-line trails covered the landscape elements in proportion to their occurrence and forced researchers to traverse steep areas and areas with tangled vegetation that they would normally avoid. In most previous studies, researchers had used areas close to rivers or roads, or followed trails made by hunters, who avoid places where it is hard to walk.

Photo 10.1 *Harpy eagle nests are enormous, but so high in the canopy that they are hard to detect from the ground. Photo by Tânia Sanaiotti.*

When we started working in Reserva Ducke, the harpy eagle was considered extinct in the area, but soon after we installed the trails a harpy-eagle nest was sighted by a botanist. Harpy eagles make huge nests of sticks, over a meter wide, high in emergent trees. They are easy to see from a plane, but only someone who habitually looks up into the canopy in search of flowers, such as a botanist, is likely to see one from ground level in dense forest. Another nest on the other side of the reserve was located soon after, and Tânia Sanaiotti started to study the eagles. She not only followed their reproduction and investigated their diets, she engaged in educational campaigns to ensure that the people around the reserve would not shoot the birds. Studies by Tânia and her students also showed the value of RAPELD for environmental-impact studies[2,155]. Using conventional methods, Tânia's compilation of several surveys indicated that only eight harpy eagles were encountered in boat surveys around the Belo Monte dam, much less than the 14 found by walking the RAPELD trails installed in the area.

The only place I have got close to a harpy eagle is in Reserva Ducke. The first time, I was alerted to its presence by the sight of a Guyanan red howler monkey falling out of a tree. The eagle flew off and I inspected the carcass. It must have weighed five kilos and the eyes stared up at me above the snarling teeth locked in a death grimace. We hoped that the eagle would come back for the body, but it never did.

A few years later, a young eagle that Tânia had been studying since it was in the nest started to hang around the reserve headquarters. It still wasn't proficient at hunting and practiced by swooping down and picking up andiroba fruits with its huge talons. I never saw it hunting an animal, but my daughter Jeni once brought her dogs with her when she came to pick me up at the reserve. The dogs jumped out of the car, but Jeni quickly bundled them back in when the eagle swooped low over them. None of this is rocket science, but interacting with the eagles was important to me to see them as mighty predators in a functioning ecosystem rather than names in a list of endangered species. I wondered whether I would have had these opportunities if we hadn't installed RAPELD and Tânia had never engaged in her campaigns to protect the Reserva Ducke eagles.

Other species were discovered as a byproduct of the trails. Spanish researchers saw a bushy tailed opossum while spotlighting[35]. There had only been 17 previous records of this species, and only three in Brazil. Species such as this, which appear to be naturally rare, are only likely to be registered where researchers have access to the forest.

After the installation of the RAPELD grid we started to get reports of a band of white-lipped peccaries in Reserva Ducke. The reserve is supposedly too small for this species, but it has been reported for the last two decades, and apparently mainly uses the northwest corner of the reserve. Almost all sightings have been on the RAPELD trails, and I was surprised when one of the guards at the park headquarters reported his sighting as being at "LO-2, 401 m", a code for the trail system that I thought only researchers would know. Apparently, the trail names and the stakes marking the distances also facilitate citizen science.

I had seen many collared peccaries in Reserva Ducke and they apparently use all the reserve. However, a sighting of white-lipped peccaries is a cause for comment. The situation is different in the RAPELD grid in the Viruá National Park, near the border

Photo 10.2 *The harpy eagle is the largest bird of prey in the New World. Photo by Bill Magnusson.*

between the states of Amazonas and Roraima. There it is common to see white-lipped peccaries and somewhat disconcerting when you find yourself in the middle of a herd, with most individuals clacking their teeth together as a warning that they are not happy with your presence.

Most of our field assistants have stories of being attacked by white-lipped peccaries when they were accompanied by dogs and having to climb trees to escape. Why the peccaries have greater animosity to dogs than humans is not immediately obvious. In fact, we know little about what triggers an attack. I had never heard of collared peccaries attacking humans in the Amazon. Perhaps their groups of 6 to 12 individuals are too small to give them courage in most situations. The situation is different in North America, however. There are many reports of collared peccaries attacking and sometime maiming people in the USA. Perhaps it is because they become more aggressive in areas that they are not hunted.

Only once I have been able to get close to collared peccaries in the wild, and that was on a RAPELD trail in the Rio Negro Sustainable Development Reserve. I saw a band of peccaries walking along a dry creek bed close to the trail, but I could not see them well enough to determine the species and I thought that they were white-lipped peccaries. As I had detected only about a dozen individuals, I assumed that there must be more coming and I positioned myself close to the creek bed where I could film passing animals.

When the band started to return, I realized that they were collared peccaries, but I was happy to get some nice footage until one of the peccaries stopped about five meters from me and raised the hairs on its back as though it was a porcupine. After watching for a while, it started to move towards me and I bent over and extended the camera, hoping to get footage at the peccary's eye level.

It was only when it got to about two meters away that I realized that it wasn't going to back off, and it was too late to avoid its rush. I jerked my hand upwards as the peccary jumped and tried to bite the camera, and it scratched my knee with its hooves as it came down. Fortunately, it was more interested in the camera than in me. If it had rushed past, ripping my leg with a side-ways slash of its tusks as peccaries have been reported to do in the USA, I would have been in a bad way.

The peccary ran off to join the rest of the band and I decided that in future I would film peccaries from a tree and not try to get any eye-level footage. Nevertheless, I did not regret my stupidity. Seeing the peccaries close up changed the way I felt about them, turning them from vague shadows and fleeting grunts into intelligent warm hairy beasts eking out a living in a landscape they know well, but one filled with dangerous predators, such as jaguars, pumas and humans.

Photo 10.3 *I should have stopped filming before the collared peccary got this close. Photo by Bill Magnusson.*

One of the reasons that we had developed the RAPELD system was to be able to study larger species that ranged over large areas. Obvious candidates were jaguars and pumas, but cat studies only came about because of initiatives by Claudia Keller. Claudia is from Rio Grande do Sul, Brazil's most southern state, but she collected data for her Doctoral thesis in the Doñana Biological Station in Spain. Her studies of tortoises there brought her into contact with the team studying the Iberian lynx, one of the best-studied cats in the World. When an opportunity arose for an integrated study involving researchers from Spain, Mexico and Brazil, Claudia suggested that they include Reserva Ducke, which was close to Manaus and had easy access.

The Iberian lynx is threatened because rabbits, its main prey, have declined due to epidemic diseases, and the species, even in the Doñana Biological Station, has low genetic variability. The Spanish researchers were therefore especially interested in the genetics of the Amazonian big cats and their prey base. Catching big cats is difficult, time consuming, and can be dangerous for both the researchers and the animals. It would be so much easier if you could tell the species just by picking up feces. The Spanish team, led by Francisco Palomares, not only developed fast methods for determining which species had produced the feces[147], they could also distinguish individuals based on the DNA of intestinal cells that mixed with the prey remains as they passed through the digestive system[148].

Claudia recruited a masters student, Denise do Prado, to study the diets and distributions of pumas, jaguars, and their prey[132]. To determine the diets of the cats, Denise and her collaborators collected feces throughout Reserva Ducke and in 25 km² RAPELD grids in Uatumã Biological Reserve, Virua National Park, and Maracá Ecological Reserve. This gave her a transect covering about 700 km through the heart of the Amazon. The feces not only provided data on diet. Severine Roques, the molecular-genetics specialist of Palomares' team, used them, together with data from Mexico and other areas in Brazil, to investigate genetic diversity in jaguars[148]. Amazonian jaguars had high genetic diversity, as did jaguars from the Pantanal. However, jaguars from Mexico and central Brazil, especially in the caatinga biome, had little genetic variability, presumably reflecting the effects of overhunting and isolation of populations by agricultural expansion.

Denise carefully picked through the feces to identify what the cats had been eating from remains of bones, fur and feathers, and the analyses by the Doñana group allowed her to ascribe feces to individual cats. By making some reasonable assumptions, Denise was able to estimate the proportions of different prey eaten by individual jaguars and pumas in each locality. There was a lot of data for Reserva Ducke, which abuts the Amazon's largest city and is heavily hunted. There was less data for the other three locations, despite Denise having surveyed them three times, but all those areas had very low densities of human hunters and we grouped them to represent what the big cats ate in relatively natural areas.

I had thought that the pumas and jaguars would differ in the mean size of prey, but they were surprisingly similar, despite the jaguars eating more white-lipped peccaries in the more natural habitats. In these areas, both species of cats ate mainly mid-sized

Photo 10.4 *Wild jaguars are extremely wary, but easily recorded in camera traps. Photo camera trap Projeto Jaguar.*

(10 – 30 kg) mammals, such as brocket deer and collared peccaries. Denise did not find any evidence of the cats eating tapirs, which are presumably too big. Despite eating mid-sized mammals, both species relied heavily on small species, such as armadillos and two-toed sloths, and this was particularly so in Reserva Ducke, where the mid-sized mammals are heavily hunted by humans.

This got me thinking about the effect of size on predation. We are used to seeing lions pulling down animals as large as they are, but lions hunt in packs. White-lipped peccaries are only about half the weight of a jaguar, but they travel in herds and are dangerous adversaries. I had seen large herds of white-lipped peccaries in Virua National Park and José Fragoso had reported even larger herds from Maracá Island[62].

You might expect the big herds to be harder to attack, but perhaps they are also harder to coordinate. Denise found no white-lipped peccaries in jaguar or puma feces in Reserva Ducke, but there is a small herd, probably less than 25 individuals, that humans see regularly. It is inconceivable the cats do not know that the peccaries are there, so they presumably consider them to be too dangerous to attack.

We did not have enough money for camera traps, so Claudia devised print traps to estimate the relative densities of cats on each grid. Most areas in the reserves had hard soil that did not record clear prints, so Claudia paid teams to carry sand from streams to be placed at one-kilometer intervals along the trails. By smoothing the sand patches and returning the next day Claudia, Denise and other team members were able to count the number of times a cat or other animal had passed. This gave an index of how much the areas were used by each species, even though we didn't know how many individuals were involved.

Denise and her team also walked the trails during the day and counted the number of prey species they encountered. As I explained before, this does not necessarily reflect very well the number of animals present, but it was the best we could do and gave a ball-park figure as to the relative abundance of prey. There are many more details about the analysis of this complex data set and the interested reader can consult Denise's dissertation[132]. The major findings for me were that there tended to be more pumas and jaguars where there were more mid-sized prey, but not where there were more small or large prey, and where there were more pumas there were more jaguars, and vice versa. That is, there was no evidence of competitive exclusion between the two large cats.

Predators probably have little effect on large herbivores, though what is large depends on whether the predator or prey also attacks or defends socially. With the extinction of the megafauna in South America, probably only tapirs are large enough to be relatively immune from attack. However, in Africa, most of the herbivores the size of buffalos or bigger are probably more limited by food or water than by natural predators[163,164]. Without Denise's studies of mammals on a large scale in the RAPELD grids, I probably would not have realized that pattern also occurs in South America.

Photo 10.5 *White-lipped peccaries live in large herds and are dangerous prey even for jaguars. Photo by Bill Magnusson.*

CHAPTER 11 - MAMIRAUÁ

Emiliano Ramalho putting a radio transmitter on a jaguar in Mamirauá
Sustainable Development Reserve. Photo by Brandi Jo Petronio Nyberg.

I would learn more about jaguars when I started to supervise students working in the Mamirauá Sustainable Development Reserve, which lies upstream of the junction of the Amazon and Japurá Rivers. It is close to Tefé, but I had not gone there on my first trips up the Amazon. The reserve was created because of lobbying by Márcio Ayres, who had studied the Bald Uakari monkey, which is restricted to forest flooded by sediment-rich waters, known in Brazil as várzea. He realized that flooded forests were underrepresented in conservation reserves and suggested a new type of state reserve modelled on the federal extractive reserves. This would allow traditional human communities to remain in the reserve while protecting biodiversity. Márcio and his collaborators also created the Mamirauá Sustainable Development Institute (IDSM), a federal-government organization to support the reserve financially and logistically. IDSM eventually took responsibility for the Amanã Sustainable Development Reserve that links Mamirauá with the Jaú National Park. These three reserves provide a corridor of wildlife habitat in central Amazonia larger than most European countries.

IDSM has supported many scientific studies and changed the way we see the várzea. Vera da Silva, one of Robin Best´s first students, and later his wife, has carried on his legacy and undertaken some of the most intensive long-term studies of river dolphins in the world. She has accompanied the growth and reproduction of many generations of botos, which she and her students can identify from their natural marks and scars. Without IDSM, this would never have been possible.

We knew that jaguar diets were different in the flooded forests of Mamirauá Reserve because Ronis Da Silveira had radio tracked caimans and recorded jaguar predation on eggs in caiman nests based on sign and camera traps[51]. Jaguars being egg predators had never been reported before and nowhere else did reptiles represent such a high proportion in jaguar diets, though subsequent video sequences made available on YouTube indicate that jaguars regularly eat caimans in the Pantanal. It made sense that jaguars would not eat mainly deer and peccaries as they do in other areas because these prey do not occur in the flooded forests. As in Reserva Ducke, the jaguars of Mamirauá ate many arboreal mammals, such as sloths.

Photo 11.1 A wattled curassow looks at the camera trap with a razor-billed curassow in the background. Photo Instituto Mamirauá.

Emiliano Ramalho studied the distribution of jaguars around lakes in Mamirauá RDS for his masters thesis[133]. He found more feces and other indications of the presence of jaguars in chavascal, which is a type of environment with short, often sparse, vegetation in the lowest areas of the reserve that flood for the longest periods[134]. Unfortunately, at that time it was not practical to identify individuals from feces, and that may have biased our conclusions.

Recognizing the importance of being able to identify individuals and to be able to record jaguar presence even in areas where it was hard to locate vestiges, Emiliano set up grids of camera traps, each covering about 100 km² in Mamirauá RDS and Amaná RDS. The grids in Mamirauá were moved over the years, so the total area surveyed was much greater. Emiliano's principal initial objective was to determine the home-range size of the jaguars, but the cameras recorded many other species as well, and Emiliano recruited students to analyze the data on other várzea animals.

Priscilla Paciullo studied the distributions of wattled and razor-billed curassows in both Mamirauá and Amaná reserves[128]. Curassows are large turkey-like birds that in most parts of South America are ecologically similar to scrub turkeys in Australia. Priscilla recorded wattled curassows only in the várzea, but the razor-billed curassows occurred in both areas. Without várzea, it is likely that the wattled curassows would go extinct, but Priscilla found different relationships between the density of the wattled curassows and flood levels than had been found in another study on the Juruá River, so not all várzea is the same from the birds' point of view. There was no relationship between the frequency of occurrence of the curassows and the frequency of registers of cats at camera-trap stations, so the birds do not seem to be avoiding potential predators. In fact, the feces studies indicate that curassows are not frequent prey of jaguars.

Daniel da Rocha analyzed the camera-trap data for Amaná, with a focus on the mammals[143]. The cameras recorded a bush dog, a species that had never before been recorded in that area[144]. As with the curassows, the herbivorous mammals did not seem to be avoiding camera-trap stations visited frequently by jaguars. However, Daniel identified a problem with the baits used to attract jaguars to the traps[145]. Comparison of stations with and without bait, indicated that jaguars were not attracted to sites with bait, though they did spend more time in front of the camera when bait was present, which increased the number of photographs with enough detail to identify the individuals. This was not a great gain, as photographs from most of the stations without bait were adequate to distinguish different animals, and the data indicated that some of the prey species were repelled by the baits. This could bias analyses of the effect of prey availability on the presence of jaguars.

Anelise Montanarin analyzed the Mamirauá camera-trap data from 2012 to 2017[123]. Because she was able to identify individuals, this study did not suffer from the same biases as Emiliano's study of vestiges published in 2020. In contrast to that study, and studies of jaguars in other regions that had not taken into account differences in behavior of individuals, Anelise found that the jaguars were generalists in the dry season, using all environments in proportion to their availability, and there was no

Photo 11.2 *Jaguars are common in the Mamirauá Sustainable Development Reserve even in areas that are submerged during much of the year. Photo Instituto Mamirauá.*

difference between males and females. It seems that much of the habitat selection of jaguars in other areas is due to avoidance of hunters and that jaguars are generally able to exploit all the habitat types in their home range when they are not persecuted.

All the camera-trap studies were undertaken in the low-water season and, although showing that jaguar diet and behavior were somewhat different in the várzea, they did not reveal the most spectacular aspect of the big cats' behavior. During the early studies, Emiliano and I had speculated about probable migrations of the jaguars from the flooded forest to higher areas during the inundation phase of the annual flood pulse, when many of the Mamirauá sites were tens of kilometer from dry land. However, Emiliano's studies showed that the jaguars remained within their home ranges, even when accompanied by cubs. They merely moved into the tops of trees, sitting calmy on horizontal branches as the flood waters raged below them[135].

The jaguars are not only arboreal, they are also aquatic, swimming from tree to tree to catch monkeys and sloths when they need food for themselves or their offspring. This behavior is not only of scientific interest. The Uakari Lodge, a tourist center run for the benefit of Mamirauá residents, offers packages to see the jaguars at high water and Brazilian and international visitors pay high prices for the privilege of seeing this spectacular wildlife phenomenon. Emiliano's patience and persistence have paid off in ways that I could not have imagined when he asked me to supervise his Masters thesis 15 years ago.

CHAPTER 12 – BATS

This bat was flying in a cave near Presidente Figueiredo, but most Amazonian bats do not live in caves. Photo by Bill Magnusson.

When I arrived in Brazil in 1979 I was mainly concerned with learning about aquatic mammals and I had little time to look for nocturnal land mammals. However, I stayed with Robin Best in his house in the suburbs of Manaus for several months and I couldn't overlook the fact that at about six in the evening hundreds of bats flew out from under the eaves of the house. I sat near the exit hole and counted the bats coming and going. As near as I could tell, they spent only about an hour foraging before returning to the roost, but some of the smaller bats only left after complete darkness had fallen. The bats did not fly outside during the greater part of the night, but I could hear them twittering and scurrying about in the roof. A few left just before dawn for another short foraging bout.

I don't know where all the bats went when they left the house, but I could see many of them flying around the street lights in front of the house and some circled a big Indian-almond tree in the front yard. The insects formed a halo around the lights and there was a layer of broken bodies and wings on the ground around the poles. Other animals, such as geckos and toads, also took advantage of the feeding site provided by humans. Many of the insect were moths and I assumed that they must have been what the bats were feeding on, but I was probably wrong.

I climbed into the cramped space between the ceiling and the roof to get a better look at the bats. There was only enough clearance to crawl and the boards were covered in several inches of bat dung. The pungent ammonia smell made it difficult to breathe and the dried feces swirled up as I moved. It was very hot during the day under the fibro-cement roofing, which was hot to touch. The heat did not seem to bother the bats though, and they had little concern for my presence; flying only if I got very close.

There were two species. The smaller had a wingspan about as long as my forearm, but the ones I captured fitted easily inside my hand when their wings were curled up. I recognized the species as the velvety free-tailed bat, a species that is often found in houses and causes commotion among humans when one falls to floor and scurries across to something climbable so that it can take off again. The other species was the black mastiff bat, similar in form and closely related to the velvety free-tailed bat, but twice the weight. Both species are known to transmit histoplasmosis, a fungal disease, as well as many viruses that are potentially lethal to humans. For this reason, and the unpleasant build up of feces, bats are usually excluded from house roofs, despite the fact that these provide excellent roosts.

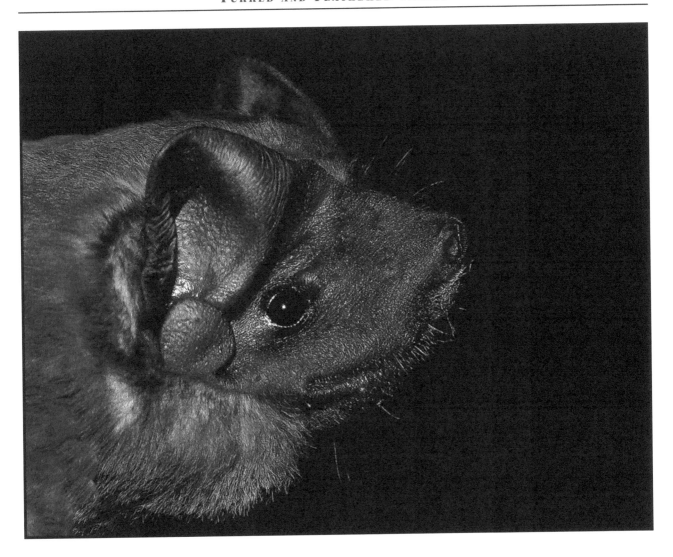

Photo 12.1 *Black mastiff bats often roost in houses. Photo by Roberto Novaes.*

Suely Marques was a masters student who entered our post-graduate program in 1980. With long dark hair and a pallid complexion, she had the austere beauty reminiscent of Caroline Jones playing Morticia Adams in the television series *The Adams Family.* Her penchant for dissecting bats added to the similarity. Suely loves bats and when studying them can be quite single minded. Paulo Vanzolini, the famous Director of the University of São Paulo Museum, had a short story about almost all the people of note that he interacted with. Dr Vanzolini encountered Suely when she was an intern at the museum and his story about her (translated from Portuguese) went something like the following. "I was suffering from a bout of malaria and lay down behind my desk to recuperate. Suely entered my office asking 'Dr Vanzolini, where are you?' When she saw me prone behind the desk, she said 'Oh, there you are', pulled up a chair, took out her notebook and proceeded to list the material she needed to buy for her project!"

Suely initially had a supervisor for her masters project who studied plants. The researcher suggested that she study the bats pollinizing trees in the canopy by observing them from ground level with binoculars. That might have been possible in Australia where most of the bats that visit flowers are at least partially diurnal, but I could not see how she could do that at night in a forest with a canopy 40 m from the ground. In any case, we didn't find out because Suely went on a field course to a biological station north of Manaus, got lost, spent the night in the forest and ended up with a case of leishmaniasis. The disease is caused by a protozoan transmitted by sandflies.

The initial stages of cutaneous leishmaniasis are usually only manifest as a small sore that does not heal, but if not treated it can invade other organs and eventually kill you. The problem is that the most effective cure is treatment with drugs based on antimony. This is a heavy metal, and if you look it up in the periodic table of elements you will see that it is adjacent to arsenic, which was also used to treat leishmaniasis in the past. There are many side effects of treatment with antimony, and Suely had to take the drugs for longer than usual to cure the disease. This meant that it would have been foolish for her to spend long periods in the forest where she might contract leishmaniasis again.

I told Suely about the bats in Robin's house and offered her the data I had already collected. Suely couldn't go into the roost because of the risk of histoplasmosis, another disease that she had already suffered, but she could count the bats as they left the roost and collect some to investigate seasonal variation in condition and reproduction. Suely accepted and I supervised her masters dissertation.

I was perhaps a little unprepared for Suely's tendency to take things at face value. At that time, our post-graduate course required that students undertake a qualifying exam. They were given a list of ten potential subjects a month before and they had to present a seminar on one of them on the day of the exam. One of the topics was sexual behavior in vertebrates and Suely asked what she should read. I considered the exam a joke and I replied that she should study the Kama Sutra. I only realized that she had taken me seriously a week later when she said in Portugues "I have been to every lab in the institute and nobody has a copy of the Kama Sutra." I guess that they were ashamed that their scientific libraries were so limited!

Photo 12.2 *Suely Marques-Aguiar studied black mastiff bats in*
Robin Best's house in Manaus. Photo by Bill Magnusson.

Suely's study revealed that some of the black mastiff bats were pregnant in all months of the year, but differences in the proportions lactating indicated that reproductive success was not constant throughout the year[114]. Pregnancies in one month did not subsequently lead to large numbers of lactating females. This was surprising because most studies of bats in the wild indicate that the females have evolved to have peaks in pregnancy that lead to the lactation and independence of young at the time of year most propitious for survival. Almost all studies of molossid bats, the group Suely studied, have been undertaken in urban settings. It would be interesting to compare those to data from more natural settings to see if they show the same tendencies.

Most studies of insectivorous tropical bats have reported that more food is available in the wet season, but based on the amount of food in stomach contents, this did not occur for the black mastiff bats. The limited evidence indicated that they ate more flying ants than moths, which I would not have expected from the proportions of bodies I found under lights, but this makes sense ecologically. Reproductive castes of ants, that is the ones that fly, have high fat content and are probably more nutritious food than moths. Also, the ants fly slowly and are easier to capture. There are probably so many insects attracted to the street lights that the bats can afford to be choosy.

After I moved to the Ecology Department I had more contact with forest bats. Several species roosted in the culverts under roads. These flew out if I approached and I generally couldn't identify them with certainty. Near rivers, I found colonies of greater bulldog bats, also known as fishing bats, in hollow trunks of trees. The bright orange color of the males made them stand out when in the roost, but at night they were just grey shadows swooping low over the water and I couldn't distinguish them from the lesser bulldog bat, a similar species that scoops insects off the water surface, but generally does not eat fish.

There were many understory palms around our camp in Reserva Ducke, and some of the leaves were bent in the middle, forming a tent because the central vein had been fractured. The little bats that nestled under the awning ignored me as I photographed them and they generally flew only if I touched their leaf. I found other bats in the furled leaves of *Heliconia* plants. These had discs on their wings and roosted head up, in contrast to all other bats I had seen. I assume that they do this so that they can quickly climb out and fly if their vegetable tubes are disturbed. They must be common because we even detected DNA from Peters disc-winged bats in water samples from Reserva Ducke streams[150].

Not all the bats roosted in confined spaces. Proboscis bats live in colonies of up to about 10 individuals and they are camouflaged to look like pieces of bark. They form a line down the trunk of a tree, often only a few meters above the ground. Proboscis bats are so well camouflaged that you often only see them when you are very close and they flutter to a nearby tree. If you back off, they generally return to their favorite tree within a few minutes. They often occur on trees over streams and their DNA was also detected in water samples from streams[150].

Photo 12.3 *Tent-making bats, such as these* Uroderma bilobatum, *bite through the midrib of leaves so that the leaves fold over and form a refuge for the bats during the day. Photo by Giulliana Appel.*

I took advantage of a conference in the State of Bahia to visit the caatinga, a very dry formation in northeastern Brazil. Despite the unpredictable rainfall regime, the caatinga has a high human density, and most of the area was covered by low thorny scrub with an abundance of cactuses. We walked to a large rock dome, perhaps covering half a hectare, to see rock paintings made by indigenous people thousands of years ago. Although the paintings were still intact, we found a man diligently breaking the boulders into hand-sized chunks to be used in road building. Presumably, this important human heritage site will eventually just be rubble.

There were boulders the size of a house piled up against the dome and I found piles of seeds under them which indicated that bats used them as feeding roosts at night. Assuming that the bats might be hiding in more concealed locations during the day, I climbed up the crevice between two boulders and I could see movement a dozen meters above. It was too far away for me to get a photograph, so I shinnied further up the crack, but the fissure was soon too narrow for my head. I had almost given up on getting a photo when I noticed that the bats were not moving away from me; several were scuttling towards me at an impressive speed considering how smooth the rocks were. I couldn't imagine why fruit eating bats would be attracted to a human, but I soon realized my mistake. These were common vampire bats, which don't usually forage during the day, but apparently were willing to have an early lunch if a big mammal decided to jam himself into their den. I got a quick photo of the nearest bat and then left the dining hall.

There were also bat colonies in the caves in the region of Presidente Figueiredo, a favorite tourist site about an hour's drive north of Manaus. These fruit-eating bats are important dispersal agents for seeds, but the seeds they dropped under their roosts in the dark caves just produced plantlets doomed to die for lack of light. I had a lot of fun identifying the seeds and trying to photograph the bats in flight as they fluttered through the circular holes in the sandstone, but I wanted to learn more about what bats do at night.

Ron, a well-known bat expert from an American museum visited Manaus and he wanted help to catch bats in the forest. I volunteered, and we camped near Acará stream in Reserva Ducke. The mist nets we strung near the stream and in clearings in the forest caught few bats. I wasn't worried because most were species I had not seen before, but Ron said that he needed larger series for the museum collection.

I suggested that we set the nets along the road through the forest. It was more a track than a road and hadn't been used by motor vehicles for some years, but it still gave easy walking through the otherwise dense undergrowth. Insectivorous bats usually detect nets with their sonar and avoid them. Most of the frugivorous species of the family Phyllostomidae use sight or smell to forage and are much more likely to fall into mist nets, but these species still use sonar with precision when they are navigating in small spaces, such as treefall gaps. If you want to catch a lot of bats, the trick is to put the nets on flyways that the bats use to transit quickly between roosts and foraging sites. In these thoroughfares that the bats know well, they only use sonar to detect large objects and are more susceptible to capture in mist nets.

Photo 12.4 *This common vampire bat scuttled towards me when I climbed into the crevice where it was roosting. Photo by Bill Magnusson.*

The nets quickly filled with Seba's short-tailed bats and I could tell that we would have trouble dealing with the dozens of bats struggling in the net. To my horror, Ron took a pair of scissors from his kit and started chopping off the bats' heads, which he dropped into a can. I asked what he was doing and he replied that there were too many bats to skin and that he would just take the heads to prepare skulls. I quickly released as many of the bats as I could, which is not easy when you don't have gloves and the bats spend most their time alternately trying to bite you and struggling so that they become more entangled.

I did not show Ron any more flyways. Bats, like most flying vertebrates[13,14], have long lives. Those tiny creatures had probably been flying down that flyway for more than a decade. I appreciate the need for zoological collections, which are especially valuable when they have small numbers of specimens from each of a large number of sites. Nevertheless, killing many animals with no convincing justification saddens me.

Ron, who saw the animals only as museum specimens couldn't understand and we never worked together again. I have been into the field with other Museum curators, such as Don Wilson of the Smithsonian Institution, so I know that many museum representatives collect responsibly.

Enrico Bernard entered our masters program in 1996. His thesis project was undertaken in the PDBFF reserves, and the PDBFF project provided the logistical support he needed to sample in both the understory and the forest canopy. This changed much of the way I thought about the bats; most species were more common in the canopy and the species caught at ground level were only a subset of the bats in the area[20]. You therefore have to be careful when talking about "communities" of bats based on mist-net captures.

In 1998, I used my research grant to take Enrico to Alter do Chão and he surveyed 25 forest fragments and 5 areas of continuous forest[21]. Most of the species were the same as those he had captured in Manaus, but the overall bat fauna in the forests at Alter do Chão was more similar to that recorded from Belém by other researchers than it was to collections near Manaus, indicating a possible east west cline in bat assemblages[22]. Although these studies were interesting, they only marginally went beyond species lists. That is, the bats were little more than names.

Enrico changed all that when he returned to Alter do Chão in 2010 to collect data for his Ph.D. thesis. Brock Fenton of York University in Toronto was his adviser, and Enrico published more on distributions[24], but he had also obtained finance to buy collars and radio transmitters to put on the bats. Most people don't bother to mark bats because the chances of a recapture anywhere but at the site that the animal was marked are remote. However, Enrico surveyed five continuous-forest sites, five sites in forest fragments and 12 savanna sites scattered over na area of about 100 km². He put collars on 3440 bats of 44 species and recaptured 159 individuals of 14 species. He also radio-tracked 23 bats of eight species. This enabled him to obtain natural history data, such as roost sites, distances moved each night, and travel routes for a wide range of species.

Photo 12.5 *This Seba's short-tailed bat was reccaptured four years after being marked in the BDFFP reserves. These small animals have long lives. Photo by Giulliana Appel.*

Enrico's publication[23], is one of the best papers on tropical bats that I have read and it brought home to me that bat assemblages are made up of individuals and species with huge variability in behavior. The Seba's short-tailed bats flew up to 3 km in a single night, but some moved so far that they went out of radio coverage. Some of the lesser bulldog bats stayed in our study area but flew around the whole peninsula. They flew back and forth when just behind the beach, but always flew north along the beach and south when returning along the eastern edge of the peninsular. Enrico recaptured a great fruit-eating bat that had been marked by another researcher 60 km away 210 days before[25]. Different bat species had different types of roosting behavior, ranging from hanging alone in foliage to large congregations in buildings. Some individuals always used the same roosts, but others moved around.

Bigger animals generally live longer than smaller animals and a bowhead whale has been estimated to have been over 200 years old when it died[66]. However, individuals of some species live much longer than expected for a terrestrial mammal of a given size[14]. Bats are long-lived animals, commonly living for decades when similar-size terrestrial mammals are lucky to make it past their first year[13]. They inherit complex instincts, which vary among species, and they complement those with extensive learning about landscape features, food sources and the behavior of predators. They are much more than vague shadows that flitter around at night, and only detailed studies like Enrico's research at Alter do Chão can reveal that complexity.

When we designed the RAPELD system we were concerned about how data collected across a landscape could elucidate the behavior of species, including bats. Most researchers that had studied bats using mist nets left them in position for five or more days. They justified this by saying that otherwise they would not catch all or most of the species that used that location. I did not believe that they had collected most of the species. In fact, I suspect that if you leave the nets in one place long enough you will catch most of the more than 70 species of bats expected to occur anywhere in the Amazon. Also, the researchers did not explain what was so important about the spot they were sampling. What if different bats used somewhere just a few hundred meters away? To understand the ecology of bats we need to know which species use a site frequently, and sampling until we have the last species that occasionally passes there does not help.

Nena Bergallo and her collaborators had shown that, in the Atlantic forest, increasing net hours at a given location was much less efficient than distributing net hours across locations[19]. For researchers sampling in the RAPELD system, I suggested that they open the nets for only one night in a given plot, then move to another plot the next night. If multiple captures were required for some analyses, it would be best if they were not on sequential days.

The same logic applied for birds and the most efficient system would be for bat biologists to use the nets at night and for ornithologists to catch the birds in the early morning and late afternoon, the nets being moved in the middle of the day. That has not happened because researchers rarely consider how planning can reduce costs, how they can help other researchers, or how the data might be used in future integrated studies.

Photo 12.6 *Enrico Bernard radio tracking bats from a hill near Alter do Chão. Photo by Enrico Bernard.*

Bats are not easy to identify, and catching them requires a lot of dedication. I probably would not have had much more to do with bat studies in the Amazon if it hadn't been for Paulo Bobrowiec, a post-doctoral researcher at our institute. Paulo carried out studies of bats in RAPELD modules used in environmental-impact studies and also in other areas, usually in collaboration with Valéria Tavares of the Federal University of Minas Gerais. Their studies showed the efficiency of the system and how data on bat assemblages from mist nets could be used to make decisions about bat ecology and conservation[27,175], and Lucas Perreira used data collected in Reserva Ducke to criticize the width of the riparian zone recognized in Brazilian legislation[129].

Paulo and I supervised a masters student, Rodrigo Marciente, who studied bats along a 512 km transect through the forest along the interfluve between the Madeira and Purus Rivers. Rodrigo surveyed bats in 80 plots distributed among eight RAPELD modules along the BR 319 Highway[113]. This area is difficult to reach, and the BR 319 is all but impassible at the height of the wet season. Although Rodrigo only opened nets for one day in each plot, the data were more than adequate to answer his primary question, which was how vegetation clutter affected the distribution of the bats?

Bat species vary in wing shape, some having wings adapted for fast flight over long distances and others are better for slow fluttering flight around obstacles. The best morphology is not always immediately apparent because some species fly quickly to get to feeding areas and then flutter around bunches of leaves looking for fruit or insects perched on the foliage. Most of the generalizations had been based on subjective categories of vegetation clutter, but Rodrigo measured the clutter around each plot by suspending a white sheet vertically and photographing it from eight meters away. The proportion of the sheet obscured by vegetation gave a sensitive index of how cluttered the vegetation would appear to a flying bat.

Species that ate insects or other small animals and understory fruit-eating bats apparently did not worry much about the degree of clutter and occurred in both cluttered and open areas, but the canopy fruit-eaters were almost always caught in the plots with the least clutter. There was little relationship between wing morphology and the mean degree of clutter in plots where a species was caught, so Rodrigo concluded that foraging strategy and diet of the bats was more important in determining their spatial distribution than the wing characteristics[113].

Ubirajara Capaverde studied the distribution of understory bats in RAPELD plots in Reserva Ducke in relation to landscape variables, such as altitude and slope, and biological variables, such as vegetation clutter and food availability[36]. The type of bat that fell into the nets was predictable from the topographic variables, but these apparently didn't affect the bats directly; they were probably responding to vegetation clutter and food availability. The fruit-eating bats responded most to fruit availability, while the bats that gleaned insects and other small animals from the foliage responded most to vegetation structure.

The mist nets captured mostly bats in the family Phyllostomidae, which holds most of the species that eat nectar, fruit or blood in South America. However, most of the insectivorous bats in other families avoided the nets. There is also a limit to what you

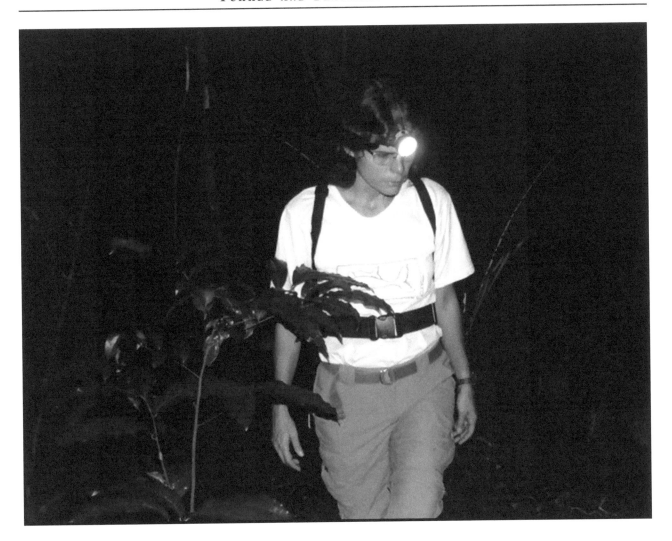

Photo 12.7 *Helena Bergallo studied protocols for catching bats in mist nets in Rio de Janeiro. Photo by Fred Rocha.*

can interpret from data on bats captured in nets. The same species might be easy to capture in one place, but avoid the nets in another. To learn more about the bats, we needed a different technique and Paulo invested in equipment to detect bat calls.

Bats vocalize for a variety of reasons. They talk to each other to show aggression or friendship, they use sonar to navigate in pitch darkness, and those that eat flying invertebrates, such as insects, also have special utterances, called feeding buzzes, that they use to home in on their prey. The chirps of phyllostomid bats are generally pretty hard to identify, but many species in other families can be distinguished by their calls. If you have good ears, younger than mine, you might be able to detect the presence of a few species by listening hard. However, most bat calls are ultrasonic, which means that they have frequencies above those that humans can hear. Therefore, several companies have developed bat detectors, which basically just lower the frequency to one that we can hear and give a digital output that allows you to analyze the sound.

It is widely believed that bats reduce their activity on moonlit nights to avoid predation by owls, and many researchers do not set mist nets on nights near the full moon. However, it is not clear whether the bats are reducing activity or are just more likely to avoid mist nets when the moon is full. Giulliana Appel used autonomous ultrasound recording stations to register the activity of bats in RAPELD plots in Reserva Ducke[9].

There are about 19 species of bats that feed on flying insects in Reserva Ducke, but Giulliana was only able to identify five of them with confidence and with high enough frequency to analyze their activity. As predicted, the riparian-myotis bats reduced their activity on bright nights and were 46 times more likely to be registered on dark nights than bright nights. However, greater sac-winged bats and chestnut sac-winged bats did not change their behavior noticeably in relation to moonlight, and lesser sac-winged bats and Parnell's mustached bats were more active on moonlit nights. It could be that increased insect availability or increased ability to catch insects on bright nights is more important for these species than increased risk of predation. In any case, moonlight only explained a small proportion of the variation in activity for all species. Most foraged mainly at the beginning and end of the night independent of moon phase, as had the urban bats studied by Suely Marques. This natural rhythm, probably related to insect activity, seems to be more important than light levels for the insectivorous bats.

Rainfall is, not surprisingly, common in rainforests, and Giulliana also checked to see whether this affected the activity of the bats, which must roost during the heaviest downfalls[10]. However, normal light rains had little effect on the bats, and they did not increase their foraging later in the night when rain fell during their normal activity peak. I was surprised by the results of both of Giulliana's studies. I had always assumed that moonlight and rainfall would greatly affect bat activity, but these little creatures are much more adaptable than I had imagined.

Photo 12.8 *Rodrigo Marciente with a captured bat during field work on the BR 319 Highway. Photo by Ocirio Pereira.*

For those species that they can detect, devices that record bat ultrasonic calls give more usable information about the ecology of the species than do captures in mist nets. Leonardo Oliveira showed this clearly for Parnell's mustached bats[126]. He used automatic recording devices in 22 RAPELD plots in Reserva Ducke. Besides recording the bats, he measured vegetation clutter and insect availability. We had assumed that insectivorous bats, such as Parnell's mustached bats, would spend most of their time near streams where there was less vegetation clutter and more flying insects, but we were very wrong.

The bats were recorded most in cluttered plots away from streams. The reason for this became clear when Leonardo looked at the distributions of the different sorts of insects. There really are more insects over streams, but they are mainly soft-bodied species, such as moths, and mayflies. The mustached bats were eating hard-bodied insects, such as beetles and bugs, that were more common away from streams in areas with greater clutter. The bats were going where their preferred food was.

Bats are by far the most common and species-diverse group of mammals in the Amazon, and they are undoubtedly the most influential insect predators and seed dispersers at night. Nevertheless, they remain one of the least-known vertebrate groups. It will only be when we have the technology to study their behavior across landscapes that we will begin to understand how they shape the ecology of the Amazon.

Photo 12.9 *Giulliana Appel used acoustic recorders to study bat activity. Photo by Giulliana Appel.*

CHAPTER 13 - THINKING BIGGER – BIRDS

Flamarion Prado Assunção (Pinduca) is one of the best Amazonian field ornithologists despite having no formal qualifications. Photo by Bill Magnusson.

I had long been advocating random or systematic surveys for biodiversity, rather than the usual method of specialists surveying the "best" places to encounter species in their group of interest. Carla S. Fontana participated in one of my courses in Rio Grande do Sul and asked me to cosupervise her Ph.D. thesis on the bird fauna of Porto Alegre, Brazil's southern-most capital city. I was apprehensive because of my lack of knowledge of birds in general and especially of the cold southern states, but I had supervised the doctoral thesis of her major professor, Maria Inês Burger[34]. I met Inês when I visited the Fundação Zoobotânica do Rio Grande do Sul, which was responsible for monitoring duck hunting in the state. When I said that Graeme Caughley had been my Ph.D. supervisor, the researchers there almost fell to their knees in awe; Graeme's publications were the basis of much of the World's wildlife management at the time.

Inês and Carla knew the natural history of the birds well, so I only had to help with the sampling design and data analysis. Carla carried out an incredibly detailed survey of the Porto Alegre birds, sampling 521 random sites across the city. It did not matter where the points fell on the map; except for military land and the airport, Carla sampled them all, even if it meant standing in the middle of a major highway or having to obtain permission to enter private gardens. Almost all previous surveys of urban birds had focused on parks and other green areas, and concluded that the urban bird fauna was depauperate. Carla's study[61] showed that the number of bird species in Porto Alegre was similar to the numbers that had been registered in forested reserves, even though the assemblages were dominated by open-area species and some introduced species were common. The bird diversity was higher where there were more trees and lower where there was more noise, but largely independent of the human density. This means that urban planning could be used to increase the conservation value of cities, even where there are a lot of people. Cities cannot replace natural areas, but they have an important role in complementing more pristine areas and buffering species against extinction.

Carla's study brought home to me the importance of surveying across the entire landscape to understand habitat preferences of animals and the installation of the RAPELD system allowed us to investigate the distribution of birds in Reserva Ducke. Over 340 species of birds have been recorded from the reserve, but there was no data on their distributions within the reserve. People often talk about habitat, but it is usually

Photo 13.1 Graeme Caughley with Maria Inês Burger (left) and Albertina Lima (right) in Manaus in 1992. Photo by Bill Magnusson.

not clear what they mean. In general, some parts of the landscape have higher densities of a given species than others, and the places where researchers encounter a species are considered its habitat. More generically, people refer to different habitats without defining the species, and they are assuming that places that look homogeneous to them will also appear homogeneous to most species in the area. This gross categorization can be useful in some cases. For example deserts have less trees than forests. However, there is little empirical justification for the "habitats" recognized by people in tropical forests.

An exception to the above-mentioned generalization is the habitat represented by riparian areas around streams. Many studies have shown that these have species assemblages different from surrounding areas, and legislation often gives special protection to the riparian zone. Vegetation often reflects this difference and riparian forest is usually distinct from surrounding areas. In the Amazon, riparian areas usually have more arborescent palms than other areas. Nevertheless, it is not obvious how wide animal species regard the riparian zone to be. Mobile species, such as birds, may be restricted to areas near streams, but wander much further from the stream than woody plants dependent on a superficial water table. To test the width of the riparian zone recognized by birds, in 2009 Anderson Bueno sampled birds in 30 uniformly-distributed and 15 riparian RAPELD plots in Reserva Ducke.

Anderson sampled the 45 plots three times and captured 1499 birds belonging to 98 species and 29 families. Some bird species, such as kingfishers and the spot-winged antbird, are almost always associated with water, but many of the species Anderson captured were more frequent near water and others only occurred at large distances. By summarizing these data, Anderson was able to show that distinct riparian assemblages extended from 90m to 140m from the streams. That is, the birds recognized riparian zones much wider than the 30m around small streams protected by Brazilian law[33].

Anderson's study revealed the general distribution of understory birds across the reserve, but I was also interested in the way individual species saw the landscape and Juliana Menger took that next step. Juliana had collected data for her masters studies in the RAPELD modules along the BR 319 highway. This road connects Manaus in the center of the Amazon with Humaitá, which is about 700 km away in the zone where the central Brazilian savannas meet the Amazon rainforest. The "highway" is little more than a dirt track in many places, and trafficking in the wet season is often difficult or impossible. The rickety wooden bridges crossing streams are hazardous and I often had a sinking feeling in my stomach when looking down on the remains of cars in the streams where other travellers had lost their lives[96].

I did not accompany Juliana in the field along the BR 319 and she was supervised by another researcher. However, I made a video of the integrated studies in the region and it can be seen on YouTube[31]. One of the students shown handling birds contracted malaria and another person featured in the filme is Flamarion Prado Assunção, better known as Pinduca, who was the most sort-after assistant for bird studies. Pinduca had lived his whole life on the BR 319 and knew it like the back of his hand. When everybody else was stalled, he would find ways to get the cars through the mud. He

Photo 13.2 *Anderson Bueno holding one of his captures in Reserva Ducke. Photo by Bill Magnusson.*

was adroit at removing birds from mist nests. In the time it took me to work out from which direction the bird had hit the net and started to untangle it, Pinduca would have the bird free and sitting calmly in his hand. Unfortunately, we could not employ him as a driver or even acknowledge that he had handled the birds. Being illiterate he cannot get a drivers licence or become an accredited birder! Juliana related the distributions of 70 species of birds to the distributions of palm species previously surveyed in the RAPELD plots by Thaise Emilio[119]. Those birds were selected based on their vocalizations, which had to be distinctive enough for Juliana to identify them in the field without seeing the caller.

For her doctoral thesis, undertaken in Reserva Ducke, Juliana focused on three species: the wedge-billed woodcreeper, the black-headed antbird and the rufous-throated antbird. For that study, Juliana had to catch the birds and she used the same methods as had Anderson Bueno five years before, except that she covered a wider area and did not sample a large number of riparian plots.

One of the biggest problems with studying population dynamics is that the organisms often have life spans much longer than the periods funding agencies normally support, and some have life spans much longer than humans. We therefore have to make conclusions based on snapshots in time. Small birds, such as those Juliana studied, often live longer than 10 years, but Anderson's and Juliana's studies had to be completed in two to three years.

Species of woodcreepers and antbirds usually have small home ranges; adults are usually territorial and avoid crossing man-made structures, such as roads, even when they are narrow. Based on the ecology of adults, researchers had assumed that these species would have little dispersal ability. We also conjectured that deforestation around the reserve would affect the direction of dispersal between the two major drainages within the reserve. The land to the west of the reserve has largely been deforested, whereas large tracts of intact forest remain to the east. We therefore expected more dispersal from the eastern drainage to the western drainage because the eastern drainage presumably would benefit from recruits moving in from the adjoining forest.

The problem was to evaluate these hypotheses about dispersal during a few years. In stable populations, each adult is substituted on average by one recruit during its lifetime. Therefore, the population does not grow or decline in numbers to any great extent. With a lifespan in excess of 10 years, that means that you can expect less than one event of dispersal and successful colonization in a decade for each adult in the population. The rest of the progeny die, so you would have to study a huge number of individuals to record a single successful recruitment event. That is clearly not viable in a huge area of tropical forest, such as Reserva Ducke.

Fortunately, there is an indirect way of attacking the problem. Individuals vary in their genetic makeup, which is necessary for evolution to occur. The more effective dispersal there is between two areas, the more similar is the genetic composition of the individuals of the same species in them. By studying the genetic structure of individuals across the landscape you can estimate the rate of effective dispersal without ever following a single individual and, more importantly, without having to extrapolate the known behavior of adults to the unknown behavior of juveniles.

Photo 13.3 *Juliana Menger capturing birds in mist nets in Reserva Ducke. Photo by Bill Magnusson.*

Wedge-billed woodcreepers are small, weighing about 15g, and you can hold one easily in one hand. Like other woodcreepers, its tail feathers have spikes on the end that can be used to give support as it perches on vertical surfaces of tree trunks, but unlike other woodcreepers, its bill is short and chisel shaped. Its home range is only about 5 ha and, after establishing territories, individuals probably stay in the same home range for the rest of their lives. Juliana recaptured one individual in the same plot in which it had been marked by Anderson five years before. If dispersal reflected the behavior of the adults, you would expect strong genetic structure to develop across the landscape, but Juliana found little spatial structure in the genes she studied and, contrary to what we expected, there was more dispersal from west to east than east to west[121]. Perhaps that is because the city is a barrier and juveniles in the western catchment had no choice but to disperse west, whereas dispersers in the eastern drainage could go either way.

The black-headed antbird weighs about twice as much as the wedge-billed woodcreeper, but also has a home range of only a little over 5 ha. Individuals of this species are thought to be specialized on foraging in treefall gaps and are not averse to crossing roads. However, Juliana found genetic structure over small distances[121], indicating that juveniles do tend to establish close to their parents. This species also showed east-west bias in dispersal, which was contrary to that of the wedge-billed woodcreepers.

Rufous-throated antbirds are more colorful, but about the same size as the black-headed antbird. There was no detectable genetic structure within Reserva Ducke for the rufous-throated antbird, and dispersal was similar from east to west and west to east[121]. However, Juliana compared individuals from Reserva Ducke and the PDBFF reserves about 50 km away, which are separated by roads and urban areas[120]. Birds from these areas differed considerably and the analyses suggested that populations in both areas had been undergoing expansion in the number of individuals over the past 50,000 years. Obviously, what we are seeing does not depend only on the ecological conditions of today, but bears a signal from past events.

The general lack of genetic structure in these species that are usually considered to have limited dispersal indicates the perils of extrapolating species dispersal from the behavior of adults. Adult trees generally move negligible distances, but this tells you nothing about the dispersal ability of the seeds! In fact, limited dispersal and territoriality of adults may be signs of high dispersal ability of juveniles in long-lived species. If the environment is filled by well-defended territories, juveniles may have to disperse long distances to find somewhere that an adult has died and they can establish. Genetic studies can help us understand much about the population dynamics of individual species, but are presently too expensive to be applied to all species in complex assemblages. Fortunately, the costs are decreasing quickly and we can expect such studies to revolutionize our understanding of dispersal in avian assemblages in the near future. For now, they tell us that we must be very careful about our assumptions in regard to the segment of the population that is most difficult to study – dispersing juveniles.

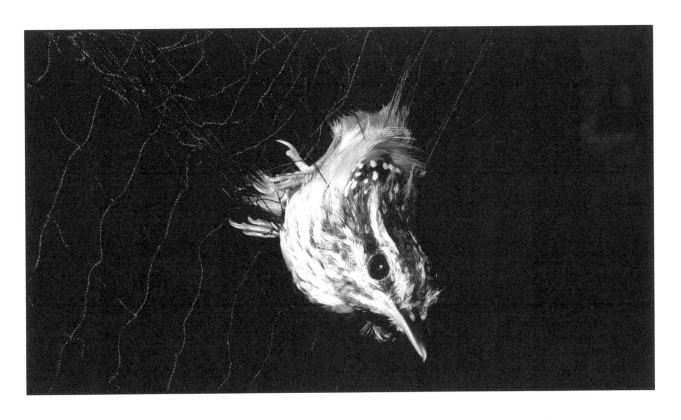

Photo 13.4 *Birds are easily captured in mist nets, but it takes skill to untangle them. Photo by Bill Magnusson.*

CHAPTER 14 - DOMESTIC ANIMALS

No fear.   No hands!

Langdon Magnusson captured on 8mm film these country lads show-jumping in the early 1950s. Photos by Langdon Magnusson.

After the pigeons I had kept as a youth, domestic animals didn't interest me. I had enough human friends and creating emotional dependence in an animal would have restricted my ability to go into the field. That changed when I was 39 years old and married. Albertina already had a daughter, Jaci, who was madly interested in horses, as are many youngsters. Louise Emmons tells me that she was also an equestrian when she was a teenager. Jaci learnt to ride with cowboys and vaquejada riders, which led to a life-long interest in horses and cows. Vaquejada originated in the northeast of Brasil and fulfils much the same role as rodeos in the USA. After finishing a degree in veterinary science, she worked for a while in pursuits related to animal husbandry, but she now lives on a ranch surrounded by her favorite animals and our discussions are often about pasture improvement.

We weren't very concerned about the time Jaci spent at vaquejadas until we happened to be at an event. She was only twelve and too young to be the principal competitor, but one of the vaquejada riders had trained her to help with bull tailing. In this typically South American competition, the rider has to wrestle the cow to the ground, but instead of grabbing it by the horns as in bulldogging, he pulls it down by the tail. This requires great strength, but perhaps the most dangerous part is done by the hazer, who rides beside the cow to keep it in a straight line after it leaves the chute and has to bend down, grab the tail and pass it to the cowboy. If the hazer makes an error, they, the steer and cowboy are likely to roll into a dangerous heap.

Although horse riding is one of the most dangerous activities humans engage in, Jaci was never badly injured and she introduced our youngest daughter, Jeni, to the sport. Jeni didn't participate in vaquejadas, but trained to compete in equestrian events, especially show jumping. None of my family was very interested in horses and I often tease Albertina that our daughters must have gotten that from her genes. Horses were never part of my upbringing, but my uncle filmed a jumping event in rural Australia in the 1950s with his 8 mm movie camera. The jumps were higher than those used in Olympic events and appeared to have been too solid to give way if a horse didn't make it over. Not only did those country bumkins make jumps higher than Olympians, they let go of the reins at the height of the jump, spread their arms and landed as though glued to the saddle. The coordination between horse and rider was incredible.

Photo 14.1 *Bull-tailing is one of the principal competions in vaquejadas. Photo by Bill Magnusson.*

There were no horses in the Americas when the first Europeans got there, but there had been when the first people colonized the New World. The horses went extinct with the rest of the megafauna and the number of species of horses in South America before the Pleistocene extinctions is debated, but morphology based on skeletons is likely to overestimate the number of species. Subfossil remains from Argentina are of a large-headed species very different in shape from modern horses. However, DNA extracted from the bones place the population with thoroughbreds, quarter and shire horses, and far from zebras, donkeys and other extinct lineages of South American equids[127]. The horses brought by the Spaniards may have just represented a reintroduction. The species-rich southern grasslands in Brazil, which are an extension of the Argentinian pampa, are being replaced by native forests in many regions with little grazing, and some researchers see an increase in horses as the most "natural" way to manage the grasslands in national parks[178].

The old obedient hacks used to train Jeni and her friends when they were small retained little of their ancestors' independent spirit. The first "jumps" were just poles laid on the ground, but Jeni soon progressed to obstacles a few handspans high. Regular tournaments allowed parents to compete vicariously as their children tried to complete the course in the shortest time without knocking a rail off an obstacle. The right clothes and posture were also an important part of this exclusive sport.

The riding school provided the horses, so whether a student won depended on the luck of the draw. If they were not in tune with the horse, the chance of winning was negligible. Jeni wanted her own horse, and one called Raio (Lightning) was available. He was not very expensive because he was temperamental and wouldn't let many people ride him. Jeni, however, won him over with gentle pats and loving looks; he became devoted to her.

Raio didn't particularly like jumping, but would try anything for Jeni. They did very well in competitions, especially with the tuition of Miguel, who had competed in the Olympics. Miguel could control horses, and also won competitions on Raio. However, he dominated Raio by force, something that Jeni would never be able to do. A sunny Sunday afternoon training session ended in one of the worst moments in my life.

Jeni had been trying some relatively high jumps that were close together and Raio balked repeatedly at an obstacle that was preceded by another barrier and a sharp turn. Miguel said that he would show Jeni how to do it and mounted Raio. As an expert rider, Miguel could sense the right moment and communicated this to Raio by flicking his boots onto the horse's belly and pulling its head up. Raio sailed over the rails with a handspan to spare.

Jeni watched attentively and followed Miguel's instructions, but she had neither the strength nor the experience to make Raio jump at the right moment. He tried, but left it a few milliseconds too late. His hooves hit the top rail and both he and Jeni somersaulted over the obstacle. They hit the ground together and Raio rolled over Jeni, breaking her hip, but that wasn't the worst moment for me. Raio was terrified and as he tried to stand he placed one hoof on Jeni's chest, right over her heart. I knew that no-one could survive the weight of a horse supported by one foot on their chest and I ran over, sure that my daughter had been killed.

Photo 14.2 *Jeni and Raio competed well when the barriers were not too high. Photo by Bill Magnusson.*

Jeni was still breathing and I pulled open her shirt. There was no mark on her chest. Even when he was confused and terrified Raio had sensed his beloved Jeni and took all the weight on his other foot. Jeni never show jumped again even though she still likes to ride. It was not as much fear of falling as having realized that horses did not evolve to jump, and forcing them to do so can damage them physically and emotionally. I still have no great attachment to horses, except of course for Raio, who gave me back my daughter. However, I learned a lot watching the interactions between huge powerful horses and the puny humans that control them. Those insights would help change the way I interacted with other people and the way I taught, but my understanding of those changes would be deepened by my interaction with another species, the domestic dog.

We already had a knee-high bitch of indeterminate parentage called Manchinha (Little Spot) and Jeni wanted a miniature pincher, so Albertina bought Minnie. I suspect that she wasn't pure bred because she had some untidy hairs around the chin. We had Minnie only a short time when she disappeared, and a week of putting up posters and asking around did not get her back. Therefore, Albertina bought Micky, a pure-bred miniature pincher to compensate. Shortly after, some friends found out who had Minnie and she was returned. That was a lot of dogs for someone like me who had never hung out with canines before.

We regularly took the dogs to a park that was a couple of blocks away and that led to me learning about street dogs. Many researchers study stray dogs[28,29], but I had never given them much thought. People often put out food for street dogs, which is a practice I don't advocate. The dogs become territorial around the food sources and attack other dogs and sometimes humans. The food supports reproduction, which makes for more stray dogs. The feeders think that they are being kind, but even with supplemental feeding, life on the street is hard and stray dogs rarely live more than two years. If the feeders really wanted to be kind they would take the dogs in or have them put down before they could breed and bring more miserable lives into the World. Feeding is evil, even though it makes the people who do it feel good. I ask myself, does an evil act become more acceptable if done by a good person?

The strays accumulated in a street halfway between our house and the park. The leader of the pack closest to us we called Captain, because he ruled the street. Although a potential threat, Captain never bothered us. When we entered his territory, he would strut beside us, barking at any dogs that came near to show that he was in charge and giving us free passage. On one occasion, the pack of five dogs from further down the street came to attack our dogs and Captain sent them packing all alone without help from his band. When we got to the road before the park, which was the limit of his territory, Captain would leave us, only to rejoin when we started back. I became very attached to Captain and was sad when he disappeared after a few years. If we hadn't so many dogs, I would have taken him in and given him the extra decade or so of life that he deserved.

Photo 14.3 *Manchinha, Micky and Minnie ready to go for a walk in the park in 2001. Photo by Bill Magnusson.*

I read a book by an illegal Mexican immigrant in the United States[122]. He had learned to interact with dogs on his grandfather's farm in Mexico and used that knowledge to good effect in his adopted country. Cesar Millan eventually became a television star and multimedia personality, visiting homes to show how to deal with troubled dogs in a still-popular reality show. Problems with Manchinha led me to try some of Cesar's techniques.

Albertina and Jeni would have let the dogs do anything, but I was a kill-joy, not letting them into the house or letting anyone feed them outside their regular meal times. Nevertheless, they coddled the dogs and rarely chastised them. This was OK until Manchina started to be aggressive, snapping at people she didn't know. When not being aggressive, she sheltered in a corner and trembled, apparently frightened of everything. These were symptoms that Cesar said were typical of a dog that had assumed pack leadership, but was insecure in that role. Instead of largely ignoring her, I started to talk to Manchinha calmly and authoritatively, reprimanding any aggression with a firm look and a hand signal for her to return to her corner.

The effect was almost instantaneous. Manchinha stopped trembling, remained calm and refrained from snapping at people she didn't know. It was a lesson for me not only in dog psychology, but also in group living. Many people do not want to be leaders and are unhappy in a leadership role. Nevertheless, they may be among the most important and productive members of a team, as long as they are secure about their position in the hierarchy and do not feel that they are obliged to lead the defense against any attack on the group. Their forte is construction, not destruction.

I realized that our good relationship with Captain was probably because we had used the same philosophy with him. We never let him question our authority or right to cross his territory. Had we run from him, he may have behaved differently. Dogs are faster than us, and the larger ones may be stronger. I see joggers carrying sticks to defend themselves from dogs and I feel sorry for them. The quickest way to show a dog that you are weak and ineffective is to start jabbing it with a stick. Once a dog closes and goes into frenzy mode there is little that you can do. Joggers would do better to carry rocks to stop an attack at a distance before the dog crosses the line, but the best thing you can hit a dog with is your attitude. Domestic dogs have been selected to like having humans as pack leaders. Imposing your leadership is the best way to make them feel good.

A dog being submissive can sometimes be very effective against a larger enemy. Jeni brought home a dog with one white paw, which we called Mãozinho (little hand). She was always nervous and showed her submissiveness by rolling on her back and exposing her neck and belly whenever she thought she was being reprimanded. I thought that level of submissiveness could never be adaptive, but one day Jeni, I and the dogs were walking down the street when a car approached. Mãozinha started to run towards us, but when the car got close she panicked and rolled onto her back. The motorist saw her and slammed on the breaks, but he was too close; the front wheel stopped on top of her belly. Jeni screamed at the driver until he drove forward, the wheel passing completely over the dog. I was sure that she had been killed, but she just got up and ran home. Lying on her back, the road had protected her spine, and the soft intestines just deformed under pressure and bounced back. Mãozinha showed no adverse effects and is with us to this day. Submissiveness can be a very effective survival strategy!

Photo 14.4 *Being submissive can be adaptive, as Māozinha showed when she was run over by a car. Photo by Bill Magnusson.*

I realized how irresponsible people can be with dogs when I took Minnie and Micky to the park by myself. There was nobody in the park except for a man on the far bench with a rottweiler on a leash. As it was a long way off and tethered I didn´t pay the dog any attention and I released my little charges to frolic in the grass. I only realized that something was wrong when I heard the man call out in Portuguese "Look out, I can´t stop him."

The rottweiler was racing towards us, so I kneeled and called my dogs. Micky ran to me immediately and I picked him up, but Minnie saw the rottweiler and was terrified. Instead of running to me, she tried to escape up the park and the rottweiler went after her. She may have been able to outmaneuver him, but when she got to the curb she apparently remembered that she was not allowed to go on the road. She turned back right into the rottweiler's jaws. He bit down with that kidney crunch that I had seen dogs use to kill small prey and threw her into the air. She fell and lay still.

By this time, I had caught up to the rottweiler and grabbed him around the neck with my left arm. I couldn't use my right hand because that was holding Micky. The rottweiler started to jump, bouncing us both up and down and making it hard to hold on. I called to the man in Portuguese "Get your dog".

By this time he was close by, but replied "I can't; I'm afraid of him."

I replied "Be afraid of me, if you don't hold your dog I'll kill you!" Pretty stupid thing to say, and obviously I wouldn't hurt him, but when you're desperate and think that you pet has just been killed, you are not very logical. In any case it worked, the man grabbed the rottweiler by the collar and I could let go. I ran to Minnie who was still breathing, though the rottweiler's teeth had ripped open her belly and exposed her intestines. I trembled as I carried her home, wondering how I was going to break the news to Jeni.

Minnie recovered. The rottweiler's teeth had broken her hip and ripped the skin, but it was just a light nip. The dog's head was as big as Minnie's body. If he had bitten seriously, she would have died almost instantly, so it was obvious that he was only playing and did not intend to hurt her. The fact that I had been able to control him with one arm showed that he was not seriously aroused and respected humans. What I couldn't understand was how a person who was afraid of a huge, potentially-lethal dog could take it to a public park. If it had killed Minnie, or me for that matter, it would have been put down through no fault of its own. If you need a dog to protect you when you're in a public area, it's a good sign that you shouldn't have a dog!

Jeni now has four dogs and we have three. We moved to a new neighborhood and there is a three-kilometer circuit that we can use to take the dogs for a walk. Both Jeni and I are adept at dominating the dogs that irresponsible owners let onto the streets, and we rarely have trouble protecting our pack. A simple command "Go home!" is usually enough to send them back into their owner's yard. The exception is when it is a female with recently born young. The instinct for maternal defense is strong and I have no respect for stupid owners that let lactating dogs onto the street.

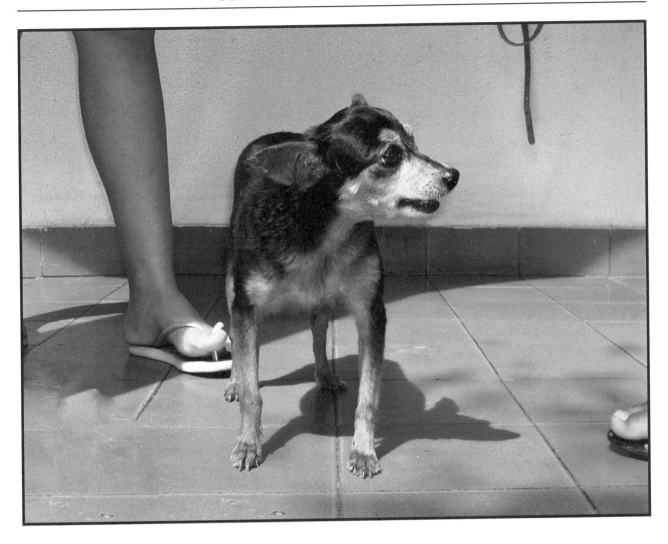

Photo 14.5 *Minnie was small, but she survived a rottweiler bite. Photo by Bill Magnusson.*

We have to be careful because Pongo, one of Jeni's dogs, is easily triggered into a frenzy. Jeni thinks that before she got him he had been used as a bait dog for training bigger animals for dog fights. Jeni only lost control of him once. We were passing a large dog, almost the size of a German shepherd, and everything seemed alright until Albertina's little house dog raced at him and started barking aggressively. When the other dog replied, Pongo slipped his leash and went after him, not fighting like most dogs do, but going straight for the throat and holding the bigger dog down, struggling in his jaws. Jeni separated them and the larger dog disappeared down a side street with Pongo hard on his heels. We didn't see that dog for quite a while after and we thought Pongo had killed him. However, he is now back and everybody respects our authority, though we have to make sure that the barky little house dog does not provoke unnecessary fights. It is strange that the tiny house dogs that receive the most coddling are the hardest to control.

When we moved to our new house, we also inherited some cats. My instinct was to get rid of them immediately, but Jeni wouldn't have that. Our dogs rarely killed native wildlife, except the occasional juvenile opossum, but domestic cats are one of the principal causes of wildlife deaths and they kill billions of animals each year on every habitable continent[112]. There is little that you can do that is more irresponsible and eviler than keeping a free-roaming cat. However, cat owners always justify their actions and say that their cat is different[50]. We were no exception. One of the cats called Fifi had a congenital hip deformation that made her a poor hunter. I have watched her unsuccessfully stalking birds and the only kills she brings home are feral rats, so we are probably justified in saying that she is not a wildlife threat.

Jeni named the other cat Confusion because she was always causing trouble. Gracile, with fine grey stripes, she was very pretty, but also a deadly hunter. A day rarely went by when she didn't bring back a live rat or a native bird and torture it by putting it in a corner and intercepting it every time it tried to escape. Even tiny lizards only the thickness of a knitting needle were open game for her, though she was more gentle with these and I managed to release most alive.

Living with the dogs and cats allowed me to see subtle differences between solitary and pack hunters. I had seen the Garfield comics and always thought that the overweight character that sat on the steps and was too lazy to move when somebody needed to walk past was pure figment of imagination. Fifi convinced me that wasn't true. She lay around in a perfect imitation of Garfield. She was only active when interacting with Pikachu, Albertina's little house dog. They played together when Pikachu was a puppy and Fifi became his surrogate mother. However, he grew up and didn't need her anymore. For a while, Fifi would grab his ears and try to induce him into puppy play, but he just ignored her. Today she still curls up beside him if she can, but he can't be induced to play.

Photo 14.6 *Walking with the pack is the highlight of a dog's day.*
Pongo is the third dog from the left. Photo by Bill Magnusson.

Confusion was somewhat un-catlike in that she would join the dog pack to walk the streets. Instead of marching parallel, she often walked between the dog's legs, and occasionally she would lead. However, we mainly saw the lack of coordination with the pack when there were dogs barking nearby. Instead of finding safety in the pack, she would slink into the forest and Jeni would have to pick her up so that she would not be left behind. Jeni thought that she could solve the problem by putting a leash on Confusion's collar. She would then be able to direct her like a dog. The result was that the cat just lay on its back and refused to move until the leash was removed. There are a lot of subtleties that go with pack behavior. Sitting on the steps because you do not predict where somewhere will tread, not respecting other's walking space and going it alone when threatened are all problems that cats have when group living that dog's generally don't. Watching my fellow scientists, I thought, "some people are cats and some people are dogs." If you don't understand that you may ask somebody to do something that does not come naturally for them. It is not a question of intelligence, it´s a matter of motivation.

We tried putting bells on Confusion's collar, but it had no effect on her hunting, and this is in line with studies that have shown that this technique is only useful to make owners feel more responsible and does not save wildlife. It became obvious that we would have to either kill Confusion or lock her up. We didn´t have to make that decision because a speeding motorist killed her as she walked on the road. Jeni now has three cats in her house, which is next door to ours, but I invested in enclosing the veranda and an outdoor play area for the cats. They are safe and happy, as is the wildlife, and my conscience is finally clear.

There is more to social interactions than dominance hierarchies and I was surprised to learn that Cesar Millan had tried to kill himself when his wife sued for divorce. As he is effective and intelligent, but was unsuccessful, I assume that the attempt was just to get attention, but it is clear that people who appear to be in control in dominance hierarchies may not be internally, even when they earn millions of dollars teaching other people to have "calm assertive energy."

Despite occasional problems, horses and large powerful dogs usually live in harmony with the species they have domesticated to look after them. This gave me clues to how to be effective in social interactions with other humans. The key was not power or weapons, but the calm assertive energy that keeps everyone feeling safe and productive. If Cesar Millan could teach it to dog owners, could I teach it to my students?

Humans, like other social animals, are always building dominance hierarchies[160], and this biological imperative also makes sense logically. Whatever the activity, you want the most competent person leading. The logic only breaks down if you try to impose a single dominance hierarchy for all situations. You may want someone to take the lead in a sexual encounter, but not want to have them telling you how to invest your money. The best fisherperson is not necessarily the best carpenter or mechanic. Leadership should be flexible depending on the objectives of the group at a given moment, and the best person to lead may change as the group composition changes and others gain experience.

Photo 14.7 *Fifi probably only caught this canopy bird because it hit a window, but domestic cats kill billions of birds each year. Photo by Bill Magnusson.*

Lack of flexibility leads to inefficient groups and we have unfortunate tendencies to classify people into different hierarchical levels independent of the situation. Worse still, we tend to accept the opinions of others and unconsciously adjust to the behavior that is expected of us. When I started to read the literature on the subconscious, I was appalled to discover that you can change how well someone will do on a test just by asking them to register their sex or ethnic background beforehand[169,170]. I always thought that people should be treated the way I would like to be treated, the proverbial golden rule, but I realized that many of the things I said could be taken very differently by members of a class. Therefore, I started to monitor what I said and modify my behavior.

After giving a class in which I thought I had been very careful to show the contributions of people of different sexes and ethnic backgrounds, and avoiding implying that some social groups were superior to others, I was content. However, a post-doctoral fellowship holder came to me afterward and said that, although she had enjoyed most of the class, she was troubled by my implication that women understood statistics less than men. In fact, I hadn't mentioned sex at all and I asked her what I had said. She asked "Don't you remember your comment about crying?"

What I had said, talking to the whole class, was that there exists a cultural paradigm in biology that "significant" results are indicated by a statistical test that generates probability values less than 0.05. This cut off is arbitrary and does not take into account the costs of possible errors, but editors and reviewers still often require it, so I suggested that the students should use an experimental design with a good chance of generating lower probabilities when appropriate. I said that if they didn't they would cry over an unjust rejection.

The student said "Everyone knows that women cry more than men, so you were inferring that mistake would be made by women." I had never thought that women might cry more than men. I am very emotional and often cry at sad scenes in films that leave my wife apparently unmoved. Many of my women friends enjoy soap operas that depict people dying slowly of terminal diseases that would bring me to tears if I were forced to watch. A sensitive person can interpret what you say almost any way they want, but I am now careful to say that rejections will result in sadness, which apparently both men and women feel, and not in tears.

This incident brought me to a quandary. Free speech is the basis of democracy, as is well explained by Michael Shermer in his book "Giving the Devil his Due"[160]. Even in the USA, which is supposed to be the bastion of free speech, universities have rules against microaggressions. I was surprised to learn that my classes were full of them. For example, at the beginning of term I ask all the students to say where they are from and what they would like to study. I thought that understanding the diversity of backgrounds in the class would be good for interactions. What I didn't know is that asking someone where they come from is considered a microaggression because they might be sensitive about it. I also lead a discussion about racism and try to convince the students that they are all unconsciously racist. I thought that might

Photo 14.8 *Confusion walked the streets with the dogs, but would not use a leash. Photo by Bill Magnusson.*

not be politically correct, but I got it backwards. Many of the students said that they did not believe in human races and I did not reprimand them for it. Apparently, it is a microaggression to say that you don't believe in races because that can be taken to imply that everyone should be the same!

Michael Shermer points out that this extreme sensitivity is recent and the "coddled generation" may have difficulty dealing with the World. I also worry about this. Humans will build hierarchies whenever they meet, it doesn't matter whether this is in a cooking class or a war zone. Women's rights are fundamental, but we shouldn't forget that male bullies hurt and kill far more men than they do women. Both sexes have to deal with the problem. Minorities will always face initial resistance. I have often represented the Ministry of Science at conservation meetings with members of the Ministry of the Environment. As I am a member of a minority group in the meeting, I have difficulty getting my points across and I am often subjected to veiled hostility.

Presumably, people from the Ministry of Environment face similar difficulties when they are a minority at meetings organized by the Ministry of Science. People can be induced to form an "us" versus "them" mentality just by assigning them randomly to groups before the interaction takes place[56], and you can reduce test performance just by asking that participants write their ethnic background on the form before taking a test[170]. Just believing in stereotypes can create sexual differences in test performance[169].

This is biology and the basic problem is not going to go away. The question is how to deal with it. Protecting students from anything that could possibly interpreted as offensive does not seem to the best way. It is a bit like joggers carrying sticks or expecting that the council officers will always be present to herd wayward dogs back into their owner's yards. The students would be better off if they really believed that "Sticks and stones can break my bones, but words can never hurt me."

People are more tolerant of, and less offended by others of their own group, whether it be based on family, religion or sport. The first thing is to promote in-group feelings and avoid anything that can be misinterpreted. I was at an international meeting when an Australian I had never met came up to me and gave me his name. I recognized the accent immediately and said "Hi, what can I do you for?"

He said "I've been looking for you since the beginning of the meeting, but I couldn't find you."

I replied "That's probaby because I saw you coming", and a delegate from the USA beside me was horrified. He asked afterward how I could insult someone I'd never met. He could not imagine that for Australians of our generation that repartee was the equivalent of saying "Words don't matter, we will respect each other no matter what you say." It only works for Australians, and only Australians of our age; the coddled generation would be crushed.

How do we teach our students to have calm assertive energy no matter what the provocation? That, and not weapons or police, is the only way they can be equals with horses, savage dogs or human bullies. I am often astounded at how quickly arrogant enemies can become humble friends when they run up against calm assertive energy, but sometimes it takes time. Like everything else in science, most of the success goes to those with patience and persistence, and not those who initially appear to be best equipped.

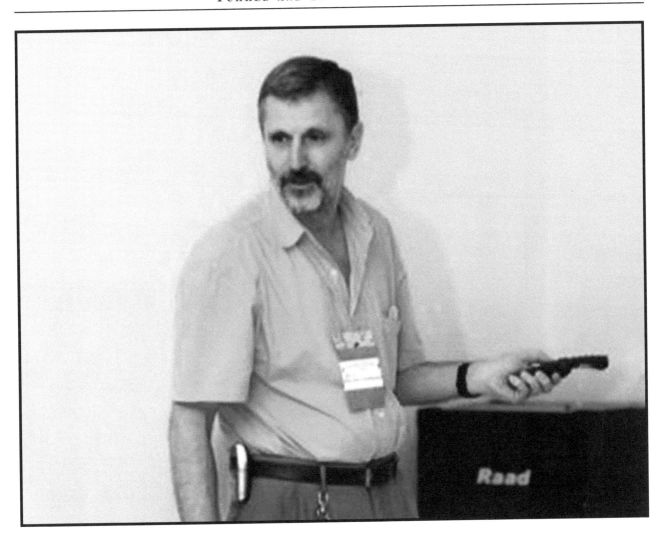

Photo 14.9 *When we teach, our words may be interpreted differently by every student. Photographer unknown.*

Getting back to my teaching, I don't think that I am going to carefully vet everything I say for microaggressions so that all the sentences consist of only "and" and "the". Teaching is about communication and group harmony. I am very careful at the beginning of my courses to avoid anything that might turn off sensitive students. This does not mean that I avoid sensitive subjects, just that I avoid implying that anything I say excludes or demeans anyone in the class. As the sense of belonging and the self-value of each student increases, I can relax my vigilance about microaggressions, and by the end of the course, I hope that they have enough confidence in the subject that they can exert calm assertive energy whenever it's needed.

Photo 14.10 *Jeni with Raio in 2011. Horses are stronger and faster than us, but respond to calm assertive energy. Photo by Bill Magnusson.*

CHAPTER 15 - WHY IS THE WORLD GREEN?

Cassowaries can be intimidating, but reports of their aggression are exaggerated; birds generally only eat small things. Photo by Bill Magnusson.

My scientific studies and the animals I kept as pets changed my views of the World, but travelling to other places during my holidays or when I was giving field courses was perhaps more important. My research has almost always been about how the environment affects organisms. I have rarely asked about organisms that change their environment – the so-called ecosystem engineers, and this reflects the places where I have worked. In those regions, humans are the most important ecosystem engineers, though most of the time they don't realize it or try to deny it. That is the situation that has held for the last 10,000 years or so, but it was not like that in the past.

In 1960, three prominent ecologists published a paper about community structure, population control and competition[72]. Although they did not mention the word green in the paper, the central question relates to why much of the World is covered by green vegetation or why is the World green? The reason follows from the following logic. Plants have plenty of light, water and nutrients available, so they can grow in most places. Plants therefore concentrate lots of nutrients in their tissues that can be consumed by animals. If there were only two trophic levels, producers and primary consumers, the plants would be in danger of all being eaten, even though they might slow the process by investing in compounds or structures that make them less palatable. That does not happen because animal tissues generally provide much better nutrition for other animals than do plant tissues. Therefore, species evolved to occupy a third trophic level, which consists of predators, or animals that eat other animals. Because meat is so much more digestible than vegetation, the predators will selectively remove the herbivores, leaving the plants largely unhindered to grow and make the World green. The Ecological Society of America has a YouTube video that illustrates this[58] that they illustrated with mammals, but I will explain below that it is probably not the mammals that make the World green.

This idea fitted nicely with all my studies. The system could be run by plants because the predators prevented the herbivores from eating them out. In some places, such as northern Australia, introduced herbivores are changing the environment. I had seen water buffalos wreaking havoc with floodplain ecosystems and I imagined that it was because tigers had not been introduced with the buffalos. It was only much later that I realized that the tigers would probably make little difference.

Photo 15.1 *This bison in Oklahoma was domesticated, but I was still nervous getting close to such a large animal. Photo by Bill Magnusson.*

The system is much more complicated than the green-world hypothesis indicates and the details all relate to size. The implications are many, including such apparently disparate questions as to why birds have beaks and mammals have teeth, or why we eat many cows and few emus. To explain how I came to my fixation with size, I will have to take you on journeys to various parts of the World that I have visited because the revelations came slowly; please bear with me.

I know little about the Northern Hemisphere, but my trips there gave an inkling to the wider story. Although I have visited Mexico, USA and Canada, I have never seen a moose or a wild bear. The largest native animal I saw was a plains bison in Oklahoma and the largest predator was a bobcat in Florida. I approached the bison nervously to get a photograph with my little digital camera without a zoom lens in 2008. It was probably a domestic animal and unlikely to charge me, but it was big and imposing to a nervous biologist from the tropics. In the recent past such an animal might have been a member of a herd many thousands strong, and getting that close would truly have been foolhardy. But going back 10,000 years the situation would have been even more impressive. Then there were many species of bison, and the one that survives today was the smallest. There were also saber-toothed cats, American lions, New World cheetahs and dire wolves, but even these large predators would have found the giant bison, let alone the mastodons and mammoths, intimidating.

I visited Thailand in 2011 and saw semi-wild red jungle fowl similar to the ancestors of modern chickens. To see wild Asian elephants I would have had to go to areas near the border with Myanmar, and that was too dangerous because of military unrest. However, I rode domesticated elephants and learned that incursions into wild areas had usually been undertaken on elephants when there were still wild tigers. Not even a tiger can take on an elephant. The same lack of large wild animals occurred in Vietnam. Some of the areas near Hanoi were spectacular, but I saw no large mammals, and most areas had few birds. The last Vietnamese rhino had been killed in 2010. Even in the remote Truong Son Range, there were no more rhinos and even the tiny Annamite rabbit was on the edge of extinction[171]. After the war with the USA, the Vietnamese government prohibited the use of rifles. Poachers therefore use wire snares which are unselective and kill everything. Local bushmeat markets provide the incentive for the common animals, and rich Chinese businesspeople pay high prices for the most endangered species.

I was eager to see fauna and the group of tourists with which I was cycling thought that I was mad when I slammed on the brakes and sat in the rain on the embankment of a rice field filming ricefield rats eating leaves and flowers. The rats are so small and the rice fields so productive that their major predator, *Homo sapiens*, cannot control them. This gave me a hint; one way to avoid predators is to be much smaller than they are.

Photo 15.2 *Ricefield rats were the only native mammals*
I saw in Vietnam. Photo by Bill Magnusson.

You look for the large animals when you travel. This is not very logical because small invertebrates are often the most numerous and spectacular animals. Nevertheless, we are humans, and tend to relate more to mammals and birds, especially the large ones. I returned to Australia in 2014 wanting to show my family some of the fauna. We went to far northern Queensland and with the help of Ceinwen Edwards we were able to find many of the iconic animals of the Australian rainforest, including four species of rainforest possums, which are herbivorous phalangers and very different from the American opossums.

I don't know anywhere else in the world where you can find four species of nocturnal arboreal herbivores so close together. Coppery brushtails are often considered a variety of the common brushtail, but have a restricted distribution in the north. We saw them both in the forest and eating oranges on Ceinwen's property. Green ring-tail possums are more yellow-brown than green, but the black lines on their back combined with the background color made them very cute as they peered down at us. They are the only ringtail not to make a nest and their color makes them inconspicuous when they curl up on a branch during the day. The Herbert River ringtail is as conspicuous as the green ringtail is camouflaged. The contrast between its black back and brilliant-white belly make it easier to find with a spotlight than the other possums. The dark grey lemuroid ringtail possums were in groups of two or three, but we often just saw their eyeshines high in the trees. Two of the ringtails can apparently occur together because the green ringtail eats high fibre, low protein leaves while most of the vegetation eaten by the Herbert River ringtail is low in fibre and high in protein. What separates the lemuroid ringtails is unknown. Ceinwen said that sugar gliders and and long-tailed pygmy possums also occur on her property, though these are not principally folivores.

I had seen captive tree kangaroos in Australia and Papua New Guinea, and we visited Lumholtz Lodge, where Margit Cianelli raises orphaned Lumholtz's tree kangaroos. They were devoted to their adopted mother, sometimes sitting poised on her shoulder and at other times diving into her shirt that served as surrogate pouch. I was intrigued by the ability of the youngsters to climb knotted ropes hung from the curtain rod. However, I wanted to see tree kangaroos in the wild, and we were lucky to find several in a small patch of forest between a road and tea plantation. One of the females had pouch young and the baby responded to our presence by first diving head-first into the pouch with its hind legs waving in the air and then wriggling around to stare over the pouch rim with huge dark eyes. I was amazed at how clumsy the kangaroos were in the trees and I assume that they escape from predators, such as eagles, by jumping to the ground.

On this trip we did not see any cuscuses or striped ringtails, or any of the species of gliders, but even including these the number of species of arboreal mammals in northern Australia is dwarfed by the number of birds in the rainforest canopy. Some are large, such as the palm cockatoos that have a huge beak capable of chopping the hardest seeds. The only parrot with a larger beak is the hyacinth macaw in South America. The smallest bird in the Australian rainforest is the weebill with a wingspan of only 15 cm.

Photo 15.3 *Herbert River ringtail possums are easy to see in Northern Australia and can regularly be found together with three other species of possums. Photo by Bill Magnusson.*

While these finds were very enjoyable, we wanted to see big dangerous wild animals, and the only species that fits that description in the Australian rainforest is the cassowary. These are beautiful birds with long, black, silky feathers, and blue and red naked skin on the neck and head. This is topped off by a high brown helmet covering the cranium. They are undoubtedly the most spectacular of the large flightless birds known as ratites that only occur on the southern continents.

Emus are taller than cassowaries, and height is important in emu social hierarchies. I remember my mother, who is not very tall, being pecked on the head by an emu, but even a small person can dominate an emu if they hold their arm high with the hand bent forward in the form of a bird's beak. Emus appear to be programmed to give way to a taller opponent. Height is not important for cassowaries. They are the World's third heaviest birds; only the two species of ostriches outweighing them. Although ostriches are formidable, they are not considered as dangerous as cassowaries, which have used their claws to kill people in at least two documented incidents, and indigenous people report many more cases.

The most famous place for seeing cassowaries is Mission Beach, a popular tourist town midway between Townsville and Cairns. On the beach in front of the car park we saw cassowary tracks, the clear outline of the three toes in the damp sand bringing images of dinosaur tracks. However, the tracks were headed down the beach and into the forest. We doubted that the bird would come back anytime soon, so went to the nearby Licuala State Forest, which has boardwalks through groves of spectacular Australian fan palms.

Signs indicated what to do if confronted by a cassowary so we were hopeful. There were many things to see and we spent hours photographing small birds, lizards and flowers, but we were starting to doubt that there were any cassowaries there when we came upon one of the most spectacular piles of feces I have seen. The base contained brightly-colored seeds the size of ping-pong balls and the rest tapered to an inverted cone a handspan high. Nothing but a cassowary could produce such spectacular excrement, but that was as close as we came to finding one that day.

The next day, we returned to Mission Beach and headed south away from the picnic areas as we assumed that the tourists would scare the cassowaries, and there it was walking over its tracks of the previous day. However, I only had time to take one reasonable photograph of the cassowary in the "wild" before it stalked into the picnic area. It went straight to a large wooden table where a family of five were eating their lunch and tried to grab fried potatoes from the plates. Someone drove it away and it went to another table. The tourists were careful not to seriously threaten it, but it was obvious that this was a daily occurrence and they had no qualms about shooing it away. We followed the bird, trying to get a photograph without tourists in the background. I had hoped that it would return to the forest, but it went into a caravan park and sat on the grass beside an almost full-grown young cassowary. It obviously considered this its home and I gave up trying to get a picture without a water tap or a caravan in the background.

Photo 15.4 *The size of cassowary dung is impressive and the huge birds must disperse seeds of many rainforest trees. Photo by Bill Magnusson.*

These birds had obviously adjusted to the urban environment and I did not feel any of the adrenalin kick I imagined I would have when getting close enough to a cassowary to photograph it. Cassowaries are obviously not that dangerous to humans, though giving them artificial food and encouraging them to hang around roads is probably not good for their long-term survival. They are thought to live 40 or 50 years in the wild, but a speeding car can cut that short.

I started to think about size and carnivory. Birds obviously can evolve to large size, and some of the moas of New Zealand and some of the elephant birds of Madagascar were much bigger; one of the elephant birds weighing over half a ton. The elephant birds went extinct when humans colonized Madagascar one or two centuries before the birth of Christ, and the Maoris were exterminating the last moas at about the time of the Italian renaissance. Although people interacted with these giant birds, and people still interact with ostriches, emus and cassowaries, there is no evidence that they were or are any great threat. Despite the large size, the elephant birds and moas had relatively small bills and probably only ingested things that they could swallow whole or small pieces of leaves. The islands of New Zealand and Madagascar were the only places that birds were the largest herbivores.

With the exception of some raptors and vultures, most birds eat small things they can swallow whole. While this might look like a limitation, beaks allow birds to selectively pick up very small prey in a way that is not possible for mammals. This innovation allowed birds to gain enough high-energy food to support flight, which lets them exploit all levels of the vegetation from the ground to the canopy. High energy demand, many species and individuals, and the ability to glean insects from foliage make birds very important in food chains. Other invertebrates also eat herbivorous insects, but these tiny predators are also eaten by birds and so are unlikely to have large effects on their prey. The adaptations that make birds great predators on invertebrates, small size and flight, however, strongly limit their activities as arboreal folivores[124].

Bats do eat a lot of insects. Nevertheless, there are many fewer species of bats that glean foliage than there are birds with this habit. Bats rely on echolocation or hearing to find their prey, which is effective in catching flying insects, but much less efficient than the acute eyesight of birds for gleaning foliage, especially for small insects. Sight is probably better than hearing even for for aerial hawkers. That is why most insects fly at night with the bats rather than flying during the day with birds. I am a keen gardener and often sit watching the bushes I planted many decades ago. Some of these seem to support few herbivorous insects, but it is rare that an hour goes past without a small bird flitting among the foliage to catch any insect that may have taken refuge there.

As far as I am aware, there is only one large-scale bird-vegetation system that has been investigated in the same detail as the studies of fish and algae in temperate lakes. I was surprised when Richard Loyn told me that the old bush tale that bell miners cause dieback in eucalyptus forests was true. Foresters had only noted that areas with the melodious calls of the bell miners had sick eucalypts, but Richard tested their hypothesis experimentally. When he removed bell miners, the forest recovered and became green again[85,86]. This has important implications for conservation and forestry, and has been examined in detail by many researchers and government agencies[162].

Photo 15.5 *Cassowaries are the largest animals in the*
Australian rainforest. Photo by Bill Magnusson.

The bell miners eat mainly psyllids, which are sap-sucking insects, often called plant lice. Many that attack eucalypt leaves produce a protective covering of crystalized honeydew called a lerp. Although it is easy to find lerps, they usually don't badly affect the trees, because many species of honeyeaters and parrots like to eat them. The parrots are particularly effective because they can hold the leaf with one foot and scrape the lerps off with their bill. Bell miners are territorial, expelling most other species of birds from their territories, which is good for the psyllids and the bell miners, but bad for the eucalypts, which become debilitated and appear brown in aerial photos.

The bell miners are like the large predatory fish that control the planktivores and let the zooplankton control the algae[37]. In this case, they are controlling the other insectivorous birds that otherwise would eat the psyllids that control the eucalypts. Noisy miners are similarly aggressive in more open eucalypt forests and suburban gardens[131], but do not affect the vegetation, possibly because there are many species of trees and psyllids usually attack only one or a few species. In most places, there is nothing to control the insectivorous birds and they glean the insects off most of the plant leaves. That is, it is the birds, and not the mammals, that keep the World green!

West Africa has rainforests similar in many respects to those of South America. The only country I have been to in this region is Liberia, a country colonized by former slaves from the USA. It is poor and has a high incidence of violent crime, so it is rarely visited by tourists. However, John Fa asked me to give a course in RAPELD methodology as part of a Center for International Forestry Research (CIFOR) project funded by US-AID. John is a specialist in the bush-meat trade and has visited markets throughout Africa, but has less experience with field studies.

I took along two young ex-students with experience in RAPELD studies. Rafael Rabelo had studied monkeys in Mamirauá for his Masters thesis and was starting a doctoral thesis on the distribution of butterflies. Rafael was dark-haired and bearded and looked a typical academic. Ramiro Melinski is a dedicated ornithologist. Also bearded, but taller and more heavily built than Rafael, Ramiro does not look like a typical university student. Numerous tatoos and a penchant for wearing sun glasses mean that he would not be out of place in the slums of Rio de Janeiro. We started ribbing him about his appearance after he was singled out "randomly" for a body search every time we went through an airport security system. The fourth member of the team was Luca Luiselli, a herpetologist with many years of experience working in Africa. He is a citizen of Nigeria and a staunch defender of the sovereignty of African nations.

The course was undertaken in the Zor community forest. Liberia has designated community forests across the country with the objective of conserving wildlife and providing local communities with subsistence and commercial opportunities. The Zor community forest is one of the largest and abuts the East Nimba Nature Reserve. We stayed in a hotel one and half hours drive from the forest, apparently because the organizers felt that would be the safest place for us. The hotel was in an enclosed compound and all the grounds had been cemented over, making it a very uninteresting place for a field biologist.

Photo 15.6 *Bell miners are aggressive and can exclude much larger species from their territories. Photo by John Barkla.*

The country we drove through reminded me much of rural Brazil, even to the presence of rubber-tree groves, but occasional roadside stalls had antelope carcasses for sale, so there must be wildlife amongst the farms. We went to a local market in one of the larger towns to see what bushmeat was on offer. There were snakes and monkeys and antelope, but the carcasses had been smoked and dried, making them appear unappetizing. They were brown and grisly, a bit like the mummified remains of children you see in Peruvian museums.

We lunched at a nearby restaurant and the forest guards were anxious that I try one of the local delicacies. The others ate more conventional fare and I probably should have too because from that day on I had a severe case of diarrhea. John kindly offered to go to a local pharmacy and buy something to control the symptoms, but the medicine the pharmacist gave him was for a bacterial infection and not for amoeba, which I assumed was the cause of my woes. There were two pieces of information on the leaflet inside the box. One was that the medication should not be taken if out of date because the result could be fatal. The second was that the medication was out of date! I put up with the diarrhea until I got back to Brazil.

The village beside the community forest consisted of about 20 palm-thatched mud-brick houses. It would have been a much nicer place to stay, but there were signs warning of a recent Ebola epidemic. I wasn't particularly worried about the Ebola, which had peaked and disappeared. However, I assumed that malaria was endemic in the village and African malaria is much more dangerous than the South American strains. African malaria has killed more biologists that I have known than any other single cause.

The people were extremely friendly and I felt more at home there than I had in the nation's capital, Monrovia, where almost nobody talked to us except when trying to sell something or swindle us with unlikely stories. The forestry officials had contracted several people to help us, but I had the impression that their curiosity would have got them involved even if there had been no cash incentive.

The forest was about a half-hour walk from the village, mainly through fallow fields. Again I had the impression of being in the Amazon, especially when we came across giant kapok trees. The same species occurs in Africa and South America. We only had four days, so we planned carefully. The RAPELD methodology is based on a system of trails and plots. The first day we showed how to make trails and the second day we showed how economically-valuable trees can be surveyed along them. The third day we taught how to install plots, with the objective of sampling them on the last day. The only vertebrates we would sample would be understory birds that can be captured in mist nets.

There are African forest elephants and pigmy hippopotamuses in Liberia, but they apparently don't occur in the part of the Zor community forest near the village. There was a chimpanzee nest in a tree near one of the trails we cut, but we did not see this species, which is the closest living relative of humans. We also found spoor of a small antelope in a patch of swampy ground, and I found tracks that looked much like those of South American coatis. When I asked what had made them, my guide replied "raccoons".

Photo 15.7 *Participants in the RAPELD course in the Zor Community Forest in 2018. Photo by Bill Magnusson.*

I was surprised by the name because there are no raccoons in Africa. However, I realized that the ex-slaves that had colonized Liberia had been raised in the USA. They gave names to the local animals based on their similarity to those they knew back home, as did colonists almost everywhere in the World. John explained that the tracks were of civets, which are species from the order Carnivora that have a generalist diet, like that of the Coatis in the New World. I had never come across a civet in the wild, so I was anxious to see one, but this was not to be in Liberia.

We were driving three hours a day, which left little time for work, and I wanted to spotlight at night, which wasn't possible in the hotel compound. I therefore proposed that the students and I camp in the forest, and John and Luca could bring us food each day. John was responsible for the course and was not comfortable about leaving us in the forest, but he eventually accepted my argument that it was much more dangerous to drive three hours each day than to sleep in the forest. I didn't mention that the most threatening thing I had encountered in Liberia was the diarrhea medicine he had bought me! We didn't have any camping gear, but it was dry season and village people said that it was unlikely to rain. The forest was also far enough from the village that we had little risk from malaria.

We had mosquito nets, but there were no biting insects. We could lie anywhere on the leaf litter without being molested by ants. In fact, we found that we could leave the chicken wraps John and Luca brought to feed us on the ground overnight without anything eating them. This may say something about the quality of the wraps, but it was in line with the rest of our experience; this forest seemed to have no insect pests, at least at that time of year.

The first night we spent in the forest was heaven in relation to the long drives and sitting around doing nothing in the hotel compound. We photographed bugs, frogs and fish, and Ramiro got some nice shots of birds in the early morning, but we saw no mammals. I wanted to see a zebra duiker and made plans for the next night, but things didn't turn out as I had expected.

By four in the afternoon we had finished putting in a demonstration plot and Ramiro had returned to get the mist nets. While we were waiting, I talked to Korkorlie who served as a go between for the Forest Service and the local communities. He was proud of his bushcraft and when he heard Black-casqued hornbills calling he took me to see them. You could hear their wing beats as they approached and they called almost constantly. We spent about half an hour trying to photograph them, but they moved too quickly and were too high in the canopy.

When we started back, Korkorlie seemed to be going in the wrong direction. I told him, but he just ignored me and kept going, so I assumed that he knew an easier trail. As I followed, I was impressed by the heavy use the people made of the forest. It was impossible to go more than 20 paces without encountering saplings that had been cut and regenerated, presumably victims of people walking around and absent-mindedly swinging a machete.

Photo 15.8 *Their tracks indicated that civets and duikers used the area around the stream, but I did not see them. Photo by Bill Magnusson.*

The forest was very dry with virtually no understory plants except juveniles of the forest trees, but it was high and imposing. There were meter-wide pinkish trunks of trees Korkorlie called redwoods rising toward the canopy. Some of the kapok trees were more than 2m in diameter and their buttress roots spread like knee-high snakes over the rocky ground.

I followed Korkorlie without paying much attention until I noticed that the sun was warming first one ear then the other; we were walking in half-kilometer circles. Korkorlie was looking around confusedly and I realized that he was lost. By that time, I had no idea of the direction back to the trail. He said "The village is east, we should go that way," but he continued to circle.

I said "Wait a minute, what direction were you going when you cut the trail?" He replied that they had been following a compass bearing of 307°, which is about North-Northwest and I said that we had to go south to pick up the stream at the edge of the forest. Nevertheless, he was adamant and wanted to go east, which by my reckoning would take us deeper into the forest.

I had drunk no water for several hours because I had expected to return to camp when the students were setting the nets, and the air was very dry. I told Korkorlie that I was not going to keep circling and that I would use the sun to follow a bearing south along the valleys, which must lead to the main stream. He said no, that we should head east. Ignoring him, I headed south, trying to cover as much ground as possible while I still had the sun to navigate. I didn't want to spend the night on the ridge top with no water because I was already dehydrated and suffering from the diarrhea.

The ground was rocky and we had to jump from one outcrop to the next as we headed downstream, but the understory was relatively open and we made good time, covering several kilometers in half an hour. Korkorlie had used his mobile phone to tell the forest guards that we were lost, but at first they thought that he was joking. He kept wanting to head east or stop and wait to be found, but I knew that the forest guards would not be able to track us in the dark and his circling would make it difficult for them to work out where we had gone. I ignored him and just kept walking; my mouth so dry that my tongue felt like it was sticking to the top of my mouth.

Korkorlie stopped, pointed uphill, and said that we had to go East. When people circle, they tend to follow some aspect of the lie of the land to orient. In Korkorlie's case it was going uphill. I said no, but as a concession, I said that we would head down the valley that was oriented about south-east. He said that we were heading further into the forest and would have stopped, but I just kept walking and he had to follow.

The rocks around the valley floor were getting bigger, which indicated to me that we were getting close to where a stream might form, and something broke cover from a cleft just two meters in front of me. It was a heavy-set animal with a black rump and lighter color towards its thickset head. Its legs were short and if I had been in the Amazon I would have thought that it was a paca. It circled around and disappeared into the undergrowth before I could get my camera out. Korkorlie gave it the local name of black but, but John Fa said that it was probably a bay duiker.

Photo 15.9 *The black bee eaters Ramiro found looked as though they had been painted against the early morning sky. Photo by Ramiro Melinski.*

I was pleased because I had seen no evidence of mammals in the three days we had been there, except for some duiker tracks in marshy areas and civet tracks around the stream. Korkorlie was becoming stressed and said "See, you only get black buts deep in the forest; we are heading the wrong way."

I ignored him and kept walking downhill. Five minutes later, the dry stream bed turned into a creek with crystal-clear water between the rocks. I still didn't want to risk drinking the water, but Korkorlie slaked his thirst. Another five minutes and we came to a straight two-meter-wide trail which Korkorlie said was the boundary to the reserve.

We could either go east or west and Korkorlie was desperate to go east. I said that would be OK, as long as he called the forest guards and told them that we were safe. I didn't mind spending a night in the forest, but I didn't want people wandering around all night looking for us.

We walked fast along the trail for about an hour until it got dark. Korkorlie was feeling the strain and after stepping over a log his leg cramped. He rolled on the ground in agony, and I tried to stretch his leg and push back on the foot as I had seen medical assistants do for football players, but it only alleviated the pain for a few minutes. Eventually, he asked me to punch the area that was cramped and that seemed to work. Within 10 minutes, he was walking again.

As the trail was straight, it went up and down hills rather than taking the easiest grades. We crossed four small streams and I drank my fill, hoping that there were no bugs in the water that might make my dysentery worse. The streams were coming out of the community forest so I was at least confident that no-one lived upstream.

We were now sure that we had gone the wrong way, and I said that we should find some flat ground with lots of leaves and spend the night in the forest. As there were no ticks, chiggers or mosquitoes, not even ants, we could lie down comfortably almost anywhere. Nonetheless, Korkorlie was desperate to get back and said that we should go back with the light of his mobile phone. That wasn't an attractive option for me. I was wearing light five-finger shoes, which are just great when you can see where you are going, but offer no protection from sprained toes if you kick straight into unseen rocks.

Korkorlie set of at a fast pace about 2m in front of me, and I tried to memorize where the rocks were from the faint light in front of me, but I was now very tired. Walking in the dark and trying to balance on one foot at a time when you are refreshed and energetic is one thing; trying to keep your balance when you are exhausted is another. After about a kilometer, which took about two hours, I told Korkorlie that I was too tired to go one. I had two sprained toes and I was feeling my years. I told him I would have to stop and rest.

Photo 15.10 *Ramiro Melinski with a freshly captured female rufous-bellied wattle-eye. Photo by Bill Magnusson.*

It would have been good to find some soft leaves to lie on, but having gotten him to stop, I was content to just lie down on the rocky ground and snooze for two hours. Korkorlie spent the time calling his wife, who didn't believe his story that he was lost in the forest with a male scientist. Afterwards, he called everybody else he could think of, effectively draining most of the charge from the battery.

After a few hours, I was feeling better, and I said that we could go on if he really wanted to. Relieved, he set off at his usual pace and I had to keep calling him back so that I could see a bit. There was no moon, but at first there was at least star light. We had not gone far, however, when the horizon was streaked by lightning strikes and the stars were covered by clouds. Walking with a light is much easier than walking in the dark, but even Korkorlie had to stop for a rest on the uphill stretches.

After we had backtracked about four kilometers and I thought we were close to where we had started, Korkorlie remembered that he had about 10 "horse peanuts" in his pocket. These are winged seeds of a leguminous tree that is dispersed by the wind. They looked identical to seeds I had seen in Brazil and Australia. Korkorlie broke open the outer shell and rubbed off the brown skin enfolding the seeds, which were about the size of a peanut, but somewhat flatter. They were sweet and I ate four, leaving the larger share for Korkorlie, who was much bigger than me. It was a rather small meal, however, for someone who hadn't eaten for 17 hours.

After dinner, Korkorlie found that his phone battery had died, so we were stuck on the top of a hill with absolutely no light. We found a relatively smooth rock platform to lie on, but it sloped downhill and I had to wrap myself in a vine so that I didn't roll into the valley. The lightning storm was in full swing, but we only got a light shower and I was able to sleep until about five in the morning. Despite the rain, it was much warmer on the hill than it had been in the valley the night before. I sat and waited for the light, which didn't come for another hour.

We hadn't walked for 20 minutes when we came to the main stream. We must have been within two hundred meters of it when we took the wrong turn the day before. I was happy to see the stream, but Korkorlie was disconsolate that the track did not continue on the other side. I said that we just had to walk up the stream, but he said "No, we'll get lost again!"

I wasn't about to let people go into the bush looking for us and I wanted to get back to camp as soon as possible, so I set off with Korkorlie following dejectedly behind. Within ten minutes I got to a part of the stream that I recognized and within another ten minutes we met the forest guards. We were back in camp in time to send Rafael and Ramiro off to check their butterfly traps and mist nets. Rafael caught only one species of butterfly in the traps, a poor catch that would never happen in Amazonian forest. In contrast, Ramiro caught as many or more species of birds than he would have with the same effort in Brazil.

Korkorlie is a great naturalist and I was impressed by his ability see birds and call them up when necessary, but I realized what a bad mistake I had made following him into the forest and assuming he would know the way out. My father had taught me to

Photo 15.11 *Four "horse peanuts" like this one represented a small dinner for someone who hadn't eaten in 17 hours. Photo by Bill Magnusson.*

always pay attention to the direction of the sun on your ear to navigate. Today, with availability of guides and GPS equipment, very few people, even good naturalists, know how to find their way around the bush. Nevertheless, when the guide makes a mistake, or the batteries run out, you can get into a distressing situation. From now on, I'll try not to forget my father's words: "Feel the sun on your ear."

I saw very little of Liberia, but the experience reinforced what I had found in South America and Australia. There are probably more than enough birds to eat most of the insects and keep the forest green, but predatory mammals are too rare or too big to have much of an effect on the hordes of herbivores trying to feast on leaves. If anything keeps the forest green, it is the birds.

The West-African rainforest was interesting, but the lack of large mammals brought home to me how different the contemporary fauna in most of the World is to that which occurred about 10,000 years ago. I remembered a trip to southern Africa in 1982. I was not thinking about ecosystem functioning and I was just enthralled by the amount of wildlife we could see during short drives through national parks in South Africa and Zimbabwe. We stopped the car when African bush elephants were crossing the road, but we felt safe ensconced in our vehicle. I only fully appreciated the power of these beasts when I went on a trip to see elephants drinking near a water hole in a Zimbabwe national park. The group consisted of 10 tourists from a diversity of countries, a driver and a naturalist guide. The driver left us near a six-meter diameter bunker sunk about a meter and a half into the ground. It had a foot-thick dome-shaped roof over the ground-level windows, so it looked more like something from a war zone than a tourist facility.

The idea was to wait for the elephants to come, at which time we would retreat to the bunker and safely watch them as they strode past. They did not appear for some time and I was enthralled by two southern ground hornbills that were foraging nearby. These large birds with spectacular red heads and necks were thigh high when walking. The two birds started to interact and I asked the English tourist sitting beside me if he had seen them. He looked up from the newspaper he was reading and said disdainfully "I'm here to see elephants!"

I wanted to see the elephants too, but other animals attracted my attention. I had never seen such a concentration of large birds and mammals. It was hard to imagine how they survived with so many predators, such as lions, leopards, cheetahs and hyenas. The Guinea fowl looked like ungainly chickens, but did not seem to be perturbed by the numerous species that could make them their lunch as they scratched the dry earth. The many vultures indicated that deaths must be common and even the giant marabou storks were scavengers. The smaller antelope regarded us with suspicion, as did the ferret-sized meerkats, but the largest animals that we seemed to make nervous

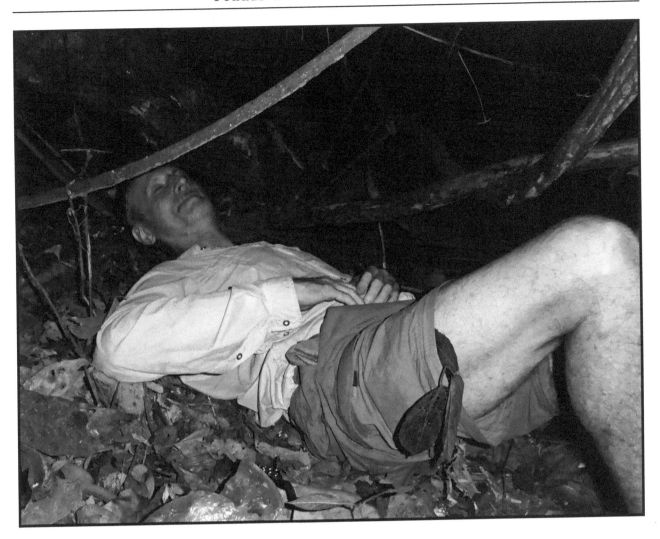

Photo 15.12 *Sleeping on the hard rock was OK, but I had to use the vines to stop rolling into the valley. Photo by Bill Magnusson.*

were the plains zebras. In contrast, the Cape buffalos just sat ruminating and didn't bother to get to their feet so that I could get an impressive photograph.

We piled into the bunker when the elephants arrived and they surrounded us with their log-like grey legs. Looking up from that position I could see why no animal on the plains could stand up to an enraged elephant. The guide was adamant that we shouldn't leave the bunker until they were long gone and told a story about a woman who had been knocked down and trampled by an elephant, which only left her because of the courageous interference of her guide, who let it chase him into the bush. The tourist survived despite having had almost all the bones in her body broken and then having to be carried for hours to get to transport. From then on I was nervous watching elephants even from the car.

One of Graeme Caughley's collaborators, Tony Sinclair, studied the mammals of the Serengeti plains and published a series of papers and a book on what controlled their numbers[163,164]. A good summary of those papers can be found in *The Serengeti Rules* by Sean Carroll[38]. Despite the green-World hypothesis, predators only controlled the smaller species. Larger herd-living species, such as the Cape buffalo are affected much more by disease or food supply than by predators, which generally find them too dangerous to attack. The population dynamics of larger species, such as rhinoceroses and elephants, are unaffected by natural predators despite the occasional death of a calf.

Being large has other advantages as well as intimidating predators. Plants tend to defend themselves by packing their most nutritious bits in a case of cellulose that is hard to digest. Small animals can be selective and only eat the most nourishing parts, leaving the less-digestible portions to fall to the ground. Slightly larger animals, such as birds, can use beaks to select unprotected fruits or seeds. The problem is that most animals have little capacity to digest thick cellulose cell walls and they rely on fungi or bacteria to transform the plant cellulose into proteins or sugars that large animals can use.

Leaf-cutter ants and some African termites eat fungi they cultivate on leaves they collect. Some termites have symbiotic microorganisms in the gut that digest even lignin found in tree trunks. These insects are regarded as herbivores or detritivores, but they should probably be regarded as predators on bacteria and fungi. This strategy is most effective if you have a large fermentation chamber, such as a leaf-cutter-ant nest. Some birds eat leaves, but they are generally selective, using their beaks to pick up only the softest and most nutritious tissue.

To eat vegetation with a minimum of selectivity you need to grind it into very small particles and put them into a large fermentation chamber. That is the specialty of mammals. They can move their jaws laterally to grind up the leaves and stalks, and if they are big they can use their stomachs or intestines as huge fermentation bins. This means that they do not have to be so selective and they mainly avoid vegetation that has secondary chemicals that would be bad for their gut flora rather than selecting only soft tissues. The advantages of being big with a mouth that can chew up anything, however, go with the disadvantage that they can't be selective and pick out only the most nutritious parts, as would a bird.

Photo 15.13 *Predators, such as this cheetah, control the numbers of only the smaller species of herbivores. Photo by Bill Magnusson.*

Savanna trees have few defenses against such big herbivores and researchers have chronicled long-term cycles of elephant densities; the populations of elephants building up until almost all the trees are eaten out, then falling in response to malnutrition until the forests can recover[42]. These megaherbivores are little affected by predators and they can eat most plants, so why don't they make the World brown? The answer is that plants have defenses against these megaherbivores and one of them is to be small. Many plants can escape the megaherbivores because they are too small for a trunk or a tongue to wrap around them and uproot them. These small plants are vulnerable to smaller species, such as sheep or grasshoppers, but they are largely protected from the small herbivores by predators, such as big cats and insectivorous birds.

The dynamics of megaherbivores in savannas are therefore very different from those of smaller species, and their effect on ecosystem functioning much more drastic. In places with megaherbivores, fires tend to be patchy and not very intense. Where the megaherbivores have been exterminated, such as South America and Australia, "natural" savanna ecosystems are dominated by fire, whereas in southern Africa it is the megaherbivores that control the system.

The story I outlined in the last paragraph is feasible for savannas, but these cover only about a third of the land surface. The forest I had been to in Liberia has been home to elephants for thousands of years, but they have never eaten out most of the trees. The Amazon rainforest was never endangered by the giant sloths or the elephant-like gomphotheres that inhabited South America. Just as herbivores can escape their predators by outgrowing them, trees can escape megaherbivores by growing very large. Big animals can't climb and tree leaves are way out of reach. It is generally assumed that trees have evolved large trunks because they compete for light, but it is possible that part of the evolutionary pressure for giant size came from the megaherbivores.

Photo 15.14 *Large herbivores are dangerous prey for predators. This Cape buffalo did not even stand to acknowledge our presence. Photo by Bill Magnusson.*

CHAPTER 16 – ARGENTINA

Magellan's penguins dominate the scene almost everywhere you go on the Patagonian coast. Photo by Bill Magnusson.

I have always liked to study diverse ecosystems so that I can see if the generalizations I get from one apply to others. For the last forty years I have been simultaneously studying rainforests, savannas, freshwater rivers and streams. Savannas are characterized by high cover of grasses. Although they occur in most terrestrial ecosystems, grasses only dominate in some areas. In general, they need plentiful water and soil nutrients. In places that have very poor soils or little rainfall, the dominant plants are bushes or small trees. An exception is the desert in central Australia, which is often dominated by spinifex grasses with stiff rolled leaves that form spikey mounds that look more like bushes than grass clumps. The problem is that bushes and trees grow quickly in areas with adequate water and nutrients and they would quickly overgrow the grasses unless something intervenes. Therefore, grasses usually only dominate the landscape in places with regular fire, megaherbivores, waterlogged soil or permafrost that prevents plants from developing deep roots. I wanted to see treeless areas different from the savannas I had studied.

There are many places on earth very different from the tropical zone in which I live and I was pleased when Albertina suggested that we visit Patagonia in 2012. It differs from Amazonia in being cold, covered in almost treeless heath and abutting the sea. It could give me clues to how mammals and birds fit into extreme ecosystems. The northern parts of Argentina are relatively humid and support productive grasslands used for cattle raising. The arid region known as Patagonia that we wanted to visit starts half-way down the country at about the level of the Colorado River. We flew to Trelew and drove to Puerto Madryn, which is the gateway to the Valdez Peninsula.

We had a diverse group. Fred and Nena with their nineteen-year-old son, Henrique, had driven their car down from Brazil. Albertina, Jeni, the same age as Henrique, and I had flown in from Brazil, and my 87-year-old mother, Dorothy, with my 33-year-old nephew known as Joe had come from Australia. We rented another car in Buenos Aires, so we ended up with a two-car, eight-person expedition.

There was a whale skeleton in the visitor's center at the entrance to the Valdez Peninsula Fauna Reserve. The whales had moved on and were not to be seen at that time of year, but the skeleton brought home to me something about baleen whales – they have no teeth! Whoever had cleaned the bones had thrown away the baleen plates that the whales use to sieve their food from the sea. Baleen whales eat a diversity of

Photo 16.1 *Our two families filled two cars. Photo by Fred Rocha.*

small creatures, including fish, but most of their nutrition comes from krill, small crustaceans that look like transparent shrimp. The krill mainly eat planktonic algae, and they are the principal herbivores in arctic and Antarctic waters.

Whales in general are big and the blue whale has the largest body size of any animal known to have existed. However, they are all carnivores in the sense that they eat other animals and it struck me as strange that the largest animals are herbivores on land, but carnivores in the sea. Aquatic mammals and birds maintain high body temperatures, which is an energetically expensive way of life that generally only pays off in the coldest oceans[68]. To see large numbers of aquatic mammals and birds, you generally have to go to cold places like Patagonia. The warmer areas have few or no seals and penguins, but large numbers of fish and other species, such as turtles, that do not need to maintain high body temperatures. This reduction in aquatic mammals from the pole to the equator is seen in both hemispheres, but even in tropical seas the largest marine animals, such as whale sharks and manta rays, are carnivores and not herbivores.

On land, plants have two size-related ways of escaping herbivores. They can become too small for large herbivores, making them vulnerable only to small herbivores that are controlled by their predators. Alternatively, they can become so tall that their leaves can only be reached by small climbing or flying animals and gravity protects them from the megaherbivores that have few effective predators. Plants in the open ocean can only use the first strategy. The light they need is near the surface and there is nowhere they can grow to that can't be reached by swimming animals. In shallow water, where plants can root in the sea floor, almost all the herbivores are small. Away from land, almost all the plants are microscopic.

Just as the plants have nowhere to hide, neither do their predators. As soon as these become big enough to be sieved from the water, something evolves to do it. In freshwater systems, the largest fish eat other fish and only the smallest species are able to eat herbivorous planktonic crustaceans, such as copepods and ostracods. Researchers have carried out famous experiments where they divide a lake in half and remove the larger predatory fish from one side[37]. This allows the smaller species to eat most of the planktonic crustaceans, which can no longer control the algae and that side of the lake becomes green. The other side remains clear because the large predators control the smaller planktivorous fish, which allows the planktonic crustaceans to multiply and control the algae. In this system, predators can make the world green or not depending on what trophic level they occupy.

In the open ocean, the giant predators can use baleen plates to sieve the small herbivores directly from the water; they are vacuum-cleaner predators. On land there are plants about the same size as any animal species, and the largest terrestrial organisms are plants, or possibly a fungus[158]. In the open ocean, just about everything that is visible to the naked eye is a predator. In the shallow waters near land, some algae and sea grasses get big enough to see, but almost none so big that you couldn't hold them easily in the palm of your hand. There are more places to hide from the vacuum-cleaner predators in shallow coastal waters, and some of the herbivorous fish and turtles get largish, but there are no giant plant eaters. There was one exception to the last sentence, but I'll leave talking about that until we get further south.

Photo 16.2 *Baleen whales are impressive, but these giant predators have no teeth! Photo by Bill Magnusson.*

Peninsula Valdez was flat and covered in bushes that ranged from knee to chest high. Most of these had a tangle of grey thorny stems with brownish-green leaves, making the landscape homogeneous and largely uninviting to tourists. The Patagonian wind blew continuously, making it cold despite the largely cloudless sky. A large hairy armadillo (that's its name, not just a description) was fossicking in the loose earth and let us get quite close before scurrying into the undergrowth. It seemed an integral part of the Patagonian landscape, so I was surprised to learn that the species only invaded Patagonia about 150 years ago[1]. A closely-related species, the dwarf armadillo colonized most of Patagonia soon after the climate warmed up about 10,000 years ago, but the invasion by the large-hairy armadillo only occurred after Europeans colonized the area.

The authors attributed the range expansion of the large hairy armadillo to the increase in productivity associated with intensive livestock raising. The only large mammals in the area previously were guanacos, which the indigenous people probably hunted intensively. Large-scale ranching lead to an enormous increase in the biomass of mammalian herbivores, which proceeded to process the vegetation into easily-digested nutrient packages called feces, which are favorite foods of many of the invertebrates that armadillos eat. The presence of the armadillos may appear unnatural to us, but that is because of the shifting baseline. If humans hadn't eliminated the giant sloths and other megaherbivores, the large hairy armadillos may have recolonized Patagonia soon after the last ice age, as much as 10,000 years ago.

The other conspicuous mammal we saw also may have increased in density since European colonization. South American grey foxes are not closely related to northern-hemisphere foxes and the common name refers to their foxlike appearance rather than genetic affinity. These small dogs have silvery-grey and black guard hairs over rufous-red underfur. The density of the guard hairs increases from back to front, so the tail is light grey with a black dorsal line and tip. The body shimmers from light grey to rufous red as the wind parts the guard hairs on the body and the head and legs are all orange red. The foxes made a pretty sight as they jumped from one side to another of the small bushes, trying to scare small animals into the open away from the sharp spines. Widescale ranching has probably increased the availability of food them as well.

The cliffs overlooking the sea on the Valdez Peninsula are favorite tourist spots. I spent a long time filming the Magellan's penguins. They are fairly big, reaching above my knee when standing, and they look as though they were painted with curved lines by an impressionist artist. They are black above and white below like most penguins, but a broad white line borders the edge of the black color on the body and a similar white line encircles the face. This meets an arc of pink skin that runs from the eye to the beak. The mating season had ended, but one couple apparently enjoyed sex and copulated passionately for over a minute, which is much longer than most birds, which

Photo 16.3 *Large hairy armadillos are common in southern Argentina, but are thought to have colonized Patagonia only within the last 200 years. Photo by Fred Rocha.*

usually spend less than a second in such matrimonial obligations. I was overjoyed because I had never spent so much time observing penguins close up, but by the end of our trip to Patagonia I had seen so many Magellan's penguins that I would come to regard them as being about as interesting as sparrows.

You can look down on the beaches below the cliffs and see creamy-brown adult sea lions lying on the beach, some suckling young as bunches of dark-colored adolescents play in the shallow water. Further down the beach the elephant seals looked like giant slugs facing the sea. These beaches are famous because a pod of orcas, which are often called killer whales, has learned to push up onto the beach to catch unwary young sea lions. This is apparently a learned behavior, the adults teaching it to the younger generations, and no other orca pod is known to hunt this way. We were about a month too late to see it, however, and the orcas had moved on.

Only two mammalian lineages have evolved to give birth in the water, the cetaceans, which includes whales, dolphins and their kin, and the sirenians, which are the dugongs and manatees. All the other marine mammals and all marine birds must come to land to give birth or lay eggs, and this probably restricts their distributions. The birds are subject to many terrestrial predators, such as foxes and armadillos, so they need places with relatively low densities of meat eaters, or places that have none at all, such as islands. The seals and sea lions are probably too big for most terrestrial predators but they too may be restricted by suitable birthing sites, which must have conditions for the newly independent young to escape from large marine predators, such as orcas and white-pointer sharks.

A short distance south of Puerto Madryn is Punta Loma, a fauna reserve famous for its sea lions, which lie around on the pebble beaches at the base of the white cliffs at low tide. It seems an idyllic place for them to lounge in the sun and look after their offspring until the tide comes in and they have to climb onto the few rock outcrops that remain above sea level. The adults don't seem to have much trouble, but the youngsters found it hard to climb the rocks and were often washed off by the waves.

I have always regarded cormorants as elegant creatures, but until I went to Argentina I thought that they came in only two basic color patterns: all black or black with white underparts. I saw one all-black Neotropical cormorant swimming close to the shore at Punta Loma, but the cliff faces were covered in rock cormorants. They were basically black above and white below, but they had a wide black stripe on the back of their legs and white patches on the cheeks. A bright orange mask of bare skin ran from under the chin, around the eye and onto the top of the beak, and pairs sat together nibbling each other's necks in a continual display of affection. Although I could get very close and had a light tripod, most of my video scenes trembled because of the unflagging Patagonian wind.

The contrast between the brown earth with grey-green shrubs and the bright blue bays was a great background to film the kelp gulls that foraged at the water's edge. Surprisingly, the gulls are thought to negatively affect the southern right whales that come to the area to give birth. Apparently, the gulls target mother-calf pairs, land on their backs and pick holes in their blubber. This is enough to severely disturb the whales, which can find no rest. It is difficult to imagine these moderate-sized birds having an effect on the mighty whales, but in some places along the Patagonian coast there were so many gulls that they covered the beaches for miles. Having tried to sleep in places with millions of mosquitoes I can testify that small creatures can make

Photo 16.4 *South American grey foxes are not closely related to northern-hemisphere foxes. Photo by Bill Magnusson.*

life a misery for much bigger animals. However, I had never thought of sea gulls as parasites rather than predators and it made me realize that size can help you escape from animals that try to kill you outright, but is an inadequate defense against tiny freeloaders.

The clear skies and contrasting colors are very attractive to tourists who will stay in the area for only a short time, but it is a harsh place for the animals and plants that spend their whole lives there. We explored the shrubland behind the beaches in search of larger animals and one of the first species we came across was the elegant crested-tinamou. These chicken-sized birds hold the spiky crest on their head high and then bob it up and down rapidly several times in a display that makes them look awkward to humans, but is probably attractive to members of their own species or has some unknown effect on potential predators. The tinamous strutted in the bare patches between the salt bushes and would have seemed very active if it wasn't for the southern mountain cavies, which despite their common name are extremely common in this arid environment near sea level.

I could see the outlines of the cavies, which are like skinny guinea pigs in size and shape, darting behind a wall of spines in the thickets that formed a patch work over the dry soil. However, it was hard to photograph one because they zipped across the open ground like balls bouncing off a tennis racket. One stopped long enough for me to see its huge head and white-rimmed eye, which seemed out of proportion to its small body and tiny legs. It ran across a clearing, entered a saltbush, then spurted back. In the process, it ran around a tinamou, which bobbed its head as if to say "What was that?" The tiny cavies are probably one of the principal herbivores in the area and provide food for many predators, though it is hard to imagine how they catch them.

Cavies are in the rodent order Caviomorpha, which includes all the New World hystricognaths, including capybaras and Patagonian maras. I always thought of hystricognaths as being slow and calm in relation to other rodents, such as murid rats and squirrels. The southern mountain cavies showed me that you should careful about generalizations. Their electric behavior was on par with any other rodent. Tinamous are palaeognaths, relatives of the rheas and cassowaries, and most of the smaller flying paleognaths are solitary, but the elegant crested-tinamous sometimes get around in flocks and act like chickens. Obviously, the native fauna of Patagonia had converged on those of other areas, with the birds pecking their way across the landscape and some of the mammals chomping their way through the vegetation.

We also saw marsupials that are carnivores in the sense that they eat other animals, though they probably don't eat many vertebrates. Albertina found two tiny white-bellied fat-tailed mouse opossums lying on the cold ground, apparently dead. They were probably young and had underestimated the dangers of straying far from their nest, or the cold wind had caught them unexpectedly. One was dead, but when I cradled the other one in my hand it warmed up and started to kick. Jeni took over as its surrogate mother and it was soon active enough to drink water and eat the banana we offered it. Tiny and delicate, it clambered over Jeni's fingers apparently without fear of its enormous benefactors.

Photo 16.5 *Sea lions must come ashore to breed. Photo by Bill Magnusson.*

We were in a dilemma as to what to do with it. We could not take it with us, which would have been illegal, and we were pretty sure that if we released it the cold wind would soon sap its strength and paralyze its muscles. Fortunately, we met two Argentinian biologists in the parking lot and they took charge of the animal, holding it so delicately that we were sure that it could not be in better hands. It would be the last marsupial we would see on the trip. Although common in the Amazon, few marsupials extend their range into southern Argentina.

The best place to see marine mammals and birds in Patagonia is probably Puerto Deseado, about 300 km south of Comodoro Rivadaria. Distances between towns are large in Patagonia, and the straight roads surrounded by low heathland provide little scenery of interest to tourists. However, all the coastal towns are well prepared for visitors and there are tourist offices that give advice on accommodation and excursions on the outskirts of most cities. Puerto Deseado is near the Deseado River estuary, which is a 40-km long drowned river valley, and famous as one of the places that Charles Darwin investigated on the voyage that resulted in his elaboration of evolutionary theory.

We arrived late in the afternoon and booked a tour of the estuary for the next day. The large open boat was full of tourists and we found seats near the bow. As in just about everywhere we visited on the coast of Patagonia, there were sea lions and Magellan's penguins, but there was also abundant bird life on the low cliffs around the bay. We saw rock, Neotropical and imperial cormorants, but the most spectacular were the red-legged cormorants. Unlike most cormorants, they only have black on the tail and flight feathers. The background color of the rest of the body is light grey, with mottled-white patches on the wings and white patches on either side of the neck. The eyes look blue, but are said to be green with blue flecks around the edges. The beak is yellow at the front and red at the base, which combines well with their bright red legs. Pairs sat together in round mud nests they had constructed on the vertical cliffs, sometimes rearranging scraps of nest material, but most of the time nibbling and caressing each other's necks in an emotional show of devotion.

White birds about the size of pigeons, but more the shape of chickens, walked among the sea lions looking for pools of liquid feces, which they scooped up with their short beaks. They are called sheathbills and belong to the Chionidae family, which is the only family of birds restricted to Antarctic waters. Although they are predators and scavengers, feces is apparently a common food because our guide said that for a long time he confused their English name and called them shitbills. Blackish oystercatchers foraged on the pebble beaches. Although we saw these birds in all the coastal areas we visited, I continued to stalk them, trying to get that perfect picture with the dark body, blood-red beak and white legs framed against the blue water.

We also got very close to Commerson's dolphins, which are called toninos by the Argentinians. These small dolphins have a broad white saddle behind the head that extends along both sides of the body under the dorsal fin, which makes them stand out at a distance even when under water. They jumped near us and swam under the

Photo 16.6 *Southern mountain cavies scurry among patches of vegetation and rarely stop to be photographed. Photo by Bill Magnusson.*

boat, apparently curious despite the fact that this boat must go through their territory almost every day of the year. There are many species of dolphins, but it is generally difficult for nonspecialists to distinguish them; toninos are an exception. This may seem unimportant, but it helped consolidate my impression of the diversity of marine mammals and birds of the southern waters.

A storm was brewing on the way back and the boat bucked as it hit the waves. Jeni loved that and sat high on prow to get the most of the action. Mum sat close behind her and the captain asked her to move back near the helm where the motion of the boat was smoother. He apparently didn't want to be responsible for damaging an 87-year-old tourist, but mum refused and sat grinning into the spray. It was an exciting end to a very productive day.

We had booked with the same company to go to Penguin Island the next day, but when we got back to town, the captain said that we would have to postpone the trip because strong winds were predicted. We asked what other tourist attractions were available that would allow us to see wildlife without stretching our budget, and he suggested that we drive to Cabo Blanco, where we could see fur seals. We took his advice and drove there the following day.

The dirt road wound through what looked like degraded sheep pasture with scattered clumps of small bushes. We didn't see any native mammals, but we stopped to photograph a herd of horses. Now just feral animals, but similar horses may have roamed these steppes 10,000 years ago. The car travel ended at the base of a steep incline leading to a lighthouse on the promontory. We pushed into a strong wind and climbed the 100 stone stairs to the base of the lighthouse, which overlooked steep cliffs to the sea below.

The waves were producing white foam as they crashed into the rocks jutting out of the water and fur seals were trying to climb the steep walls. This was difficult because, unlike the round boulders used by the sea lions at Punta Loma, the rocks at Cabo Blanco formed pinnacles with small flat-topped turrets that were only a few handspans wide. The seals used the waves to push them up the almost vertical rock walls, grabbing the sharp rocks with their flippers as the waves retreated. Their skin must be very tough and their bones resilient because I would have been cut to bits and suffered broken legs and arms if I had been hurled onto the rocks by the waves the way they were.

Space was at a premium on the tops of the rocks and the seals vied for position on the uppermost turrets, biting at each other and swinging around balanced only on their fore flippers, much as circus seals do on upturned tubs. The dark seals were silhouetted against the bluish-grey sea and the white spray that blew over their heads occasionally reached as high as we were, making everything salty and cold. The agility of the fur seals on the rocks was impressive considering their size; males only reach the size of female sea lions, but they still may weigh as much as 200 kg. Imagine a sumo wrestler scrambling up a near vertical cliff and balancing on his hands with body held horizontal into the howling wind!

Photo 16.7 *Pairs of red-legged cormorants spend a lot of time caressing each other. Photo by Bill Magnusson.*

The wind decreased, but never stopped, as we walked to the ruins of the post office and warehouse near the beach that are the only remains of a once-thriving town in the area. A black-faced ibis was foraging in the grass and I sat still to allow it to approach. These beautiful birds, the size of a goose with buff-colored necks and long curved beaks, have a misleading common name; apart from a small mask around the eyes, they don't have black faces! The ibis's behavior reinforced what I had come to recognize as a bird specialty. Although quite a large animal, it used its long, curved beak to probe into the grass and capture small animals that it could swallow whole; it was eating with chop sticks.

The rocks near the beach served as perches for cormorants and gulls, but the most interesting birds were a pair of flying steamer ducks that were bobbing in the waves just offshore. Their generally grey color made them hard to see against the grey-green water, but the female's orange beak contrasted with the rest of the nondescript coloration. Most ducks and related species dabble in shallow water and are never seen in the open sea. Steamer ducks have apparently evolved to take advantage of the abundant shellfish and crustaceans that are found in the frigid waters off the southern continents. They live in pairs and dive to catch their prey, which can't be all that abundant because they are said to be territorial, sometimes killing steamers and other species they see as competitors. Three of the four species have lost the capacity for flight, which is why the ability to fly stands out enough to have been included in the common name of the fourth species. Penguins did not evolve from ducks and their closest living relatives are thought to be albatrosses. Nonetheless, steamer ducks may give us clues as to why flightless marine birds have only evolved in the coldest seas.

We had seen a lot of cormorants during our travels and they no longer evoked enough interest for me to spend long periods trying to film them close up. However, one bird imposed itself on us. My mother was walking along the beach dressed in navy-blue coat and trousers, topped off by a white balaclava, and an imperial cormorant was walking beside her. Imperial cormorants mainly have black upperparts and white underside, the only exceptions being a fine white line on the wing, black on the rear parts of the legs, a small orange fleshy area at the base of the beak and blue eyes. I thought that the cormorant must have mistaken mum for a giant black and white cormorant, but it also sought out Jeni's company.

Jeni was wearing a red parka and dark pants with pink lines down the side, so she didn't look like a cormorant. When she was sitting on the beach, the cormorant came up behind her and pecked on her back to get her attention. Later, she was walking on the beach and tried to dig something out of the sand. The cormorant first pecked at her hand and then walked into the pit she had dug. Jenny thought that the bird might be hungry and offered it strips of chicken that had been our lunch, but it didn't show any interest. Either if wasn't hungry or didn't consider the chicken as food. I cannot imagine how a cormorant in such a remote place would come to be so trusting around humans. Many years ago, Konrad Lorenz showed that newly-hatched geese will imprint on the first moving thing they see, even if it is a human. I wonder if a human might have been present when our bird hatched, making it confused from then on as to what species it belonged?

Photo 16.8 *The fur seals balanced on rock pinnacles. Photo by Bill Magnusson.*

We stopped watching the birds when a fine icy drizzle started to fall and by the time we reached the car the rain covered the landscape in a grey shroud. We weren't concerned because it had been a great day, but when we drove up the slight incline behind the beach the car initially fishtailed as though there was no tread on the tires and then started to drag, as if the handbrake was on. Eventually, it just stopped and I got out into the freezing drizzle to see what was wrong. The sticky brown mud had built up on the rear wheels to the point where it jammed on the chassis, stopping all motion. We tried pushing, but it was to no avail. I had to kneel in the cold slush and scrape the mud off the wheel until it was free to turn again. This allowed us to drive several hundred meters before the process had to be repeated. The whole 90 km trip should have taken about two hours, but we only travelled about 30 km in that time. I was imagining spending most of the night immersed in mud and rain when the road turned to gravel and we were able to drive normally.

Back at our hostel, we enjoyed warm showers, and were sitting around the table imbibing hot coffee when there was a knock on the door. We knew no-one in Puerto Deseado, so I couldn't imagine who would be knocking at that time of night and I was surprised to see the tourist agent who had booked our tour for the next day standing in the downpour. He explained that he noted the heavy rain and was worried that we had taken his advice and gone to Cabo Blanco, because the road becomes untrafficable for small vehicles and perhaps we were trapped there. He had thought of going to rescue us, but first had gone around all the hostels in Puerto Deseado to see if he could find us. That sort of responsibility and dedication are hard to find in most places and reflected the quality of the tour guides we found everywhere in Argentina.

The next day dawned sunny and bright with little wind and we took the tour to Penguin Island, which is close to the coast, but about 25 km from Puerto Deseado. The captain of our large inflatable boat remembered my mother from our trip two days before and said "Lady, I'm only going to let you onto this boat if you promise to sit near the helm and not in bow!" She agreed and we set off for the island in good spirits. The waves were high enough make the trip interesting, but not uncomfortable. We were accompanied in parts by almost all-black melanistic Commerson's dolphins and by a pair of what the guide identified as austral dolphins.

Penguin Island is basically just flat rock with no beaches or wharves. The captain nudged the boat up against the rock wall and we jumped off, which was not all that difficult, even for my 87-year-old mother. There were the usual sea birds and seals we had seen in many other places, and we were able to get close to most. I even filmed many more of the ubiquitous Magellan's penguins. These breed in large groups in the center of the island and the lines of penguins marching in after foraging at sea is a spectacular sight. The young penguins were covered in thick down, which made them look much larger than their parents. Chilean skuas, which look like large brown sea gulls, sat among the penguins and did not appear to concern their neighbors. However, they are apparently one of the main predators on penguin eggs and chicks, and parents need to be constantly on guard.

Photo 16.9 *The steamer ducks foraged in the sea just beyond where the waves were breaking. Photo by Bill Magnusson.*

Our main reason to go to Penguin Island was to see the rock-hopper penguins. These iconic birds completely ignore humans as they sit on the rocky shore, often with wings outstretched and the deep blue water behind, as though they just wanted their photos taken. They are black on the back and white underneath like most penguins, but they distinguish themselves by the yellow eyebrow, which looks as though it is painted over the eyes, but turns into protruding tufts above the ears. The beak is light orange, but the most notable feature when you get close is the deep red eyes. Probably no other penguin is so photogenic.

Their beauty when still is offset by their strange mode of locomotion on land. Most penguins look clumsy as they waddle along, but rockhoppers, true to their name, rarely waddle; they jump from place to place. Small hops on flat ground do not seem ungainly, but when the penguin wants to go a dozen meters it jumps as though being chased by a predator, gaining momentum until it falls, crashes into a rock, or knocks over another penguin. It is as though they perfected forward velocity at the expense of the brakes. Such tumbling on hard rocks would be disastrous for us, but, like the fur seals, they seem immune to effects of having their legs and bodies thrown randomly at hard surfaces.

The trip back from Penguin Island in the open boat would have been uneventful, but a storm came up and hail battered us as we neared the port. Everybody bowed over and tried to adjust the hoods of their parkas to avoid the stinging ice and the agony only lasted about 10 minutes. Afterwards, a beautiful rainbow formed behind us and made a fitting backdrop to the end of a very special day.

Nena, Fred and Henrique left us in Rio Gallegas; they would explore Terra del Fuego, but we couldn't take our rented car into Chile. We headed to Cabo Virgenes, which is the southeastern tip of continental Argentina. Most of the way was bordered by ankle-high sheep pasture, which was not inspiring and it was very cold. The thermometer in Rio Gallegas had registered seven degrees centigrade at 10 pm the night before, and it seemed even colder in the incessant Patagonian wind. As usual, the most prominent inhabitants of the seashore were Magellan's penguins. Here they nested among bushes or frolicked in the waves that pounded the beaches. I thought that I had filmed everything of interest about Magellan's penguins on land, but I regarded them as being largely silent. The pairs at Cabo Virgenes proved me wrong; they bayed like donkeys, pointing their heads vertically and convulsing their bodies in movements that appeared more conducive to vomiting than to singing. Despite fumbling with thick gloves, I was able to film them close enough to record their vocalizations over the drumming of the wind.

We climbed the light house and looked out to sea, which brings me to our first Patagonian forest, not on land, but in the sea. The grey water was streaked with black lines that oscillated in the swell. The lines only appeared black because of our angle of vision. They were formed by leaves of giant kelp, which can be over forty meters long; as high as the canopy in an Amazonian rainforest. You probably remember that I said that plants can't outgrow the herbivores in the sea, which is why most of them

Photo 16.10 *This imperial cormorant followed Jeni around and posed for a photograph. Photo by Bill Magnusson.*

are small. How then can forests of kelp live along the shores of the coldest oceans? The story is complex, and we have only a few of the answers. Kelp are technically not plants and are closely related to a variety of micro-organisms that do not photosynthesize. Nevertheless, they play the major role of plants in cold seas.

Kelp forests maintain complex communities of fish and invertebrates, and many other algal species grow on the kelp fronds. However, there are surprisingly few species that can subsist on kelp alone. The kelp beds off western North America are grazed by sea urchins and these denude the sea floor if not controlled by sea otters. We only know this because sea otters were hunted to near extinction for their pelts in the early years of the last century. The kelp beds disappeared and only reappeared after the sea otters were protected and their numbers increased. Surprisingly, it is not only humans that can eliminate sea otters. In the area around the Aleutian Archipelago, orcas hunt sea otters, resulting in an increase in sea urchins and the loss of kelp forests. The situation may be even more complicated and I recommend that you read James Estes account of his 40 years studying the Aleutian Archipelago[59]. Whales and seals are alternative prey for orcas, so their effect on sea otters may depend on what happens to other marine mammals. Even the terrestrial systems of the Aleutian Islands are affected by predators. The presence of introduced arctic foxes on the islands changes the distributions and densities of nesting sea birds, which changes the availability of nutrients and the growth of plants.

Sea urchins are not very big and so can be controlled by larger predators, but what about mammalian megaherbivores? The only marine mammals that might fall in this category belong to the Sirenia, which includes the dugongs and manatees. Manatees generally remain in rivers, so they are only occasionally marine. Dugongs live in the sea, but only in areas near the coast that support sea-grass beds. Sea grasses are flowering plants, which unlike algae are restricted to shallow sheltered areas with muddy or sandy bottoms. Dugongs are the largest herbivores in these areas and are sometimes preyed upon by orcas[7] and sharks[179], but there is no evidence that these predators control their numbers. In fact, dugongs move into deeper water when densities of tiger sharks are high[179] so they are probably able to take care of themselves if they have sufficient space to maneuver.

One species of sirenian, Steller's sea cow, evolved to eat kelp, and it grew to such a large size, nine meters long and eight to ten tons, that it was largely immune to natural predators. However, it was positively buoyant and could not fully submerge. Although it had a much wider range in the Pleistocene, something, probably humans, had reduced its distribution to a small area around the Commander Islands at the end of the Aleutian Archipelago in the Bering Sea between Alaska and Russia by the 1700s. In less than 30 years after its discovery by Europeans it had been hunted to extinction. The size of the kelp provided a protection from this megaherbivore. Because Steller's sea cow couldn't dive, it could only browse the tops of the kelp, which kept growing from below, attached to rocks dozens of meters below the surface.

What is it that controls the sea urchins and other invertebrates that can eat kelp in areas without sea otters? I don't think that anybody knows, but it is likely that in

Photo 16.11 *Rock-hopper penguins are photogenic, but ungainly when they move on land. Photo by Bill Magnusson.*

many areas it is marine mammals or birds. The circle closes, the marine vertebrates protecting the kelp forests that support the varied biodiversity that supports them and a multitude of other species. What we don't know is how many pieces we can take out of this complex ecosystem before it collapses. If I wasn't so old, and the water wasn't so cold, I'd probably go there to try to find out!

The eastern part of Patagonia is very flat, but it is lined on the west by higher country that is the tail of the Andes. Most Patagonians obviously aren't used to hilly country and I photographed a road sign indicating a steep grade where the incline was almost imperceptible. We travelled west to Rio Turbio, a coal-mining town that is also a ski resort in winter. Fortunately, there was no snow when we were there and the Antarctic beech forests provided a welcome relief to the flat terrain of the east. I was surprised to see austral parakeets in this cold dry region. The species has the most southerly range of any parrot and stays in the snow country throughout winter. Their green plumage with dull red on the belly and tail camouflaged them among the beech leaves.

There isn't a lot to see in Rio Turbio, but as we left we came on a large concentration of southern crested caracaras feeding on carrion beside the road and a shallow lake had

many Chilean flamingos. These pinkish-white birds with orange on the folded wings would be spectacular at any time, but the lake acted as a mirror in the early morning sun and each bird had a perfect reflection below it.

The flamingos were shuffling in shallow water in what looked like a circular dance. I have seen other birds, such as sea gulls, use the same technique to stir up small animals that they can grab with their beaks. However, a sea gull has to be exact about where it snaps with the tip of its beak, which is not easy in murky water. The flamingo's answer to the problem is to have a down-curved beak armed with tiny hair-like structures that have the same function as the baleen plates of whales. When the flamingo's head is pointing down, the curved beak is parallel to the bottom and the bird can filter out any tiny animals that try to escape from its shuffling feet. As the beak has a large area and is touch sensitive the technique works even in murky water.

The feeding birds are beautiful, but when a flock takes off you can see that the whole upper surface of the wings is bright orange, except for the flight feathers, which are black. One of the most spectacular scenes I have filmed was of a flock of flamingos feeding on the shore of a lake in the late evening. I had no sooner set my camera on the tripod and started filming than the flock took off. First one bird, then another until the entire scene was filled with flashing orange and black wings propelling pinkish-white bodies. Had I started filming a few seconds later I would have missed it. Evolution results in convergent solutions, such as a flamingo's beak and a whale's baleen plates, but flight restricts the options and no flying bird approaches the size of a small dolphin, much less that of a baleen whale.

Photo 16.12 *The Magellan's penguins brayed like donkeys. Photo by Bill Magnusson.*

About 240 km north of Rio Turbio is El Calafate, the gateway to Argentina's glaciers. We went to see the ice by boat and land, and both trips were worthwhile. The highlight of the boat trip was the floating islands of blue ice that appeared to have been sculpted in the most weird and wonderful ways. From the land, seeing the tourist boats passing the Perito Moreno glacier gave an idea of its immense size, and walking over it was an adventure. However, the only wildlife that caught my attention was a lone black-chested buzzard-eagle that circled above the ice. To see wildlife, we drove to El Chaltén, which is within the Glaciares National Park. We photographed the Fitz Roy and Torre mountain spires and views along the Rio de las Vueltas. The images were spectacular, but comparing them with those I found on the internet indicated that many thousands of tourists must have taken photographs from the same spots as I had.

There are long trails through Galciares National Park, but we only took some that were indicated as relatively easy in deference to my mother's age. In fact, she had no trouble with the steep inclines, but she is small and often had to hold on to Joe to avoid being swept away by the strong wind, which buffeted us and often made us stumble as though drunk on Argentinian wine. The more sheltered valleys had Antarctic beech forests, and the trees often had large trunks almost an arm-span wide. Nevertheless, they usually had few leaves and many broken branches, and most were hollow. The only mammal we saw was a domestic llama carrying two large boxes that was being led by one of the park guards, but there were many birds.

In most places I have been, the most common birds either glean insects off foliage or fossick among low vegetation for seeds. In the Glaciares National Park, most of the birds foraged on dead wood. I followed a sparrow-sized thorn-tailed rayadito that was foraging on a beech trunk. It had a blackish head with broad brown bands running over the eyes. Its underparts were light grey and the body mainly brown. The lateral feathers on its tail ended in two sharp spikes that allowed it to prop itself on the trunk as though it had a third leg. The other shorter tail feathers also have spines on the tips, but they apparently are used in sexual displays rather than for climbing. It was similar to the treecreepers I had seen in the Amazon, but then it surprised me by going into a hole in the trunk and only appearing again about a meter higher.

A magellanic tapaculo, slightly larger than the rayadito and without the spiky tail feathers, also disappeared into trunks for long periods. Almost all the birds we saw seemed to be foraging in the hollow trunks, a behavior I have not seen in birds anywhere else. Of course, it is the woodpeckers that are most famous for trying to get into tree trunks, though they only use their bills and not the whole body. All woodpeckers are photogenic, but I have always had trouble getting a good picture because they are skittish and remain high in the trees. Magellanic woodpeckers were different. At first I got close enough to photograph the mainly black and white females from a distance of about six meters and thought I was doing well. Then I started to follow a male with a bright red head that contrasted with the black and white body.

The bird seemed to be avoiding me and moved to the other side of the trunk when I got close. However, when I circled the tree he just kept hammering the bark and

Photo 16.13 *Sea otters are highly social and control sea urchins that would otherwise eliminate northern-hemisphere kelp forests. Photo by Bill Magnusson.*

I got some nice footage looking up at him. I thought I wouldn't be able to do any better, but that was before he descended the trunk and started to hammer a rotten log on the ground. I sat beside him as he pecked into the soft wood and I was so close that I sometimes had to move the camera back so that he wouldn't bump into it as he swiveled around. If you want to film birds that eat insects on tree trunks, I recommend the Los Glaciares National Park!

The only bird I noted that didn't forage in tree trunks was a black-throated huet huet. The rotund little bird about the size of a small dove was foraging among the moss-covered rocks in a stream and it let me get very close. Its mainly black coloration diffused with brown made it hard to see among the round stones and its feet seemed disproportionately large, but well adapted for clinging to the rocks. It balanced on one leg while stretching the other forward to rake the moss and leaf litter in the stream, stopping occasionally to peck at the tiny invertebrates it scratched up.

Back in El Calafate, we walked to Laguna Nimez in the late afternoon. The lake is a famous for watching waterfowl and the small café with large windows beside the lake even provides binoculars for customers. There were large numbers of ducks, geese, coots, lapwings and other waterbirds. It is the only place that I have seen two species of native swans side by side, though the smaller all-white coscoroba swan may be as closely related to geese as it is to other swans. I always remember an embarrassing moment when I first saw black-neck swans in Brazil's southernmost state, Rio Grande do Sul. The locals were very proud when they showed it to me and were not amused when I asked if it were a hybrid.

Although some water birds dive to catch fish, those that eat vegetation generally do so from the surface, hence the utility of a long neck. Being the largest South American waterfowl, the black-necked swan can reach deeper than any other species, though all the birds that grazed underwater looked ungainly when they turned head down with only their tails and splashing legs above water. Red shoveler ducks foraged in pairs in the deeper water. Although they could not reach the bottom, the pairs swam around each other creating whirlpools which brought up small prey that they could sieve from the water with their broad beaks.

More than 50 species of birds regularly forage in the water around Laguna Nimez and I have seen similar concentrations in other small temperate lakes. It gives the impression of a smaller avian replica of the concentrations of mammals in the Serengeti of Africa. However, there are few mammals in such places. I have filmed small rats eating the reeds in the Pantanal, on the shores of Lake Titicaca and in rice fields in Vietnam. The swamp rats I tried to study for my honors thesis have similar habits in Australia. However, in most marshes, mammals are incredibly rare in comparison with the birds. I suspect that this might be because small productive lakes tend to be ephemeral over geological time and being able to fly is a great advantage when trying to locate them. Surprisingly, I have never seen such concentrations of birds in the upper

Photo 16.14 *Flamingos shuffle to stir up invertebrates that they filter from the water with special structures on their bills. Photo by Bill Magnusson.*

Amazon, despite the fact that it is arguably the World´s largest wetland and has huge numbers of shallow productive lakes.

The El Calafate region was not always dominated by small flying dinosaurs. We visited the local museum, which had bones of giant sloths that had roamed the area just ten thousand years ago. I wondered if they might have waded into the shallow lakes to eat the emergent vegetation and made the place less attractive to birds. The museum also had bones of carnivorous dinosaurs that inhabited the area more than 60 million years ago. They were much bigger than the sloths, and presumably only the very biggest herbivorous dinosaurs would have been immune to their attacks.

We headed north to see the Cueva de las Manos. In a straight line it was only about 300 km, but the road distance was 730 km and we had underestimated the amount of fuel we would need. We made it, but only by driving economically and coasting downhill when possible. Large flocks of Darwin's rheas grazed the salt bushes and fossicked among the short grass. Much smaller than the rheas I had seen in the Pantanal, they only stood about a meter high.

The only other large herbivores we saw were guanacos. Most people associate camels with North Africa and Eurasia, but there were species in the camel family in North and South America when the first people arrived. Two wild species, the guanaco and the vicuña, and their domesticated derivatives, the llama and the alpaca, survive today. Guanacos are now the largest herbivores in Patagonia and can weigh up to 140 kg, though they are small in comparison with the megaherbivores that were their companions more than 10,000 years ago.

Guanacos have the general camelid shape: long legs, long neck and short tail. However, they appear much more delicate than the Old-World camels. When you are near or mounted on an Arabian or Bactrian camel you feel insignificant in relation to these megaherbivores. In contrast, guanacos are smaller and more slightly built. Their orange brown upper parts contrast with the white on their bellies, and inner legs, and with their grey heads. They generally walk delicately as though choosing where to put each foot, though they can run quickly and even jump fences; abilities at a premium if pursued by a puma. I filmed many with young at foot and the juveniles make a pretty sight following the herd or copying their mother rolling in a dust bath. I am surprised that no children's-film producer has used them as models for a cartoon character. Although we saw guanacos almost everywhere we went, domestic sheep are now the principle mammalian herbivores in Patagonia.

We arrived at the Cueva de las Manos in the early morning. It lies in a dry steep-sided valley and the park headquarters looked out of place as the European-style high-roofed buildings accompanied by tall introduced pines made it appear more like a ski resort than an archeological site. Small trees in the dry stream bed below provided the only greenery in the desert landscape. I had hoped to see a mara, one of the largest Patagonian rodents, but our trip was nearing an end and I still hadn't found one. The

Photo 16.15 *Birds, such as this magellanic tapaculo, foraged in as well as on the trunks of the southern beech trees. Photo by Bill Magnusson.*

difference in attitude towards wildlife between anthropologists and biologists was brought home to me when the guide said that a Patagonian mara had often been seen near the tourist trail, but she thought that the cats might have killed it. There were cats almost everywhere we looked, sitting under bushes or on the ledges that lined the cliffs. I asked her whether there were any cat-control efforts under way and she was shocked. She said that the park guards maintained the cats to control an outbreak of southern mountain cavies. I cannot imagine why park guards would want to control a harmless native animal with an introduced predator, but it was obvious that her expertise laid with the conservation of human artifacts and not biological species.

The Cueva de las Manos is in fact a series of rock shelters along the valley that people used as a canvas for painting between 9,000 and 4,000 years ago. Most of the designs were made by blowing red, black or white pigments onto an outstretched hand. The significance of these is uncertain. There was also the outline of a rhea foot done in the same style. We could identify paintings of guanacos, pumas, pools, frogs and even something that might have been a scorpion. However, there were no giant sloths or mastodons, so these must have been extinct by the time the cave came to be used to record the lives and beliefs of the people.

The Bosques Petrificadas National Monument lies to the east of Cueva do las Manos just inland of Puerto Deseado. The area between the coast and the mountains has few tourist attractions and the small towns are associated with sheep ranching or oil production. The contrast between the oil towns and the towns supported mainly by tourism was glaring. The land around the oil towns was strewn with plastic bags and other refuse that accumulated along the fence lines. We stayed overnight in a hotel worse than any I have seen in the Brazilian interior. The doors didn't shut, there were no windows and the shower cubicle was permanently awash with water that could not escape through the blocked drain. We didn't note any bed bugs, but I wouldn't have been surprised!

The only live animal we saw on this section of the trip was a large hairy armadillo. I was interested to see two roadkills. One was a European hare, a supposedly common species, but we didn't see any live animals. The other was a Humboldt's hog-nosed skunk. I have never seen a skunk in the wild and I fantasized about filming these beautiful black and white animals, but that will have to wait for a future opportunity.

Bosques Petrificadas means petrified forests in Spanish, and there are many in Patagonia, though the one we visited is the most famous as it lies near the main road linking Comodoro Rivadavia and San Julian. We could get close to guanacos and I spent time filming Patagonia's largest living herbivores, but it was the fossilized trees that set me thinking about the herbivores of the past. Some of the trunks of the trees were wider than we here tall, which means that they would have been as large or larger than trees found in forests anywhere in the World today. I have seen estimates of the ages of petrified trees in Patagonia spanning 50 to 150 million years, which means that most of them would have flourished during the reign of the dinosaurs.

Volcanic activity did in the trees before the aridity of the changing climate had time to eliminate them and I started to think about the dinosaur fossils I had seen in El Calafate and the petrified forests. What were the implications of living with dinosaurs for the trees? The dinosaur fossils I had seen were not the largest from Patagonia. One species, *Gigantosaurus*, may have stood about 6m high and had a bite force three times

Photo 16.16 *This young magellanic woodpecker let me sit beside it as it excavated a fallen tree trunk. Photo by Bill Magnusson.*

that of the famous *Tyranosaurus rex*. That species probably preyed on or scavenged *Argentinosaurus*, possibly the largest known land herbivore that has ever existed. It stood around 20 m high.

What does this have to do with the trees? Until about 10,000 years ago, the megaherbivores probably controlled the distribution of forests, as they do in some parts of Africa until now. Trees need to be very tall to escape from large mammals. Giraffes stand about six meters tall and an elephant's trunk can reach about that high. If it can't reach the leaves, an elephant will push over the tree. Giant sloths probably pulled rather than pushed over trees, as has been suggested for the giant extinct palorchestid marsupials[142]. The only escape from this is for the tree to grow so big that its leaves are out of reach and its trunk so thick that it is not worthwhile for a megahervivore to try to knock it down. Trees can only get that big under favorable growing conditions, so the distribution of forests probably resulted from an interplay between large mammals and climate until humans with axes and fire changed the rules.

Six meters is now very tall for a mammalian herbivore, but the largest carnivorous dinosaurs were as high. To escape their predators, herbivorous dinosaurs had to be even bigger, standing more that three times that height. If the herbivorous dinosaurs could reach 20 m, the trees would have had to have been much larger than today to escape the megaherbivores. Presumably, the distribution of forests during the age of dinosaurs was much more restricted than it is now, even given that there were higher concentrations of CO_2 then, which presumably promoted plant growth. If the feces of mammalian megaherbivores is important today in determining food chains, and ultimately biodiversity, dinosaur poo must have been an incredible ecological force!

As we headed back to Trelew to catch our return flight I was disappointed in only one aspect. We had seen most of the major groups of Patagonian birds and mammals, but one special group was missing. The hystricomorph rodents have evolved grazing and browsing species that only occur in the arid areas of southern South America and we had seen none of them. We were only a few hundred kms from our destination when I saw what looked like two small wallabies in the bushes beside the road. I was concentrating on driving and it took a second to remember that there are no wallabies in Patagonia. I drove back in time to see two Patagonian maras walking sedately among the bushes. About the size of a hare, they had the round head and compact body of a rodent, but long antelope-like legs and largish, rabbit-like ears. The grey on the upper part of the body merged into a black band across the buttocks, which was outlined by a white belt below. Most of the underside was a light orange brown. The black and white emphasized the rear, which appeared to be overhanging and this was the last part I saw as they passed into the distance.

As we had time before the flight, we drove to Gaiman, which is not far from Trelew. The town doesn't have much to distinguish itself, except that it was founded by Welsh immigrants, some of whom still speak the Welsh language. The people take advantage of the difference from the surrounding Spanish culture to promote tourism,

Photo 16.17 Laguna Nimez has many species of waterbirds, including white and black-knecked swans. Photo by Bill Magnusson.

principally through their tea houses. We went to the most famous, which advertised that it had been visited by Lady Diana, Princess of Wales, but it was too expensive for our end-of-trip budget. We found another, much cheaper, establishment on a side road that seemed even more traditional than the first. Soon after we sat down to enjoy the Welsh afternoon tea, Fred, Henrique and Nena walked in. We had been travelling independently for over a week and it was pure coincidence that they had stopped there at that time on their way back. It was good to catch up and I took advantage of the opportunity to rub it in to Nena that I had filmed Patagonian maras and she had not. Her rejoinder was that she had filmed North American beavers in Ushuaia!

The short film sequence of maras I obtained on that trip did little to satisfy my desire to see the hystricomorphs of arid southern South America. Patagonian maras are in the same family as the smaller cavies, but the Chinchilla family also has grazing and browsing species. I especially wanted to see viscachas, which were very common before human persecution and purportedly a major prey of Argentinian pumas. I thought I saw viscachas when I visited Peru in 2013. They were sitting on the rocks around the famous Inca ruins at Machu Pichu, but I later learned that they were mountain viscachas, only remotely related and morphologically very different from the plains viscacha of Argentina. Like their close relatives, the chinchillas, the mountain viscachas look like squirrels, though their sluggish behavior and gregarious habits reveal their very different ancestry.

My chance to see the Argentinian large hystricomorphs came in 2018 when Ana Ochoa, better known as Kitty, invited Nena and me to give a course on multivariate statistics in San Luis, which is north of Patagonia on the border between arid steppe and desert. Kitty took us on a quick tour of central Argentina before the course. We drove over 1800 km to give a one-hour talk! In the Sierra de las Quijadas National Park, we saw guanacos and Patagonian maras, but to see viscachas, we had to go to a ranch run by the family of Maximiliano Pardo, better known just as Max, who was a university student and friend of one of Kitty's students. Shortly before we arrived at the ranch, we saw Chacoan maras, which looked like a cross between the Patagonian maras that I had seen and southern mountain cavies. Before Kitty showed me, I didn't realize that this smaller species of mara existed.

The Patagonian maras we saw were always in pairs, and apparently they mate for life, the male following the female anywhere she goes. However, many pairs raise their young together in communal warrens. I had never heard of this combination of monogamy and communal raising of offspring in mammals, which further emphasized their unique ecology.

I had seen the maras and the mountain viscachas during the day, but plains viscachas are strictly nocturnal. We wandered over the almost bare ground of the ranch between scattered trees until we cane to large holes and trenches in the ground, which Max said were viscacha warrens, but we saw no foraging animals. The trenches were so deep that Kitty almost disappeared when she crouched in one. Many of the entrances

Photo 16.18 *Guanacos are now the largest native herbivores in Patagonia. Photo by Bill Magnusson.*

were protected by a tangle of fallen branches that had obviously been dragged there by the burrow's inhabitants. Overhead, large numbers of burrowing parrots chided us, and the huge stick nests of the monk parrots covered the trees and even the ranch water tower. Bright red scarlet flycatchers and black-crested finches fossicked in the trees and it was obvious that birds were the dominant native vertebrates during the day.

When we returned at night, there seemed to be a heavy silence after all the bird songs of the daylight hours. However, we could hear the strangest wailing and growling from deep in the viscacha burrows. The sweep of our headlights revealed animals near the entrances to some burrows, but they were skittish and I could only film them from far away. The images were grainy due to the weak light, but I could tell that these creatures were like none I had seen before. They had big heads and relatively small bodies followed by a short tail. The closest general shape in mammals I had seen was that of a Tasmanian devil and they moved in a similar trot on their short legs.

The strangest thing about them was their color; the head had a broad black band accompanying the mouth and light bands above and below. The contrast between the black and white was similar to that of the Patagonian maras, but the pattern was on the front rather than the rear of the animal. I would love to know what selective pressure results in these strange patterns in Patagonian maras and plains viscachas. The smaller Chacoan maras do not have them, but have a white ring around the eye, as does the southern mountain cavy.

Although not considered endangered, the viscachas are heavily hunted and ranchers less conscientious than Max's family destroy the burrow systems to avoid competition with cattle. Although maras and viscachas are often compared to hares, antelopes and rabbits, and the viscachas could possibly be compared to wombats, these animals and the role they play in Argentinian ecosystems is so unique that such comparisons demean them. I wished that I had more time to follow them and learn about their ecologies.

The animals of Argentina were very different from those I had seen on other continents, but the changes from 10,000 years ago to the present were similar; the megaherbivores were gone and only the fast-running medium-sized mammals, burrowing mammals, and small species were left. The birds were less affected and they still keep the World green.

Photo 16.19 *People have been registering their presence at Cueva do las Manos for about 9000 years. Photo by Bill Magnusson.*

Photo 16.20 *Giant trees like these that were petrified must have coexisted with dinosarurs that could reach leaves more than 20 m above ground . Photo by Bill Magnusson.*

Photo 16.21 *Maras look like a cross between a rabbit and a deer. Photo by Bill Magnusson.*

Photo 16.22 *The plains viscachas only left their warrens at night and would not let us get close. Photo by Bill Magnusson.*

CHAPTER 17 – INDONESIA

The effect of aggression can be deceptive. These sea eagles over
Rinca were apparently just playing. Photos by Bill Magnusson.

The last place I want to take you is Flores Island and the islets around it. None of these now has large native mammalian herbivores or predators, but the situation was different around 50,000 years ago. At that time, Flores was the home of tiny human-like people and small elephants[174]. There is dispute as to whether these people belonged to our species, *Homo sapiens*, or a closely related sister clade, though the consensus seems to be coming down in favor of the latter. Elephants and their relatives are good swimmers and fossils of dwarf elephants and mammoths have been found on islands throughout the World.

Species tend to become smaller or larger than their ancestors on islands, but it is not known how big the ancestors of the Flores people were. In any case, they were probably replaced by our species, either because of competition or through predation. There were no large mammalian predators on these islands, but giant lizards, now known as Komodo dragons, got to the islands, probably from Australia, and still occur there today[161]. The dragons were probably both prey and predators for the little people of Flores.

The elephants were gone by the time the present colonists of Flores and surrounding islands arrived, so they brought pigs, descendants of wild boar, water buffalos and rusa deer to provide meat. There is evidence that people have been taking pigs to islands in the region for about 7000 years, but it is not clear when the rusa deer and buffalo arrived, possibly only in the last few hundred years[174]. Flores is heavily populated, but the neighboring islands of Komodo and Rinca have low population densities and most are park employees who provide for the huge numbers of tourists that visit the islands to see the Komodo dragons.

We stopped in Bali on the way to Flores. There are not many large animals on Bali because it is densely populated and tourists mainly go there to immerse in the Indonesian culture or partake of water sports, such as surfing and scuba diving. Of interest to me though was a visit to a coffee plantation, which was more a tourist park in the middle of the suburbs. We were offered over a dozen different types of coffee, but the premium was Kopi Luwak, which is made from coffee beans that have been partially fermented in palm-civet guts. The digestive juices of the palm civet permeate the beans and are said to reduce acidity, though I suspect that there may be another reason for the quality of the coffee.

Photo 17.1 *Captive palm civets are used to produce Kopi Luwak coffee. Photo by Bill Magnusson.*

When humans harvest coffee, they run their hands down the branches to release the ripe fruits. Big clumsy humans also knock off the almost-ripe fruits that are mixed with mature beans. Smaller animals, like civets, are more selective, only picking the fully ripe beans and avoiding any that have been attacked by insects. Therefore, the beans are of better quality even before the civet swallows them. I suggest that this may be important because the most expensive coffee in Brazil is jacu coffee, which is obtained from the feces of guans, which are large chicken-like birds in the cracid family. The guans carefully select the ripe fruit, but their digestive juices do not enter the seeds. Kopi Luwak was originally obtained from the feces of wild civets. Now, it mainly comes from the dung of captive civets that are fed coffee fruits that have been harvested by humans. I bet that the wild dung, which contains only premium ripe beans, is better than the dung of captive animals for producing Kopi Luwak, but you would have to ask a coffee connoisseur about that. On a more general level, I think that this illustrates the difference in the quality of food obtained by a big mammal, a small mammal and a bird. Bulk processing by big animals comes at the cost of loss in nutritional value.

The coffee plantation also provided an opportunity to see some of the Indonesian flying foxes. We climbed steps beside a grove of banana plants and I noticed that some of the leaves were bent over in the form of a tent. I don't know if they were responsible for the tent, but two light-brown bats were hanging from its ceiling in the same manner as the tent-making bats in the Amazon. They were small enough that one with folded wings would have fitted in my hand. That is fairly large as insectivorous bats go, but small for a fruit-eating megachiropteran. They had rounded noses and I assume that they were Indonesian short-nosed fruit bats.

I had seen a long-tongued nectar bat in Papua New Guinea when Terry Frohm and Ian Games took me bat netting near Madang in 2008. That is also a small megabat, but most of my remembrances of that night relate to a bridge and a car. There were tiny plank bridges across the streams and the car fell off one of them and ended up suspended over the stream; the back wheels on solid ground, one front wheel still on the bridge and the the other front wheel balanced on the top of a pylon that had supported a former bridge. There was a meter of nothing between that pylon and the bank and I couldn't see how the car could be moved without it tumbling into the stream. However, Terry gunned the motor, put the car in reverse and jumped it back onto the road. I think that all that adrenalin covered my memories, because I remember the bats mainly because of the pictures I took.

A world where even the smallest fruit- and nectar-eating bats are large is very different from that in South America, where even the frugivorous bats are tiny. I wonder what would happen if these two faunas ever come into contact. As we were leaving the coffee plantation come tourist trap, we passed a large flying fox hanging on a shrub beside the path. I don't know what species it was, but it was about the size of Fang and covered in black fur with silvery guard hairs. It obviously liked company and used the hook on its wing to intercept me as I walked past. When I bent over to look at it more closely it pulled off my hat. It didn't appear to have any injuries so I don't know why it remained in the coffee plantation. Keeping it was probably illegal and tourists

Photo 17.2 *Some megachiroptera, such as this* Macroglossus *from Madang, are relatively small. Photo by Bill Magnusson.*

would probably worry that it might carry viruses that could be transmitted to people. Some researchers believe that the virus responsible for COVID-19 was transmitted to people from bats by first contaminating palm civets. Nevertheless, that friendly little animal probably did a lot to make tourists more tolerant of bats.

A black-crowned night-heron in the hotel courtyard reminded me of how often we underestimate the intelligence of other species. It was standing in a pool in the garden and appeared to be having trouble with a piece of bread it had stolen from the restaurant. It repeatedly flicked the bread into the water and remained motionless watching it for a while before picking it up and throwing it to another place in the pool. I have seen herons swallow much larger pieces of food and I couldn't understand why it had so much trouble with the soft bread. Then I saw that the fish in the pond were attracted to the bread and the heron was concentrating on them when it remained motionless. Rather than being clumsy, it was using the bread as bait for the fish!

We almost ended our trip on Bali because our flight to Flores was delayed and we had a few hours to spare in the airport. I photographed the huge orchid displays and thought that Jeni and Albertina had wandered off to inspect the duty-free shops. They did not respond to the "last call" for our flight and I ran madly through the airport trying to find them, but to no avail. I asked the Nam Air attendants to hold the flight, but they could only do so for a short time. I had just about given up when I saw them huddled together sleeping, not 10 meters from the gate.

Flying over Flores I could see the brown grasslands and the jagged peninsulas jutting into the blue sea that are typical of the eastern Indonesian islands, and I imagined how it might have been with meter-high people stalking dwarf elephants 50.000 years ago. Once we had landed, however, the mystique was lost. Labuan Bajo was just a small Indonesian village heavily modified by the intense tourist trade. The ugly brick buildings reminded me of the favelas around many Brazilian ports and I was pleased that we would be spending our time on a boat.

I had arranged the trip through Ruchira Somaweera, who is a scientist with Australia's national research institution, CSIRO. He grew up in Sri Lanka, but has extensive experience in Indonesia, wrote *A Naturalist's Guide to the Reptiles & Amphibians of Bali*[165] and *Amphibians and Reptiles of Komodo National Park*[166], and co-manages a specialized, science-based wildlife-expedition venture – Aaranya Wildlife Odysseys. I chose to go with Ruchira's company because I knew that he would provide well-trained guides and make sure that the local people benefited from the tourism. The trip exceeded my expectations.

The boat was about 10 m long, with a wooden hull, low cabins and an upper deck covered by a canvas awning. It was the sort of small boat that might have been used by local fishermen or traders. The crew consisted of the captain, who doubled as cook, and a first mate. Our guide was experienced and knew where to find animals, both during the day and at night. There were no other tourists, just Albertina, Jeni and me.

We slept on mats in the cabin and awoke to a fine Indonesian breakfast. We had tried "traditional" food in Bali, but it was obviously heavily modified for western

Photo 17.3 *This black-crowned night-heron used bread as bait for fish. Photo by Bill Magnusson.*

tastes. The dishes the captain served were varied and I am sure that they were the same as his family ate at home; delicious and authentic. The crew didn't speak English, but our guide translated as Jeni and Albertina tried to decipher the recipes.

We first went to Rinca Island, which is smaller and much less impacted by tourist facilities than Komodo Island. It was dark when we set off and I was impressed by the number of snakes we saw as we walked along the boardwalk through the mangroves, especially the highly-venomous, bright-green island pit-vipers. I assumed that so many vipers meant many rodents, though the snakes probably also eat many of the giant tokay geckos that we encountered everywhere on the islands. There were civet tracks in the mud and I wanted very much to see one. I had seen similar tracks in Liberia, but had not been able to find their makers. The captive palm civets on Bali had been interesting, but seeing an animal in a cage is not the same as seeing it in the wild.

The grasslands behind the mangroves were spotted with dark shadows, some of which I recognized as wild boar. Their large heads sloping down to their tusked muzzles made them look sinister, but they moved off when we got closer. The other dark smudges turned into rusa deer as we approached and our headlights pierced the gloom. They were much less skittish and the males looked regal with their sweeping antlers and large dark eyes.

We passed them and moved into the forest where water buffalos had churned up the earth around the almost-dry bed of a small stream. Walking at night would give me an opportunity to see palm civets in the wild, but they looked almost all black as they climbed among the branches in the dry forest. I could make out the black face mask and spots on the body, but only when very close. The civets stared down at us with their huge eyes, giving the same impression as possums in Australia and kinkajous in South America.

I was surprised by the number of species that the dry forest supported. We found more species of snakes and geckos, an enormous variety of invertebrates and several species of frogs. One scene that particularly impressed me was of a scorpion sitting on a tree trunk with a centipede suspended from its mouth. This for me was an example of an apex predator. People call lions apex predators, but they are on very short food chains with only three levels: plants, herbivores, such as antelopes, and lions. In contrast, the scorpion was a hyperpredator on a food chain with at least five levels: plants, herbivorous invertebrates, spiders, centipedes and scorpions. Mammals are generally parts of simple systems, and we know very little about the roles of invertebrates, which represent the greater part of biodiversity.

The fauna active during the day was just as diverse on both islands. The lizards were represented by several species of skinks on the ground and *Draco* flying lizards on the trees. The flying lizards didn't fly, but spent their time eating ants and displaying their yellow dewlaps, which they expanded in twitches as though opening a soft fan attached to a stick. Although the Komodo dragons accounted for most of the kilograms of lizard on the island, the skinks and flying lizards were much more numerous. We saw fewer insects during the day, but that is probably because they have to hide from the birds.

Photo 17.4 *The wild boars on Rinca were just vague shapes in the night. Photo by Bill Magnusson.*

Some of the birds, such as the green imperial pigeons and the critically endangered yellow-crested cockatoos, eat mainly fruits and seeds directly from the vegetation. However, others, such as the black drongos and large-billed crows, are further up the food chain. There were also avian predators of vertebrates in abundance. Even before we set off to explore the island, two sea eagles gave a display of aerobatics over the boat, diving and tumbling in what I assume was a mock fight. There were many Brahminy kites in the forest and a pair had constructed a nest in one of the larger trees. The adults were orange brown on top with brilliant white underparts, but the juvenile that had just left the nest was dull mottled brown. The crows didn't like the Brahminy kites and one spent a long time dive bombing them and not letting them leave their perches. A variety of small blue, yellow and brown birds foraged in the undergrowth.

The eastern Indonesian islands have been colonized by animals from both Asia and Australia. The mammals, such as the rusa deer, buffalos, pigs and crab-eating macaques, come from Asian stock. Many of the birds, such as the brown-capped woodpecker and the green jungle fowl also come from that region. Other species, such as the Komodo dragons and orange-footed scrubfowl, originated from lineages in Australia and New Guinea. I was pleased to see the green jungle fowl. Although I saw red jungle fowls in Thailand, I was never sure how pure they were because they gave rise to domestic chickens thousands of years ago and continue to interbreed with them.

Green jungle fowl have apparently contributed some genes to domestic chickens, but there is no evidence of gene flow in the other direction. Female green jungle fowl are camouflaged in speckled brownish grey with grey bare patches around the face. In contrast, the males have iredescent blue feathers on much of the body and tail, orange and black tassels over the wings, and scintillating feathers that make a scale-like pattern on the back. Bright-pink bare flesh forms a crest on the head and extends across the face. It also forms a gular flap under the beak that grades into yellow near the body. Although they are not very cryptic, we did not see many.

The orange-footed scrubfowls were much more common and scratched through the leaf litter beside the trails. They were chicken sized with a short tail and a tuft of feathers that looks like a helmet on the back of the head. Their thick orange legs were their most distinctive feature. I had seen orange-footed scrubfowls in Papua New Guinea and northern Australia, and was surprised at how well they adapt to a variety of situations. It is a megapode and incubates its eggs in huge mounds that are warmed by the decomposing vegetation. Newly-hatched megapodes are precocious, dig themselves out of the mound after hatching and run off to fend for themselves with no help from the parents. I would have expected the eggs to be susceptible to predators that use the sense of smell to hunt, the adults subject to predation while attending the huge nests, and the solitary young vulnerable until they can fly. However, the system must be very effective because they do very well for themselves. Sometimes, theory is not much good for predicting evolutionary potential; what works, works!

The density of large animals was surprising considering the dry semideciduous forest and savanna that covers most of Rinca and Komodo Islands. Rusa deer were everywhere and I filmed two young bucks sparing on the beach. Their antlers were

Photo 17.5 *Mammals and birds rarely act above the third trophic level. This scorpion was at least at the fifth trophic level. Photo by Bill Magnusson.*

well developed, but nowhere near as big as the racks carried by some of the older males. An adolescent animal with horns only a handspan long circled the two, sometimes approaching so close that it was almost touching their interlocked antlers. I don't know if it was just looking to get tips on fighting or it really wanted to get into the competition. Crab-eating macaques strolled across the ground in a manner reminiscent of baboons in Africa and gave chirping warning cries when we approached too close. We saw few pigs during the day, and only a couple of buffalo.

I had seen several documentaries that portrayed Komodo dragons killing goats, deer and even a buffalo, but none of the mammals or birds seemed particularly concerned about the huge lizards that were lying around or strolling through the forest. Komodo dragons can easily kill humans, and sometimes do. Nevertheless, the only protection our guides used consisted of strong forked sticks that can be used to pin the dragon's neck if it gets too close. My impression was that, although they can be effective hunters if need be, the dragons prefer not to spend a lot energy to obtain their food.

One published paper says that Komodo dragons are not apex predators, as are lions in Africa, because they do not control the population dynamics of the herbivores[74]. That is, it is the herbivores that determine the energy flow in the system, and they depend on the plants. This type of system is called "bottom-up" because it is the organisms low on the food chain that control the ecological processes. The alternative system is "top-down", in which the predators control the herbivores, and hence the potential for energy flow up the food chain. That is what happens when predatory fish are excluded from a lake and it turns green[37]. Top-down control seems to be fairly common in aquatic ecosystems, but how frequent is it on land? It may be in forests, where predators, especially birds, glean the foliage and allow the megaplants to dominate the landscape, but it may not be where the animals can get bigger than the plants, such as in savanna systems.

The classic example of lions as apex predators in Africa is not as simple as it appears. Yes, lions may be able affect the numbers of, and sometimes control, the population dynamics of small to medium-sized herbivores, but Tony Sinclair's studies have shown that predation has little effect on the population dynamics of herbivores that weigh more than 150 kg[163]. There are many such species in African savannas and a bit over 10,000 years ago there were megaherbivores on all the continents except antarctica. In terms of predation, lions may be at the tops of short food chains involving medium-sized mammals, but the overall dynamics of African savannas and dry forests is determined by the megaherbivores; that is, the system is controlled by bottom-up processes. Rather than use lions as a symbol of how African savannas work, maybe we should use a pile of elephant dung!

Komodo dragons can maintain much higher biomass than mammalian predators[74], and this occurs with some other reptilian predators[97]. That is because you can contribute more offspring to the next generation if you conserve energy. Why don't the dragons bother to hunt intensively when they are capable of killing any of the mammals on their islands? I did a few back-of-the-envelope calculations based on what is known of the densities of the larger mammals on Komodo and Rinca. Researchers have

Photo 17.6 *The green jungle fowl has contributed few genes to domestic chickens, but is very similar. Photo by Bill Magnusson.*

estimated the densities of rusa deer and pigs in many sites in the region[11,12]. Sometimes they counted animals, but most of the estimates are based on the relationship between the number of fresh dung piles and the number of animals. That is, the researchers recognize that the density of mammalian herbivores, and presumably their effect on the ecosystem, can be estimated from their feces output.

Taking the middle values based on these studies, a reasonable estimate of the number of rusa deer on Komodo Island would be about 32,000 animals, and about 16,000 for Rinca. Using the same calculations, there would be about 5,000 pigs on Komodo and 2,500 on Rinca. How long can a pig or a deer live? Most indications are that an individual is unlikely to pass five years in the wild, but that reflects disease and predation. In captivity, and very occasionally in the wild, rusa deer can live 20 years, and a similar age is estimated for pigs. Therefore, if the population remains stable, about 1 in 20 animals should die of old age each year if a predator doesn't get it first. Based on this, we would expect about 1,600 rusa deer and about 251 pigs to die on Komodo each year. The equivalent numbers for Rinca are 800 and 125.

These estimates are very rough and probably wild underestimates of the number of carcasses that would be available even if the dragons did not kill any deer or pigs, but you can see why it would make more sense for a dragon to conserve energy and scavenge, rather than trying to run down healthy deer and pigs. In fact, there is an even greater "excess" than this. In a stable population, during its lifetime, each animal only successfully produces one individual to replace it. The rest, which in the case of a female pig that lived five years would be more than 20, die young while still feeble and easy prey for predators.

I suggest that this is typical of a bottom-up grassland system. The megaherbivores are important for maintaining the diversity of other animals by producing huge quantities of highly nutritious feces for the invertebrates, which sustain many species further up the food chain, especially birds, and they also provide regular meat dishes in the form of carcasses and vulnerable young for the vertebrate carnivores. Are lions so different from Komodo dragons? They can kill animals as large as adult buffalo, giraffes and elephants, but Tony Sinclair's studies show that they do not control the population dynamics of any of those species. The cost of hunting these megaherbivores, which often includes a high probability of death, has apparently resulted in the lions evolving to concentrate on smaller prey, or to only crop off the young, disabled or senile animals, just like Komodo dragons.

Humans now control the populations of herbivores almost everywhere in the World[26]. It therefore appears to be a predator-controlled top-down system, but people control the herbivores by manipulating the vegetation, usually to produce a savanna-like system of grasslands. Alternatively, humans act as megaherbivores and bulldoze the woody vegetation to make the land more suitable for herbs, such as soybeans, or grasses, such as wheat. The vegetation they displace is not converted into feces, but vaporized in fire. Unlike the megaherbivores, humans usually do not distribute their feces to support a varied fauna, but concentrate them in places with other pollutants where only microorganisms can live. That is, the system we have produced had no known analogue in the past.

We are fast losing the only places on earth dominated by megaherbivores, most of which are in Africa. For us to get a glimpse into the way a large part of the World functioned since the age of dinosaurs we will soon have to go to a few unique places, like the islands of Komodo and Rinca, to see in miniature how biodiversity was maintained by the action of large mammalian herbivores.

Photo 17.7 *The rusa deer sparred with each other, but largely ignored the Komodo dragons. Photo by Bill Magnusson.*

I am going to end the book here. I know that much of what I have said is personal and anecdotal, but I hope that I have explained to you my fixation on the sizes of mammals and birds, and why I am so sad that the next generation will probably have no chance to stand next to a megaherbivore that is not imprisoned in a zoo or preserved in a museum. They will never appreciate the biodiversity that exists in a poo paradise!

Photo 17.8 *Komodo dragons largely ignore potential prey, such as this medium-sized mammal. Photo by Bill Magnusson.*

Photo 17.9 *The bones of giant extinct mammals tell us little about the huge effects their browsing and dung must have had on ecosystems. Photo by Helena Bergallo.*

REFERENCES

[1] Abba, A. M., S. Poljack, M. Gabrielli, P. Teta & U. F. J. Pardiñas. 2014. Armored invaders in Patagonia: recent southward dispersion of armadillos (Cingulata, Dasypodidae). Mastozoologia Neotropical 21:311-318.

[2] Aguiar-Silva, F. H., T. G. Junqueira, T. M. Sanaiotti, V. Y Guimarães, P. V. C. Mathias & C. V. Marnsonça. 2015. Resource availability and diet in harpy eagle breeding territories on the Xingu River, Brazilian Amazon. Brazilian Journal of Biology 75:S181-S189.

[3] Albernaz, A. L. 2001. Zoneamento ecológico da região de Alter do Chão, Pará: um exercício de planejamento para uma Unidade de Conservação de uso direto. Doctoral Thesis, Instituto Nacional de Pesquisas da Amazônia, Manaus.

[4] Albernaz, A. L. & W. E. Magnusson. 1999. Home-range size of the bare-eared marmoset (*Callitrix argentata*) at Alter do Chão, central Amazonia, Brazil. International Journal of Primatology 20:665-677.

[5] Almeida-Santos, S. M., M. M. Antoniazzi, O. A. Sant'Anna and C. Jared. 2000. Predation by the opossum *Didelphis marsupialis* on the rattlesnake *Crotalus durissus*. Current Herpetology 19: 1-9.

[6] Alvarez, L. W., W. Alvarez, F. Asaro & H. V. Michel. 1980. Extraterrestrial Cause for the Cretaceous-Tertiary Extinction. Science 208:1095-1108.

[7] Anderson, P. K. & R. I. T. Prince. 1985. Predation on dugongs: attacks by killer whales. Journal of Mammalogy 66:554-556.

[8] Andrewartha, H. G. & L.C. Birch. 1964. The distribution and abundance of animals. University of Chicago Press, Chicago.

[9] Appel, G., A. López-Baucells, W. E. Magnusson & P. E. D. Bobrowiec. 2017. Aerial insectivorous bat activity in relation to moonlight intensity. Mammalian Biology 85:37–46. DOI:10.1016/j.mambio.2016.11.005.

[10] Appel, G., A. López-Baucells, W. E. Magnusson & P. E. D. Bobrowiec. 2019. Temperature, rainfall, and moonlight intensity effects on activity of tropical insectivorous bats. *Journal of Mammalogy* 100:1889–1900 DOI:10.1093/jmammal/gyz140.

[11] Ariefiandy, A., D. M. Forsyth, D. Purwandana, J. Imansyah, C. Ciofi, H. Rudiharto, A. Seno, & T. S. Jessop. 2016. Temporal and spatial dynamics of insular Rusa deer and wild pig populations in Komodo National Park. Journal of Mammalogy 97:1652–1662.

[12] Ariefiandy, A., D. Purwandana, G. Coulson, D. M. Forsyth, & T. S. Jessop. 2013. Monitoring the ungulate prey of the Komodo dragon Varanus komodoensis: distance sampling or faecal counts? Wildlife Biology 19: 126-137. DOI: 10.2981/11-098.

Austad, S. N. 2010. Methusaleh´s zoo: how nature provides us with clues for extending human health span. Journal of Pathology 142(Suppl. 1):S10-S21. DOI: 10.1016/j.jcpa.2009.10.024.

Austad, S. N. & K. E. Fischer. 1991. Mammalian aging, metabolism, and ecology: evidence from the bats and marsupials. Journal of Gerontology 146:B47-53. DOI: 10.1093/geronj/46.2.b47.

Bannister, J., D. Barwick, P. Best, S. Brown, D. Cato, M. Cawthorn, G. Chittleborough, R. Gambell, P. Gill, R. Paterson & B. Warneke. 2006. William H. Dawbin. Marine Mammal Science 14:904-907.

Bates H. W. 1892. The Naturalist on the River Amazons, With a Memoir of the Author by Edward Clodd. Murray, London.

Bergallo, H. G. & W. E. Magnusson. 1999. Effects of climate and food availability on four rodent species in southeastern Brazil. Journal of Mammalogy 80:472-486.

Bergallo, H. G. & W. E. Magnusson. 2004. Factors affecting space by two rodent species in Brazilian Atlantic forest. Mammalia 68:121-132.

[13] Bergallo, H. G., C. E. L. Esbérard, M. A. R. Mello, V. Lins, R. Mangolin, G. G. S. Melo & M. Baptista. 2003. Bat Species Richness in Atlantic Forest: What Is the Minimum Sampling Effort? Biotropica 35:278–288.

[14] Bernard, E. 2001a. Vertical stratification of bat communities in primary forests of central Amazon, Brazil. Journal of Tropical Ecology 17:115-126. DOI: 10.1017/S0266467401001079.

Bernard, E. 2001b. Species list of bats (Mammalia, Chiroptera) of Santarém area, Pará State, Brazil. Revista brasileira de Zoologia 18:455-465. DOI 10.1590/S0101-81752001000200016.

Bernard, E., A. L. K. M. Albernaz & W. E. Magnusson. 2001. Bat species composition in three localities in the Amazon Basin. Studies in Neotropical Fauna and Environment 36:177-184.

Bernard, E. & B. Fenton. 2003. Bat mobility and roosts in a fragmented landscape in central Amazonia, Brazil. Biotropica 35:262-277.

Bernard, E., & B. Fenton. 2011. Species diversity of bats (Mammalia: Chiroptera) in forest fragments, primary forests, and savannas in central Amazonia, Brazil. Canadian Journal of Zoology 80:1124-1140. DOI: 10.1139/z02-094.

Bernard, E. & L. N. Saldanha. 2004. Anilhamento de morcegos: um registro de deslocamento no Pará. XXV Congresso Brasileiro de Zoologia - Resumos, Brasília, p.235.

[15] Bocherens, H. 2018. The rise of the Anthroposphere since 50,000 years: An ecological replacement of megaherbivores by humans in terrestrial ecosystems? Front. Ecol. Evol. 6:3 DOI: 10.3389/fevo.2018.00003.

Bobrowiec, P. E. D. & V. C. Tavares. 2017. Establishing baseline biodiversity data prior to hydroelectric dam construction to monitoring impacts to bats in the Brazilian Amazon. PLoS ONE 12: e0183036. DOI:_10.1371/journal.pone.0183036.

Boitani, L. & P. Ciucci. 1995. Comparative social ecology of feral dogs and wolves, Ethology Ecology & Evolution 7:49-72.

Bonano, R. & S. Cafazzo. 2014. The social organization of a population of free-ranging dogs in a suburban area of Rome: a reassessment of the effects of domestication on dog's behaviour. Pp 65-104 *In* J. Kaminski & S. Marshall-Pescini (eds) The Social Dog. Academic Press, Amsterdam.

Borges-Matos, C., S. Aragon, M. N. F. da Silva, M.-J. Fortín & W. E. Magnusson. 2016. Importance of the matrix in determining small-mammal assemblages in an Amazonian forest-savanna mosaic. Biological Conservation 204:417-425.

BR-319 https://www.youtube.com/watch?v=rNkiv1appOY.

Buechley, E. R. & Ç. H. Şekercioğlu. 2016. The avian scavenger crisis: Looming extinctions, trophic cascades, and loss of critical ecosystem functions. Biological Conservation 198: 220-228. DOI: 10.1016/j.biocon.2016.04.001.

Bueno, A. J., R. S. Bruno, T. P. Pimentel, T. M. Sanaiotti & W. E. Magnusson. 2012. The width of riparian habitats for understory birds in an Amazonian forest. Ecological Applications 22:722–734.

[16] Burger, M. I. 1996. Os Efeitos de Habitat e Variacoes Climaticas Na Densidade de *Dendrocigna viduata* no Rio Grande do Sul. Doctoral Thesis, Instituto Nacional de Pesquisas da Amazônia, Manaus.

[17] Calzada, J., M. Delibes, C. Keller, F. Palomares & W. E. Magnusson. 2008. First record of the bushy-tailed opossum, *Glironia venusta*, Thomas, 1932, (Didelphimorphia) from Manaus, Amazonas, Brazil. Acta Amazonica 38:807-810.

[18] Capaverde, U. D., L. G. A. Pereira, V. C. Tavares, W. E. Magnusson, F. B. Baccaro & P. E. D. Bobrowiec. 2018. Subtle changes in elevation shift bat-assemblage structure in Central Amazonia. Biotropica 50: 674–683. DOI: 10.1111/btp.12546.

[19] Carpenter S. R., J. F. Kitchell, J. R. Hodgson, P. A. Cochran, J. J. Elser, M. M. Elser, D. M. Lodge, D. Kretchmer, X. He & C. N. von Ende. 1987. Regulation of lake primary productivity by food web structure. Ecology 68:1863-1876.

[20] Carroll, S. B. 2017. The Serengeti Rules. Princeton University Press, Princeton.

[21] Carvalho, E. A. R. 2003. Efeitos da fragmentação florestal sobre a composição e abundância de lagartos de serrapilheira e sub-bosque em fragmentos associados a uma savana amazônica. Masters Thesis, Instituto Nacional de Pesquisas da Amazônia, Manaus.

[22] Caughley, G. 1983. The Deer Wars. Heinemann, Portsmouth, New Hampshire, USA.

[23] Caughley, G. 1987. Ecological relationships. Pp. 159–187 *In* G. Caughley, N. Shepherd & J. Short (eds) Kangaroos: Their Ecology and Management in Sheep Rangelands of Australia. Cambridge University Press, Cambridge.

Caughley, G. 1976. The elephant problem - an alternative hypothesis. African Journal of Ecology 14:265-283. DOI:10.1111/j.1365-2028.1976.tb00242.x.

Caughley, G. 1977. Analysis of Vertebrate Populations. John Wiley & Sons, Hoboken, NJ, USA.

Chemin, Norma. 1999. O uso de microhábitat de forrageio por *Lepidocolaptes angustirostris*. Masters Dissertation, Instituto Nacional de Pesquisas da Amazônia, Manaus.

Cintra, R. 1990. Black-eared Fairy (*Heliothryx aurita*, Trochilidae) using a gliding flight like falling leaves when leaving nest. Journal of Ornithology 131, 333–335. DOI:10.1007/BF01641006.

[24] Cintra, R. 1997. Spatial Distribution and Foraging Tactics of Tyrant Flycatchers in Two Habitats in the Brazilian Amazon. Studies on Neotropical Fauna and Environment 32: 17-27. DOI: 10.1076/snfe.32.1.17.13459.

Cintra, R. & T. M. Sanaiotti. 2005. Fire effects on the composition of a bird community in an Amazonian savanna. Brazilian Journal of Biology 65: 29-41. DOI:10.1590/S1519-69842005000400016.

Cintra, R., W. E. Magnusson & A. Albernaz. 2013. Spatial and temporal changes in bird assemblages in forest fragments in an eastern Amazonian savannah. Ecology and Evolution. 3: 3249-3262. DOI: 10.1002/ece3.700.

[25] Coelho, L. A. 2011. Dinâmica e composição da avifauna do sub-bosque sob influência de diferentes históricos de queimada em uma região de savana amazônica. Masters Dissertation, Instituto Nacional de Pesquisas da Amazônia, Manaus.

[26] Crowley, S. I., M. Cecchetti & R. A. McDonald. 2020. Diverse perspectives of cat owners indicate barriers to and opportunities for managing cat predation of wildlife. Frontiers in Ecology and Environment 18:544-549. DOI: 10.1002/fee.2254.

[27] Da Silveira, R., E. E. Ramalho, J. B. Thorbjarnarson & W. E. Magnusson. 2010. Depredation by jaguars on caimans and importance of reptiles in the diet of the jaguar. Journal of Herpetology 44:418-424.

Dambros, C., G. Zuquim, G. M. Moulatlet, F. R. C. Costa, H. Tuomisto, C. C. Ribas, R. Azevedo, F. Baccaro, P. E. D. Bobrowiec, M. S. Dias, T. Emilio, H. M. V. Espirito-Santo, F. O. G. Figueiredo, E. Franklin, C. Freitas, M. B. Graça, F. d'Horta, R. P. Leitão, M. Maximiano, F. P. Mendonça, J. Menger, J. W. Morais, A. H. N. de Souza, J. L. P. Souza, V. C. Tavares, J. D. do Vale, E. M. Venticinque, J. Zuanon & W. E. Magnusson. 2020. The role of environmental filtering, geographic distance and dispersal barriers in shaping the turnover of plant and animal species in Amazonia. Biodiversity and Conservation 2020: DOI: 10.1007/s10531-020-02040-3.

Dankers, N. M. J. A. 1977. The Ecology of an Anuran Community. Ph. D. Thesis, University of Sydney, Sydney, Australia.

[28] Dantas, S. M., T. M. Sanaiotti & A. L. K. M. Albernaz. 2005. Effects of fragmentation on *Thamnophilus stictocephalus* (Aves, Thamnophilidae) in semideciduous forest of Alter-do-Chão, Pará. Brazilian Journal of Biology 65:423-430.

[29] Dawbin, W. H. & E. J. Eyr. 1991. Humpback whale songs along the coast of Western Australia and some comparison with East Coast songs. Memoirs of the Queensland Museum 30:249-254.

[30] Doise, W., G. Csepeli, H. D. Dann, G. Gouge, K. Larsen & A. Odell. 1972. An experimental investigation into the formation of intergroup representations. European Journal of Social Psychology 2:202-204.

[31] Domning, D. P. 2012. The Early Years of the Amazonian Manatee Project at INPA, Manaus, Brazil. Aquatic Mammals 38:204-222, DOI 10.1578/AM.38.2.2012.204.

[32] Ecological Society of America <https://www.youtube.com/watch?v=bLs2dZvJQX4>.

[33] Estes, J. A. 2010. The Aleutian Archipelago. Pp 155-176 In Billick, I. & M. V. Price (Eds). The Ecology of Place. University of Chicgo Press, Chicago.

[34] Fadini, R. & R. Cintra. 2015 . Modeling Occupancy of Hosts by Mistletoe Seeds after Accounting for Imperfect Detectability. Plos One 10: e0127004-11.

[35] Fontana, C. S. 2011. Bird diversity in a subtropical South-American city: Effects of noise level, arborisation and human population density. Urban Ecosystems 14:341-360.

Fragoso, J. 1998. Home range and movement patterns of white-lipped peccary (*Tayassu pecari*) herds in northern Brazilian Amazon. Biotropica 30:458-469. DOI: 10.1111/j.1744-7429.1998.tb00080.x.

[36] Fragoso J. M. V., T. Levi, L. F. B. Oliveira, J. B. Luzar, H. Overman, J. M. Read & K. M. Silvius. 2016. Line transect surveys under detect terrestrial mammals: implications for the sustainability of subsistence hunting. PLoS ONE 11:e0152659. DOI: 10.1371/journal.pone.0152659.

[37] Fragoso J. M. V., F. Gonçalves, L. F. B. Oliveira, H. Overman, T. Levi & K. M. Silvius. 2019. Visual encounters on line transect surveys under-detect carnivore species: Implications for assessing distribution and conservation status. PLoS ONE 14:e0223922. DOI: org/10.1371/journal.pone.0223922.

[38] Francisco, A. L., W. E. Magnusson & T. M. Sanaiotti. 1995. Variation in growth and reproduction of *Bolomys lasiurus* (Rodentia, Muridae) in an Amazonian savanna. Journal of Tropical Ecology 11:419-428.

[39] George, J. C., J. Bada, J. Zeh, L. Scott, S. E. Brown, T. O'Hara & C. R. Suydam. 1999. Age and growth estimates of bowhead whales (*Balaena mysticatus*) via aspartic acid racemization. Canadian Journal of Zoology 77:571-580.

[40] Ghizoni, I. R., V. M. G. Layme, A. P. Lima & W. E. Magnusson. 2005. Spatially explicit population dynamics in a declining population of the tropical rodent, *Bolomys lasiurus*. Journal of Mammalogy 86:677-682.

[41] Grady, J. M., B. S. Maitner, A. S. Winter, K. Kaschner, D. P. Tittensor, S. Record, F. A. Smith, A. M. Wilson, A. I. Dell, P. L. Zarnetske, H. J. Wearing, B. Alfaro & J. H. Brown. 2019. Metabolic asymmetry and the global diversity of marine predators. Science 363:eaat4220.

[42] Green, K. 2002. Selective predation on the broad-toothed rat, *Mastacomys fuscus* (Rodentia: Muridae), by the introduced red fox, *Vulpes vulpes* (Carnivora: Canidae), in the Snowy Mountains, Australia. *Austral Ecology* **27**:353–359.

[43] Grigg, G. C. 2018. A sorry tale of sheep, kangaroos and goats. Pp 1-9 In G. Baxter, N. Finch & P. Murray (eds) Advances in Conservation Through Sustainable Use of Wildlife. University of Queensland, Brisbane.

[44] Grigg N. P., J. M. Krilow, C. Gutierrez-Ibanez, D. R. Wylie, G. R. Graves & A. N. Iwaniuk. 2017. Anatomical evidence for scent guided foraging in the turkey vulture. Scientific Reports 7: 17408. DOI:10.1038/s41598-017-17794-0.

[45] Hairston, N. G., F. E. Smith & L. B. Slobodkin. 1960. Community structure, population control, and competition. American Naturalist 94:421-425.

[46] Hamilton, C. A. 1981. Rusa deer in the Royal National Park: dietary overlap with *Wallabia bicolor*, influence on the vegetation, distribution and movements. M.Sc. Thesis, Sydney University, Sydney.

[47] Jessop, T. S., A. Ariefiandy, D. M. Forsyth, D. Purwandana, C. R. White, Y. J. Benu, T. Madsen, H. J. Harlow & M. Letnic. 2020. Komodo dragons are not ecological analogs of apex mammalian predators. Ecology 101:e02970.

[48] Kaluza J., R. L. Donald, I. C. Gynther, L. K.-P. Leung & B. L. Allen 2016. The distribution and density of water mice (*Xeromys myoides*) in the Maroochy River of Southeast Queensland, Australia. PLoS ONE 11: e0146133. DOI: 10.1371/journal.pone.0146133.

[49] Kaspari, M. 2020. The seventh macronutrient: how sodium shortfall ramifies through populations, food webs and ecosystems. Ecology Letters 23:1153-1168. DOI: 10.1111/ele.13517.

[50] Layme, V. M. G., A. P. Lima & W. E. Magnusson. 2004. Effects of fire, food availability and vegetation on the rodent *Bolomys lasiurus* in an Amazonian savanna. Journal of Tropical Ecology 20:183-187.

[51] Leuchtenberger, C., C. Ribas, W. E. Magnusson & G. Mourão. 2012. To each his own taste: latrines of the giant otter as food resources for vertebrates in Southern Pantanal. Studies on Neotropical Fauna and Environment 47: 81-85. DOI: 10.1080/01650521.2012.697690

[52] Leuchtenberger, C., L. G. R. Oliveira-Santos, W. E. Magnusson & G. Mourão. 2013a. Space use by giant otter groups in the Brazilian Pantanal. Journal of Mammalogy 94: 320-330. DOI:10.1644/12-MAMM-A-210.1

Leuchtenberger, C., C. A. Zucco, C. Ribas, W. Magnusson & G. Mourão. 2013b. Activity patterns of giant otters recorded by telemetry and camera traps. Ethology, Ecology and Evolution 26: 19-28. DOI: 10.1080/03949370.2013.821673.

Leuchtenberger, C., R. Sousa-Lima, N. Duplaix, W. E. Magnusson & G. Mourão. 2014. Vocal repertoire of the social giant otter. Journal Acoustic Society of America 136: 2861-2875. DOI: 10.1121/1.4896518.

Leuchtenberger, C., W. E. Magnusson & G. Mourão. 2015. Territoriality of giant otters in an area with seasonal flooding. PLoS ONE 10:e0126073. DOI: 10.1371/journal.pone.0126073.

Leuchtenberger, C., R. Sousa-Lima, C. Ribas, W. E. Magnusson & G. Mourão. 2016. Giant otter alarm calls as potential mechanisms for individual discrimination and sexual selection. Bioacoustics 25: 279-291. DOI: 10.1080/09524622.2016.1157704.

Leuchtenberger, C., M. L. Rheingantz, C. A. Zucco, A. C. Catella, W. E. Magnusson & G. Mourão. 2020. Giant otter diet differs between habitats and from fisheries offtake in a large Neotropical floodplain. Journal of Mammalogy 101:1650–1659. DOI: 10.1093/jmammal/gyaa131.

Loyn R. H. 1995. Bell miners and the farming hypothesis – a comment. Emu 95:145-146.

Loyn, R. H., R. G. Runnalls, G. Y. Forward, & J. Tyers. 1983. Territorial bell miners and other birds affecting populations of insect prey. Science 221:1411-1413. DOI:10.1126/science.221.4618.1411.

Lyson, T. R., I. M. Miller, A. D. Bercovici, K. Weissenburger, A. J. Fuentes, W. C. Clyde & J. W. Hagadorn, J. W. Hagadorn, M. J. Butrim, K. R. Johnson, R. F. Fleming, R. S. Barclay, S. A. Maccracken, B. Lloyd, G. P. Wilson, D. W. Krause & S. G. B. Chester. 2019. Exceptional continental record of biotic recovery after the Cretaceous–Paleogene mass extinction. Science 366:977-983. DOI: 10.1126/science.aay2268.

Macêdo, R. H. & M. A. Mares. 1987. Geographic variation in the South American cricetine rodent *Bolomys lasiurus*. Journal of Mammalogy 68:578-594.

[53] Magnusson, W. E. 1974. Water Balance of *Rattus fuscipes* (Waterhouse 1839). Honors Thesis, Sydney University, Sydney.

[54] Magnusson, W. E. 1979. Nesting Ecology of *Crocodylus porosus*, Schneider, in Arnhem Land, Australia. Ph.D. Thesis, Sydney University, Sydney.

[55] Magnusson, W. E. 1984. Urine urea concentrations in *Rattus fuscipes*. Australian Mammalogy 8:61-63.

[56] Magnusson, W. E. 1987. Reproductive cycles of teiid lizards in Amazonian savanna. Journal of Herpetology 21:307-316.

[57] Magnusson, W. E. 2001. Standard errors of survey estimates: what do they mean? Neotropical Primates 9:53-54.

[58] Magnusson, W. E. 2015. The Eye of the Crocodile. Open Science Publishers, New York.

[59] Magnusson, W. E. 2016. The Fish and the Frogs. Open Science Publishers, New York.

[60] Magnusson, W. E. 2019. Diversity, Freedom and Evolution. Cambridge Scholars, Cambridge: p79 Death on the BR 319.

[61] Magnusson, W. E. & A. P. Lima. 1991. The ecology of a cryptic predator, *Paleosuchus trigonatus*, in a tropical rainforest. Journal of Herpetology 25:41-48. DOI: 10.2307/1564793.

[62] Magnusson, W. E. & A. P. Lima. 1993. Black vultures (*Coragyps atratus*): a side benefit for trees with buttress roots? Biotropica 15:216.

[63] Magnusson, W. E. & T. M. Sanaiotti. 1987. Dispersal of *Miconia* seeds by the rat *Bolomys lasiurus*. Journal of Tropical Ecology 3:277-278.

[64] Magnusson, W. E., G. J. W. Webb & J. A. Taylor. 1976. Two new locality records, a new habitat and a nest description for *Xeromys myoides* Thomas (Rodentia: Muridae). Australian Wildlife Research 3:153-157.

[65] Magnusson, W. E., G. J. Caughley & G. C. Grigg. 1978a. A double-survey estimate of population size from incomplete counts. Journal of Wildlife Management 42:174-176.

[66] Magnusson, W. E., G. C. Grigg & J. A. Taylor. 1978b. An aerial survey of potential nesting areas of the saltwater crocodile, *Crocodylus porosus* Schneider, on the north coast of Arnhem Land, northern Australia. Australian Wildlife Research 5:401-415.

[67] Magnusson, W. E., G. C. Grigg & J. A. Taylor. 1980a. An aerial survey of potential nesting areas of *Crocodylus porosus* on the west coast of Cape York Peninsula. Australian Wildlife Research 7:465-478.

[68] Magnusson, W. E., R. C. Best & V. M. F. da Silva. 1980b. Numbers and behavior of Amazonian dolphins, *Inia geoffrensis* and *Sotalia fluviatilis fluviatilis*, in the Rio Solimões, Brasil. Aquatic Mammals 8:27-41.

[69] Magnusson, W. E., E. V. da Silva & A. P. Lima. 1987. Diets of Amazonian crocodilians. Journal of Herpetology 21:85-95.

[70] Magnusson, W. E., A. L. Francisco & T. M. Sanaiotti. 1995. Home-range size and territoriality in *Bolomys lasiurus* (Rodentia: Muridae) in an Amazonian savanna. Journal of Tropical Ecology 11:179-188.

[71] Magnusson, W. E., M. C. de Araújo, R. Cintra, A. P. Lima, L. A. Martinelli, T. M. Sanaiotti, H. L. Vasconcelos & R. L. Victoria. 1999. Contributions of C_3 and C_4 plants to higher trophic levels in an Amazonian savanna. Oecologia 119:91-96.

[72] Magnusson, W. E., V. M. G. Layme & A. P. Lima. 2010. Complex effects of climate change: population fluctuations in a tropical rodent are associated with the southern oscillation index and regional fire extent, but not directly with local rainfall. Global Change Biology 16:2401–2406.

[73] Magnusson W. E., R. Braga-Neto, F. Pezzini, F. Baccaro, H. Bergallo, J. Penha, D. Rodrigues, L. Verdade, A. Lima, A. Albernaz, J.-M. Hero, B. Lawson, C. Castilho, D. Drucker, E. Franklin, F. Mendonça, F. Costa, G. Galdino, G. Castley, J. Zuanon, J. Vale, J. Santos, R. Luizão, R. Cintra, R. Barbosa, A. Lisboa, R. Koblitz, C. Cunha & A. Mendes Pontes. 2013. Biodiversity and Integrated Environmental Monitoring. Áttema Editorial, Manaus. <http://ppbio.inpa.gov.br/sites/default/files/Biodiversidade%20e%20monitoramento%20ambiental%20integrado.pdf>.

Magnusson. W. E., C. Rosa, V. Layme, I. R. Ghizoni & A. P. Lima. 2021. Local effects of global climate on a small rodent *Necromys lasiurus*. Journal of Mammalogy 102:188–194, https://doi.org/10.1093/jmammal/gyaa140.

Magnusson. W. E., C. Rosa, V. Layme, I. R. Ghizoni & A. P. Lima. 2021. Local effects of global climate on a small rodent *Necromys lasiurus*. Journal of Mammalogy. – Supplement [https://academic.oup.com/jmammal/article/102/1/188/6039962#supplementary-data]

[74] Mara, P. P. & C. Santella. 2016. Cat Wars. Princeton University Press, Princeton, USA.

[75] Marciente, R., P. E. D. Bobrowiec & W. E. Magnusson. 2015. Ground-vegetation clutter affects phyllostomid bat assemblage structure in lowland Amazonian forest. PLoS ONE 10: e0129560. DOI: 10.1371/journal.pone.0129560.

[76] Marques, S. A. 1986. Activity cycles, feeding and reproduction of *Molossus ater* (Chiroptera: Molossidae) in Brazil. Boletim do Museu Paraense Emilio Goeldi Zoologia 2:159-179.

Martin, P. S. 2005. Twilight of the Mammoths: Ice Age Extinctions and the Rewilding of America. University of California Press. Berkeley.

Mauro, R. A., G. M. Mourão, M. P. Silva, M. E. Coutinho, Tomás, W. M. & W. E. Magnusson. 1995. Influência do habitat na densidade e distribuiçãode cervo (*Blastoceros dichotomus*) durante a estação seca, no Pantanal mato-grossense. Revista Brasileira de Biologia 55:745-751.

Mauro, R. A., G. M. Mourão, M. E. Coutinho, M. P. Silva & W. E. Magnusson. 1998. Abundance and distribution of marsh deer *Blastocerus dichotomus* (Artiodactyla: Cervidae) in the Pantanal, Brazil. Revista de Ecologia Latinoamericano 5:13-20.

McHarg, I. 1979. Design with Nature. The Natural History Press. New York.

[77] Menger, J. S. 2011. Fatores determinantes da distribuição de aves no interflúvio Purus-Madeira. Masters Dissertation, Instituto Nacional de Pesquisas da Amazônia, Manaus.

[78] Menger, J., K. Henle, W. E. Magnusson, A. Soro, M. Husemann & M. Schlegel. 2017. Genetic diversity and spatial structure of the Rufous-throated Antbird (*Gymnopithys rufigula*), an Amazonian obligate army-ant follower. Ecology and Evolution 7:2671–2684. DOI: 10.1002/ece3.2880.

[79] Menger, J., J. Unrein, M. Woitow, M. Schlegel, K. Henle & W. E. Magnusson. 2018. Weak evidence for fine-scale genetic spatial structure in three sedentary Amazonian understorey birds. Journal of Ornithology 159:355–366. DOI 10.1007/s10336-017-1507-y.

[80] Millan, C. & M. J. Peltier. 2006. Cesar's Way. Harmony Books, New York.

[81] Montanarin, A. Efeito de variáveis ambientais e antrópicas na seleção de habitat por machos e fêmeas de onça-pintada (*Panthera onca*) em uma área de várzea do Médio Solimões. Masters Dissertation, Instituto Nacional de Pesquisas da Amazônia, Manaus.

[82] Morton, E. S. 1978. Avian arboreal folivores: Why not? Pp 123-130 In Montgomery, G. G. (ed.). The Ecology of Arboreal Folivores. Smithsonian Institution Press, Washington, D.C.

[83] Mourão, G., M. Coutinho, R. Mauro, Z. Campos, W. Tomás & W. Magnusson. 2000. Aerial surveys of caiman, marsh deer and pampas deer in the Pantanal Wetland of Brazil. Biological Conservation 92:175-183.

[84] Oliveira, L. Q., R. Marciente, W. E. Magnusson & P. E. D. Bobrowiec. 2015. Activity of the insectivorous bat *Pteronotus parnellii* relative to insect resources and vegetation structure. Journal of Mammalogy 96: 1036–1044. DOI: 10.1093/jmammal/gyv108.

[85] Orlando, L., D. Male, M. T. Alberdi, J. L. Prado, A. Prieto, A. Cooper & C. Hänni. 2008. Ancient DNA Clarifies the Evolutionary History of American Late Pleistocene Equids. Journal of Molecular Evolution 66:533-538. DOI 10.1007/s00239-008-9100-x.

[86] Paciullo, P. R. M. 2019. Padrão de atividade temporal e uso do habitat por *Crax globulosa* e *Pauxi tuberosa* em floresta de várzea e terra firme na Amazônia brasileira. Masters Dissertation, Instituto Nacional de Pesquisas da Amazônia, Manaus.

[87] Pereira, L. G. A., U. D. Capavede, V. C. Tavares, W. E. Magnusson, P. E. D. Bobrowiec & F. B. Baccaro. 2019. From a bat's perspective, protected riparian areas should be wider than defined by Brazilian laws. Journal of Environmental Management 232:37–44. DOI: 10.1016/j.jenvman.2018.11.033.

[88] Pickrell, J. 2017. Weird Dinosaurs. Columbia University Press, New York.

[89] Piper, S. D. & C. P. Catterall. 2003. A particular case and a general pattern: hyperaggressive behaviour by one species may mediate avifaunal decreases in fragmented Australian forests. Oikos 101:602-614.

[90] Prado, D. M. 2010. Dieta e relação de abundância de *Panthera onca* e *Puma concolor* com suas espécies-presa na Amazônia central. Masters Dissertation, Instituto Nacional de Pesquisas da Amazônia, Manaus.

[91] Ramalho, E. E. 2006. Uso do habitat e dieta da onça-pintada (*Panthera onca*) em uma área de várzea, Reserva de Desenvolvimento Sustentável Mamirauá, Amazônia Central, Brasil. Masters Dissertation, Instituto Nacional de Pesquisas da Amazônia, Manaus.

[92] Ramalho, E. E. & W. E. Magnusson. 2008. Uso do habitat por onça-pintada (*Panthera onca*) no entorno de lagos de várzea, Reservade Desenvolvimento Sustentável Mamirauá, AM, Brasil. Uakari 4:33-39.

Ramalho, E. E., M. B. Main, G. C. Alvarenga & L. G. R. Oliveira-Santos. 2021. Walking on water: the unexpected evolution of arboreal life style in a large top predator in the Amazon flooded forests. Ecology e03286, DOI: 10.1002/ecy.3286.

[93] Read, J. M., J. M. V. Fragoso, K. M. Silvius, J. Luzar, H. Overman, A. Cummings, S. T. Giery & L. F. de Oliveira. 2010. Space, Place, and Hunting Patterns among Indigenous Peoples of the Guyanese Rupununi Region. Journal of Latin American Geography 9:213-243.

[94] Redhead, T. D, & J. L. McKean. 1975. A new record of the false water-rat, *Xeromys myoides*, from the Northern Territory of Australia. Australian Mammalogy 1:347-354.

[95] Reich, D. 2018. Who We Are and How We Got Here. New York: Pantheon Books, New York.

[96] Ribas, C., A. V. Vasconcellos, G. Mourão, W. Magnusson, A. M. Solé-Cava & H. A. Cunha. 2011. Polymorphic microsatellite loci from the endangered Giant

Otter (*Pteronura brasiliensis*). Conservation of Genetic Resourses 3:769–771. DOI 10.1007/s12686-011-9454-z.

[97] Ribas, C., G. Damasceno, W. E. Magnusson, C. Leuchtenberger & G. Mourão. 2012. Giant otters feeding on caiman: evidence for an expanded trophic niche of recovering populations. Studies on Neotropical Fauna and Environment 47: 19-23. DOI: 10.1080/01650521.2012.662795.

[98] Ribas, C., H. A. Cunha, G. Damasceno, W. E. Magnusson, A. Solé-Cava & G. Mourão. 2016. More than meets the eye: kinship and social organization in giant otters (*Pteronura brasiliensis*). Behavioral Ecology and Sociobiology. 70: 61-72. DOI: 10.1007/s00265-015-2025-7.

[99] Richards H. L., R. T. Wells, a. R. Evans, E. M. G. Fitzgerald & J. W. Adams. 2019. The extraordinary osteology and functional morphology of the limbs in Palorchestidae, a family of strange extinct marsupial giants. PLoS ONE 14(9): e0221824. DOI: 10.1371/journal.pone.0221824

[100] Rocha, D. G.. 2015. Padrão de atividade e fatores que afetam a amostragem de mamíferos de médio e grande porte na Amazônia central. Masters Dissertation, Instituto Nacional de Pesquisas da Amazônia, Manaus.

[101] Rocha, D. G., E. E. Ramalho, G. C. Alvarenga, D. M. Gräbin & W. E. Magnusson. 2015. Records of the bush dog (*Speothos venaticus*) in central Amazonia. Journal of Mammalogy 96:1361–1364.

[102] Rocha, D. G., E. E. Ramalho & W. E. Magnusson. 2016. Baiting for carnivores might negatively affect capture rates of prey species in camera-trap studies. Journal of Zoology 300:205–212.

[103] Rocha, D.G., K. M. P. M. de Barros Ferraz, L. Gonçalves, C. K. W. Tan, F. G. Lemos, C. Ortiz, C. A. Peres, N. Negrões, A. P. Antunes, F. Rohe, M. Abrahams, G. Zapata-Rios, D. Teles, T. Oliveira, E. M. von Mühlen, E. Venticinque, D. M. Gräbin, D. Mosquera B., J. Blake, M. G. M. Lima, R. Sampaio, A. R. Percequillo, F. Peters, E. Payán, L. H. M. Borges, A. M. Calouro, W. Endo, R. L. Pitman, T. Haugaasen, D. A. Silva, F. R. de Melo, A. L. B. de Moura, H. C. M. Costa, C. Lugarini, I. G. de Sousa, S. Nienow, F. Santos, A. C. Mendes-Oliveiras, W. Del

Toro-Orozco, A. R. D'Amico, A. L. Albernaz, A. Ravetta, E. C. O. do Carmo, E. Ramalho, J. Valsecchi, A. J. Giordano, R Wallace, D. W. Macdonald & R. Sollmann. 2020. Wild dogs at stake: deforestation threatens the only Amazon endemic canid, the short-eared dog (*Atelocynus microtis*). Royal Society Open Science 7:190717.

[104] Roques, S., B. Adrados, C. Chavez, C. Keller, W. E. Magnusson, F. Palomares & J. A. Godoy. 2011. Identification of Neotropical felid faeces using RCP-PCR. Molecular Ecology Resources 11:171–175.

[105] Roques, S., R. Sollman, A. Jácomo, N. Tôrres, L. Silveira, C. Chávez, C. Keller, D. Mello do Prado, P. C. Torres, C. J. dos Santos, X. B. G. da Luz, W. E. Magnusson, J. A. Godoy, G Ceballos & F. Palomares. 2016. Effects of habitat deterioration on the population genetics and conservation of the jaguar. Conservation Genetics 17:125–139.

[106] Rosenberg, K. V. A. M. Dokter, P. J. Blancher, J. R. Sauer, A. C. Smith, P. A. Smith, J. C. Stanton, A. Panjabi, L. Helft, M. Parr & P. P. Marra. 2019. Decline of the North American avifauna. *Science* 366:120-124. DOI: 10.1126/science. aaw1313.

[107] Sales, N. G., M. C. Kaiser, I. Coscia, J. C. Perkins, A. Highlands, J. P. Boubli, W. E. Magnusson, M. N. F. da Silva, C. Benvenuto & A. D. McDevitt. 2020. Assessing the potential of environmental DNA metabarcoding for monitoring Neotropical mammals: a case study in the Amazon and Atlantic Forest, Brazil. Mammal Review 50:221-225.

[108] Sampaio, R, A. P. Lima, W. E. Magnusson & C. A. Peres. 2010. Long-term persistence of midsized to large-bodied mammals in Amazonian landscapes under varying contexts of forest cover. Biodiversity Conservation 19:2421-2439. DOI: 10.1007/s10531-010-9848-3.

[109] Sanaiotti, Tânia Margarete. 1986. Área de vida de *Formicivora rufa* em savana amazônica, Alter do Chão - PA. Masters Dissertation, INPA/UFAM, Manaus.

Sanaiotti, T. M. & R. Cintra. 2001. Breeding and Migrating Birds in an Amazonian Savanna. Studies on Neotropical Fauna and Environment 36:23-32. DOI: 10.1076/snfe.36.1.23.8878.

Sanaiotti, T. M. & W. E. Magnusson. 1995. Effects of annual fires on the production of fleshy fruits by birds in a Brazilian Amazonian savanna. Journal of Tropical Ecology 11: 53-65.

[110] Sanaiotti, T. M.,T. G. Junqueira, V. Palhares, F. H. Aguiar-Silva, L. M. P. Henriques, G. Oliveira, V. Y. Guimarães, V. Castro, D. Mota, D. F. Trombin, D. N. A. Villar, K. M. Lara, D. Fernandes, L. Castilho, E. Yosheno, R. M. Alencar, L. Cesca, S. M. Dantas, T. O. Laranjeiras, P. C. Mathias & C. V. Mendonça. 2015. Abundance of harpy and crested eagles from a reservoir-impact area in the low- and mid-Xingu River. Brazilian Journal of Biology 75:S190-S204.

[111]Sasse, D. B. 2003. Job related mortality of wildlife workers in the United States, 1947-2000. Wildlife Society Bulletin 31:1000-1003.

[112] Schaller, G. B. & J. M. C. Vasconcelos. 1978. A marsh deer census in Brazil. Oryx 14:345-351.

[113] Schmitt, C. L. & M. L. Tatum. 2008. The Malheur National Forest: Location of the World's largest living organism. United States Department of Agriculture Forest Service, Washington, DC, USA.

[114] Shapin, S. 1989. The Invisible Technician. American Scientist 77: 554-563.

[115] Shermer, M. 2020. Giving the Devil His Due. Cambridge University Press. Cambridge.

[116] Shine, R. & R. Somaweera, 2019. Last lizard standing: the enigmatic persistence of the Komodo dragon. Global Ecology and Conservation 18:e00624.

[117] Silver, M. J. & A. J. Carnegie. 2017. An independent review of bell miner associated dieback. Final report prepared for the Project Steering Committee: systematic review of bell miner associated dieback.

[118] Sinclair, A., S. Mduma, and J. S. Brashares. 2003. Patterns of predation in a diverse predator–prey system. Nature 425:288.

[119] Sinclair, A. R. E. 2012. Serengeti Story. Oxford University Press, Oxford, UK.

[120] Somaweera, R. 2018. A Naturalist's Guide to the Reptiles & Amphibians of Bali. John Beaufoy, Oxford, England.

[121] Somaweera, R., A. Asiz, E. Resa, M. Panggur, D. Saverinus & K. Muga. 2018. Amphibians and Reptiles of Komodo National Park. Aaranya Wildlife Odysseys, Perth, Australia.

[122] Souza, C. M. 2002. Ocorrência e Distribuição de Pequenos mamíferos em Fragmentos Florestais Naturais Inseridos em uma Matriz de Savana Amazônica. Masters Dissertation. Instituto Nacional de Pesquisas da Amazônia, Manaus.

[123] Souza, M. 2007. Silvino Santos: o Cineasta do Ciclo da Borracha. 2nd Edition. EDUA, Manaus.

[124] Spencer, S. J., C. M. Steele, & D. M. Quinn. 1999. Stereotype threat and women's math performance. Journal of Experimental Social Psychology 35:4–28.

[125] Steele, C. M., & J. Aronson, J. 1995. Stereotype threat and the intellectual test performance of African Americans. Journal of Personality and Social Psychology 69:797–811.

[126] Sterling, E. J., M. M. Hurley & L. D. Minh. 2006. Vietnam: A Natural History. Yale University Press, New Haven.

[127] Stouffer, P. C., V. Jirinec, C. L. Rutt, R. O. Bierregaard Jr, A. Hernández-Palma, E. I. Johnson, S. R. Midway, L. L. Powell, J. D. Wolfe & T. E. Lovejoy. 2020. Long-term change in the avifauna of undisturbed Amazonian rainforest: ground-foraging birds disappear and the baseline shifts. Ecology Letters 24:186-195. DOI: 10.1111/ele.13628.

[128] Sutherland, S. K. 1999. A Venomous Life. Highland House, Melbourne.

Sutikna, T., M. W. Tocheri, J. T. Faith, Jatmiko, R. D. Awe, H. J. M. Meijer, E. W. Saptomo & R. G. Roberts. 2018. The spatio-temporal distribution of archaeological and faunal finds at Liang Bua (Flores, Indonesia) in light of the revised chronology for *Homo floresiensis*. *Journal of Human Evolution 124:52-74. DOI:* 10.1016/j.jhevol.2018.07.001.

[129] Tavares, V. C., C. C. Nobre, C. F. S. Palmuti, E. P. P. Nogueira, J. D. Gomes, M. H. Marcos, R. F. Silva, S. G. Farias & P. E. D. Bobrowiec. 2017. The bat fauna from southwestern Brazil and its affinities with the fauna of western Amazon. Acta Chiropterologica 19:93-106. DOI: 10.3161/15081109ACC2017.19.1.007.

[130] Troughton, E. 1953. Furred Animals of Australia, 2nd Edition. Angus & Robertson, Sydney.

[131] Tyndale-Biscoe, C.H. 1999. Biographical Memoirs: Graeme James Caughley 1947–1994. Historical Records of Australian Science 12:363-381.

[132] Vélez-Martin, E., L. Chomenko, M. Madeira & V. P. Pillar. 2015. Políticas públicas para os campos. Pp 169-173 *In* V. P. Pillar & O. Lange (eds). Os Campos do Sul. Rede Campos Sulinos – UFRGS, Porto Alegre.

[133] Wirsing, A. J., M. R. Heithaus & L. M. Dill. 2007. Fear factor: do dugongs (*Dugong dugong*) trade food for safety from tiger sharks (*Galeocerdo cuvier*)? Oecologia 153:1031-1046. DOI: 10.1007/s00442-007-0802-3.

GLOSSARY OF SCIENTIFIC NAMES

African bush elephant, *Loxodonta africana*.

African forest elephant, *Loxodonta cyclotis*.

Alpaca, *Vicugna pacos*.

Amazon royal flycatcher, *Onychorhynchus coronatus*.

Amazonian manatee, *Trichechus inunguis*.

Amazonian pigmy owl, *Glaucidium hardyi*.

Andean condor, *Vultur gryphus*.

Andiroba, *Carapa guianensis*.

Antarctic beech forests are dominated by several species of the genus *Nothofagus*, especially *Nothofagus antarctica*.

Arabian camel, *Camelus dromedarius*.

Arapaima, *Arapaima gigas*. Recent studies indicate that there may be more species.

Asian elephant, *Elephas maximus*.

Austral parakeet, *Enicognathus ferrugineus*.

Australian *Fan Palm*, *Licuala ramsayi*.

Bactrian camel *Camelus bactrianus*.

Bald Uakari monkey, *Cacajao calvus*.

Bay duiker, *Cephalophus dorsalis*.

Bell miner, *Manorina melanophiys*.

Black-casqued hornbill, *Ceratogymna atrata*.

Black-chested buzzard-eagle, *Geranoaetus melanoleucus*.

Black-crested finch, *Lophospingus pusillus*.

Black drongo, *Dicrurus macrocercus*.

Black-faced ibis, *Theristicus melanopis*.

Black flying fox, *Pteropus alecto*.

Black-footed tree rat, *Mesembriomys gouldii*.

Black-headed antbird, *Percnostola rufifrons*.

Black mastiff bat, *Molssus ater*.

Black-neck swan, *Cygnus melancoryphus*.

Black-throated huet huet, *Pteroptochos tarnii*.

Black vulture, *Coragyps atratus*.

Blackish oystercatcher, *Haematopus ater*.

Blue whale, *Balaenoptera musculus*.

Bobcat, *Lynx rufus*.

Boto, *Inia geoffrensis*.

Bottlenose dolphin, *Tursiops truncatus*.

Brahminy kite, *Haliastur indus*.

Brazil nut, *Bertholletia excelsa*.

Brazilian squirrel, *Sciurus aestuans.*

Broad-snouted caiman, *Caiman latirostris.*

Broad-toothed rat, *Mastacomys fuscus.*

Brown antechinus, *Antechinus stuartii.*

Brown-capped woodpecker, *Dendrocopos moluccensis.*

Brown-crested flycatcher, *Myiarchus tyrannulus.*

Budgerigar, *Melopsittacus undulatus.*

Burrowing owl, *Athene cunicularia.*

Burrowing parrot, *Cyanoliseus patagonus.*

Bushdog, *Speothos venaticus.*

Bush rat, *Rattus fuscipes.*

Cape buffalo, *Syncerus caffer.*

Capybara, *Hydrochoerus hydrochaeris.*

Cassowary, *Casuarius casuarius.*

Chacoan mara, *Dolichotis salinicola.*

Chestnut sac-winged bat, *Cormura brevirostris.*

Chimpanzee, *Pan troglodytes.*

Chilean flamingo, *Phoenicopterus chilensis.*

Chilean skua, *Stercorarius chilensis.* There is confusion as to the taxonomic distinction of the various skua species that occur in the Southern Hemisphere and these may have been another species or hybrids.

Chinchilla is the common name for two species: *Chinchilla chinchilla* and *Chinchilla lanigera* from the Andes of South America.

Cockatiel, *Nymphicus hollandicus*.

Collared anteater, *Tamandua tetradactyla*.

Collared peccary, *Pecari tajacu*.

Commerson's dolphin, *Cephalorhynchus commersonii*.

Common brushtail possum, *Trichosurus vulpecula*.

Common dunnart, *Sminthopsis murina*.

Common mouse opossum, *Marmosa murina*.

Common opossum, *Didelphis marsupialis*.

Common vampire bat, *Desmodus rotundus*.

Coppery brushtail, *Trichosurus johnstonii*.

Coscoroba swan, *Coscoroba coscoroba*.

Crab-eating fox, *Cerdocyon thous*.

Crab-eating macaque, *Macaca fascicularis*.

Crab-eating raccoon, *Procyon cancrivorus*.

Crested eagle, *Morphnus guianensis*.

Crimson rosella, *Platycercus elegans*.

Currawong, *Strepera graculina*.

Darwin's rhea, *Rhea pennata*.

Delicate slender opossum, *Marmosops parvidens*.

Diamond dove, *Geopelia cuneata*.

Diamond spotted pardalote, *Pardalotus punctatus*.

Double-barred finch, *Stizoptera bichenovii*.

Dugong, *Dugong dugon*.

Dusky antechinus, *Antechinus swainsonii*.

Dusky rat, *Rattus colletti*.

Dwarf armadillo, *Zaedyus pichiy*.

Eastern pigmy possum, *Cercartetus nanus*.

Echidna, *Tachyglossus aculeatus*.

Elegant crested-tinamou, *Eudromia elegans*.

Elephant birds, large extinct flightless birds from Madagascar related to New Zealand
   kiwis (genus *Apteryx*).

Emu, *Dromaius novaehollandiae*.

European hare, *Lepus europaeus*.

European fox, *Vulpes vulpes*.

European rabbit, *Oryctolagus cuniculus*.

Fallow deer, *Dama dama*.

False water rat, *Xeromys myoides*.

Feathertail glider, *Acrobates pygmaeus*.

Flying lizards of the genus *Draco* have been divided into many species, but under the
   old classification the species we saw was *Draco volans*.

Flying steamer duck, *Tachyeres patachonicus*.

Funnel-web spider, *Atrax robustus*.

Fur seal, *Arctocephalus australis*.

Giant anteater, *Myrmecophaga tridactyla*.

Giant armadillo, *Priodontes maximus*.

Giant otter, *Pteronura brasiliensis*.

Grassland sparrow, *Ammodramus humeralis*.

Great fruit-eating bat, *Artibeus lituratus*.

Great tinamou, *Tinamus major*.

Greater bulldog bat, *Noctilio leporinus*.

Greater grison, *Galictis vittata*.

Greater long-nosed armadillo, *Dasypus kappleri*.

Greater potoo, *Nyctibius grandis*.

Greater sac-winged bat, *Saccopteryx bilineata*.

Greater yellow-headed vulture, *Cathartes melambrotus*.

Green imperial pigeon, *Ducula aenea*.

Green jungle fowl, *Gallus varius*.

Green ring-tail possum, *Pseudochirops archeri*.

Green vine snake, *Oxybelis fulgidus*.

Grey-headed flying fox, *Pteropus poliocephalus*.

Guanaco, *Lama guanicoe*.

Guinea fowl, *Numida meleagris*.

Guyanan red howler monkey, *Alouatta macconnelli*.

Hairy-tailed bolo mouse, *Necromys lasiurus*.

Harpy eagle, *Harpia harpyja*.

Herbert River ringtail, *Pseudochirulus herbertensis*.

Hornbill, species of the family Bucerotidae.

House rat, *Rattus rattus*.

Humboldt's hog-nosed skunk, *Conepatus humboldtii*.

Humpback whale, *Megaptera novaeangliae*.

Hyacinth macaw, *Anodorhynchus hyacinthinus*.

Iberian lynx, *Lynx pardinus*.

Imperial cormorant, *Leucocarbo atriceps*.

Indian almond, *Terminalia catappa*.

Indian mynah, *Acridotheres tristis*.

Indonesian short-nosed fruit bat, *Cynopterus titthaecheilus*.

Island pit-viper, *Trimeresurus insularis*.

Jabiru stork, *Jabiru mycteria*.

Jaguar, *Panthera onca*.

Jaraqui, name given to *Semaprochilodus insignis and related species*.

Java finch, *Lonchura oryzivora*.

Kaypok tree, *Ceiba pentandra*.

Kelp are macro-algae in the order Laminariales. They are technically heterokonts rather than plants, but ecologically they function as plants.

Kelp gull, *Larus dominicanus*.

King quail, *Coturnix chinensis*.

King vulture, *Sarcoramphus papa*.

Kingfishers are birds in the family Alcedinidae, many of which eat few or no fish.

Kinkajou, *Potos flavus*.

Koala, *Phascolarctos cinereus*.

Komodo dragon, *Varanus komodoensis*.

Kookaburra, *Dacelo novaeguineae*.

Lance-head viper, highly venomous vipers, mainly of the genus *Bothrops*.

Large-billed crow, *Corvus macrorhynchos*.

Large hairy armadillo, *Chaetophractus villosus*.

Lesser bulldog bat, *Noctilio albiventris*.

Lesser elaenia, *Elaenia chiriquensis*.

Lesser sac-winged bat, *Saccopteryx leptura*.

Lesser yellow-headed vultures, *Cathartes burrovianus*.

Lion, *Panthera leo*.

Little red flying fox, *Pteropus scapulatus*.

Llama, *Lama glama*.

Long-tongued nectar bat, *Macroglossus minimus*.

Lumholtz's tree kangaroo, *Dendrolagus lumholtzi*.

Lyrebird, *Menura novaehollandiae*.

Macquarie perch, *Macquaria australasica*.

Magellan's penguin, *Spheniscus magellanicus*.

Magellanic tapaculo, *Scytalopus magellanicus*.

Magellanic woodpecker, *Campephilus magellanicus*.

Magpie, *Gymnorhina tibicen*.

Marabou stork, *Leptoptilos crumenifer*.

Marsh deer, *Blastocerus dichotomus*.

Meerkat, *Suricata suricatta*.

Moa, common name for large flightless birds from New Zealand, related to the tinamous of South America.

Monk parrot, *Myiopsitta monachus*.

Moose, *Alces alces*.

Mountain viscacha, *Lagidium viscacia*.

Nankeen night heron, *Nycticorax caledonicus*.

Neotropical cormorant, *Phalacrocorax brasilianus*.

Neotropical otter, *Lontra longicaudis*.

Noisy miner, *Manorina melanocephala*.

North American beavers (*Castor canadensis*) have been introduced to Patagonia and are now considered and invasive species.

Northern quoll, *Dasyurus hallucatus*.

Ocelot, *Leopardus pardalis*.

Orange-footed scrubfowl, *Megapodius reinwardt*.

Orca, *Orcinus orca*.

Ostrich is the common name for two species in the genus *Struthio*.

Pale-throated three-toed sloth, *Bradypus tridactylus*.

Palm civet, *Paradoxurus hermaphroditus*.

Palm cockatoo, *Probosciger aterrimus*.

Parma wallaby, *Macropus parma*.

Parnell´s mustached bat, *Pteronotus parnellii*.

Patagonian mara, *Dolichotis patagonum*.

Peters disc-winged bat, *Thyroptera discifera*.

Pigmy hippopotamus, *Choeropsis liberiensis*.

Plains bison, *Bison bison*.

Plains zebra, *Equus quagga*.

Plains viscacha, *Lagostomus maximus*.

Platypus, *Ornithorhynchus anatinus*.

Proboscis bat, *Rhynchonycteris naso*.

Puma, *Puma concolor*.

Rainbow lorikeet, *Trichoglossus moluccanus*.

Rakali, *Hydromys chrysogaster*.

Rat kangaroo, *Aepyprymnus rufescens*.

Razor-billed curassow, *Mitu tuberosum*.

Red acouchi, *M. acouchi*.

Red-bellied titi monkey, *Plecturocebus moloch*.

Red brocket deer, *Mazama americana*.

Red deer, *Cervus elaphus*.

Red jungle fowl, *Gallus gallus*.

Red-legged cormorant, *Phalacrocorax gaimardi*.

Red-necked pademelon, *Thylogale thetis*.

Red-knecked wallaby, *Macropus rufogriseus*.

Red-rumped agouti, *Dasyprocta leporina*.

Red shoveller duck, *Spatula platalea*.

Red-tailed black cockatoo, *Calyptorhynchus banksii*.

Ricefield rats in Vietnam, probaby *Rattus argentiventer*.

Ring-tailed possum, *Pseudocheirus peregrinus*.

Riparian-myotis bat, *Myotis riparius*.

Rock cormorant, *Phalacrocorax magellanicus*.

Rock dove, *Columba livia*.

Rock-hopper penguin, *Eudyptes chrysocome*.

Rough tree fern, *Cyathea australis*.

Rufous-throated antbird, *Gymnopithys rufigula*.

Rusa deer, *Rusa timorensis*.

Rusty-backed antwren, *Formicivora rufa*.

Scarlet flycatcher, *Pyrocephalus rubinus*.

Schneider's dwarf caiman, *Paleosuchus trigonatus*.

Scrub turkey, *Alectura lathami*.

Sea eagle, *Haliaeetus leucogaster*.

Sea lion, *Otaria flavescens*.

Sea otter, *Enhydra lutris*.

Seba's short-tailed bat, *Carollia perspicillata*.

Sewer rat, *Rattus norvegicus*.

Sheathbill, *Chionis albus*.

Short-eared dog, *Atelocynus microtis*.

Silky anteater, *Cyclopes didactylus*.

Silvery marmoset, *Mico argentatus*.

Soft tree fern, *Dicksonia antarctica*.

South American coati, *Nasua nasua*.

South American grey fox, *Lycalopex griseus*.

South American rattle snake, *Crotalus durissus*.

South American tapir, *Tapirus terrestris*.

Southern beech, *Nothofagus moorei*.

Southern crested caracara, *Caracara plancus*.

Southern elephant seal, *Mirounga leonine*.

Southern ground hornbill, *Bucorvus leadbeateri*.

Southern mountain cavy, *Microcavia australis*.

Southern right whale, *Eubalaena australis*.

Southern two-toed sloth, *Choloepus didactylus*.

Sparrow, *Passer domesticus*.

Spectacled owl, *Pulsatrix perspicillata*.

Spinifex, common name used in Australia for desert grasses of the genus *Triodia*. A coastal grass goes by the same name.

Spot-winged antbird, *Myrmelastes leucostigma*.

Spotted dove, *Spilopelia chinensis*.

Star finch, *Bathilda ruficauda*.

Starling, *Sturnus vulgaris*.

Steller's sea cow, *Hydrodamalis gigas*.

Striped ringtail, *Dactylopsila trivirgata*.

Stygian owl, *Asio stygius*.

Swamp rat, *Rattus lutreolus*.

Swamp wallaby, *Wallabia bicolor*.

Tasmanian devil, *Sarcophilus harrisii*.

Tawny frogmouth, *Podargus strigoides*.

Thorn-tailed rayadito, *Aphrastura spinicauda*.

Thylacine, *Thylacinus cynocephalus*.

Tokay gecko, *Gekko gecko.*

Tucuxi, *Sotalia fluviatilis.*

Tuft grasses – the commonest small tuft grass near Alter do chão is *Paspalum carinatum.*

Turkey vulture, *Cathartes aura.*

Two-toed sloth, *Choloepus didactylus.*

Velvety free-tailed bat, *Molossus molossus.*

Vicuña, *Vicugna vicugna.*

Vietnamese rhino, *Rhinoceros sondaicus annamiticus*, a subspecies of the javan rhino.

Virginia opossum, *Didelphis virginiana.*

Wallaroo, *Macropus robustus.*

Water buffalo, *Bubalus bubalis.*

Water rat, *Hydromys chrysogaster.*

Wattled curassow, *Crax globulosa.*

Wedgebilled woodcreeper, *Glyphorynchus spirurus.*

Wedge-tailed eagle, *Aquila audax.*

Weebill, *Smicrornis brevirostris.*

West-Indian manatee, *Trichechus manatus.*

White-bellied fat-tailed mouse opossum, *Thylamys pallidior.*

White-cheeked spider monkey, *Ateles marginatus.*

White-fringed antwren, *Formicivora grisea.*

White-lipped peccary, *Tayassu pecari.*

White-nosed saki, *Chiropotes albinasus*.

White-pointer shark, *Carcharodon carcharias*.

White-throated toucan, *Ramphastos tucanus*.

White-winged parakeet, *Brotogeres versicolurus*.

Wild boar, *Sus scrofa*.

Wombat, *Vombatus ursinus*.

Yapok, *Chironectes minimus*.

Yellow-bellied elaenia, *Elaenia flavogaster*.

Yellow-bellied glider, *Petaurus australis*.

Yellow-crested cockatoo, *Cacatua sulphurea*.

Zebra duiker, *Cephalophus zebra*.

Zebra finch, *Taeniopygia guttata*.

Lightning Source UK Ltd.
Milton Keynes UK
UKHW051255051021
391677UK00002B/112